C0-AQI-643

Seizo Sekine
Philosophical Interpretations of the Old Testament

Beihefte zur Zeitschrift für die alttestamentliche Wissenschaft

Edited by
John Barton, Reinhard G. Kratz
and Markus Witte

Volume 458

Seizo Sekine

Philosophical Interpretations of the Old Testament

Translated by J. Randall Short,
in collaboration with Judy Wakabayashi

GTU
LIBRARY
GRADUATE THEOLOGICAL UNION
1962

DE GRUYTER

BS
1110
Z37
v.458
GTU

G

ISBN 978-3-11-034015-0
e-ISBN 978-3-11-034076-1
ISSN 0934-2575

Library of Congress Cataloging-in-Publication Data
A CIP catalog record for this book has been applied for at the Library of Congress.

Bibliographic information published by the Deutsche Nationalbibliothek
The Deutsche Nationalbibliothek lists this publication in the Deutsche Nationalbibliografie;
detailed bibliographic data are available in the Internet at http://dnb.dnb.de.

© 2014 Walter de Gruyter GmbH, Berlin/Boston
Printing: Hubert & Co. GmbH & Co. KG, Göttingen
♾ Printed on acid-free paper
Printed in Germany

www.degruyter.com

MIX
Papier aus verantwor-
tungsvollen Quellen
FSC
www.fsc.org
FSC® C016439

b14992486

Contents

Preface —— 1
Part I   The Old Testament and Philosophy —— 1
Part II   Old Testament Thought and the Modern World —— 1
Part III   The Prophets and Soteriology —— 2
Part IV   Old Testament Studies in Japan —— 2

Explanatory Notes —— 5

Abbreviations —— 6
    Abbreviations for Hebrew Bible / Old Testament Books —— 6
    Abbreviations for New Testament Books —— 7
    Abbreviations for Bible Versions —— 7
    Ancient Versions —— 8

Introduction
Philosophical and Historical Interpretations —— 9
    Historical Interpretation —— 9
        Examples of Historical Interpretation —— 10
    Philosophical Interpretation —— 11
        Examples of Philosophical Interpretation —— 12
    The Relationship between the Two Approaches and the Task at Hand —— 13
    Monotheism in the Context of Contemporary Challenges —— 14

Part I   The Old Testament and Philosophy —— 17

Chapter 1
Philosophical Interpretations of the Sacrifice of Isaac: Inquiring into the True Significance of the Akedah —— 19
    Introduction —— 19
1   An Evaluation of Kierkegaard's Interpretation —— 20
1.1   Kierkegaard's Interpretation —— 20
1.2   Westermann's Critique —— 21
1.3   Questions for Westermann —— 22
2   Interpretations by Kant, Buber, Levinas, Derrida, and Miyamoto, and
            a Critical Summary —— 23
2.1   Kant's Interpretation —— 23
2.2   Buber's Interpretation —— 24
2.3   Levinas's Interpretation —— 25

2.4   Derrida's Interpretation —— **26**
2.5   Miyamoto's Interpretation —— **27**
2.6   Critical Summary —— **30**
3   Examining the Theory that Treats Verses 15–19 as a Later
         Accretion —— **35**
3.1   Translation of Verses 15–19 and Notes —— **35**
3.2   Grounds for Treating Verses 15–19 as a Later Accretion —— **36**
3.3   Examining the Theory that Treats Verses 15–19 as a Later
         Accretion —— **37**
3.4   The Theory that Treats Verse 19 as a Later Accretion —— **40**
4   A Reconstruction of the Dialogue among God, Abraham, and Isaac,
         and their States of Mind —— **41**
4.1   Silence or Dialogue —— **41**
4.2   Translation of Verses 2–4 and Verse 9 with Notes —— **42**
4.3   When Was Abraham "Told" about "the Place"? —— **42**
4.4   Toward Understanding the Characters' States of Mind —— **43**
5   Isaac's Feelings —— **44**
5.1   The Father's Love —— **44**
5.2   Translation of Verses 7–8 with Notes —— **45**
5.3   Isaac's Self-sacrifice —— **45**
5.4   Why Did Isaac Not Run Away? —— **46**
6   Abraham's Feelings —— **47**
6.1   In His Relationship with Isaac —— **47**
6.2   Abraham's Logic and Conviction: With Reference to Josephus —— **47**
6.3   Abraham's Statement: Returning to the Akedah —— **48**
6.4   The True Meaning of Abraham's Statement —— **48**
6.5   Faith and Unbelief —— **51**
6.6   Contradictory Views of the Talkative Abraham —— **51**
6.7   The One Who is Weak and the One Who Fears God —— **52**
7   God's Self-Denial —— **53**
7.1   Doubts about "God" —— **53**
7.2   Criticism from Philosophy of a Personal God, and its
         Outcome —— **57**
7.3   Nishida's Understanding of the Akedah —— **58**
7.4   Abraham's Evil and God's Love —— **59**
7.5   Summary —— **59**
7.6   Self-Negation within the Creator God —— **60**
7.7   Self-Negation within the Ethnic God —— **61**
7.8   The Meaning of Self-Negation —— **63**

7.9   Additional Comments on *Agape*: *Agape* in the Old and New
             Testaments —— **63**
7.10   The Meaning of *be-har yahwe yera'e* —— **65**
      Conclusion —— **67**
             A Retrospect of the Main Points Concerning "the True Significance of the
             Akedah" —— **67**
             Prospects for Collaboration Between Old Testament Studies and
             Philosophy —— **70**

Chapter 2
The Paradox of Suffering: Comparing Second Isaiah and Socrates —— 73
      Introduction —— **73**
1   Theodicy of Suffering in Israelite Religion —— **74**
1.1   Suffering of the Righteous in the Book of Second Isaiah —— **74**
1.2   Max Weber's Interpretation and its Merits —— **75**
1.3   Despair in Life —— **77**
2   Egoism of Suffering in Greek Philosophy —— **80**
2.1   The Execution of Socrates —— **80**
2.2   The Relationship between Love and Suffering in Aristotle —— **81**
2.3   Hope in Life —— **83**
3   Suffering as the Starting Point of Liberation from Egoism —— **84**
3.1   Abandonment of Egoism —— **84**
3.2   Devotion —— **85**
3.3   The Paradox of Suffering —— **88**

Chapter 3
Reconstructing Old Testament Monotheism: A Dialogue between Old Testament
Studies and Philosophy —— 90
      Introduction —— **90**
1   What is Problematic about Monotheism? —— **91**
2   Various Views of God in the Old Testament's Self-
             Understanding —— **93**
2.1   The God Who Directs Israel's Wars —— **93**
2.2   The God Who Uses Other Nations to Punish Israel's Sins —— **95**
2.3   The God Who Does Not Guide History —— **95**
3   Various Views of God Classified in Terms of Religious
             Studies —— **97**
3.1   The Relationship with Polytheism —— **97**
3.2   The Law of Monolatry —— **99**
3.3   The Formation and Significance of Monotheism —— **101**

4   Philosophical Reflections about the Concept of God ── 107
5   The Anthropological Significance of Atonement Faith ── 109
5.1   Atonement of the Righteous in Judaism and Christianity ── 110
5.2   Egoism of Suffering in Greek Philosophy ── 110
5.3   Atonement as the Starting Point of Liberation from Egoism ── 111
    Conclusion ── 113

Part II   Old Testament Thought and the Modern World ── 117

Chapter 4
Modern Aspects of the Old Testament Understanding of God: Qohelet,
Schoenberg, Jung ── 119
1   Suspicions, Criticisms, and Verbal Attacks against the Old
           Testament God ── 119
1.1   Qohelet's Suspicions of the God who Requites Good and
           Evil ── 119
1.2   Schoenberg's Criticism of the God who Rejects Idols ── 120
1.3   Jung's Statement that "Job's God is a Fool" ── 121
2   A Response from the Old Testament ── 123
2.1   The Nihilism of Qohelet and his Triumph Over It: The Ontological
           Personal God and the Non-ontological Transcendent One ── 123
2.2   Schoenberg's Uncertainty: Toward the Idea of Atonement
           Thought ── 125
2.3   What Jung Missed: Demythologizing the Creation Story ── 128
3   How Does the Old Testament Understanding of God Challenge the
           Modern World? ── 129
3.0   What Kind of Age is this Modern Period? ── 130
3.1   Doubts about the Concept of God ── 130
3.2   Sensitivity to Suffering ── 131
3.3   The Givenness of Existence ── 132

Chapter 5
Toward Regenerating Ethics: Seeking an Ordered Path of Joyful
Coexistence ── 134
    Introduction ── 134
1   Two Attitudes Toward Ethics ── 136
1.1   Emotional Draconianism and Ethical Education ── 136
1.2   Theoretical Ethical Relativism and Skepticism ── 136
1.3   Aphasia and Working to Overcome It ── 137
2   Two Grounds for Rejecting Murder: Awareness of Order (Ri) ── 139

2.1   A Ktisiological Reason (*Ri*) — **139**
2.2   A Soteriological Reason (*Ri*) — **142**
2.3   Summary — **144**
3   Seven Paths (*Ro*) for Arriving at the Two Understandings of
          Order (*Ri*) — **144**
3.1   Religion — **145**
3.2   Philosophy — **146**
3.2.1   The Philosophical Hermeneutics of Gadamer and Ricœur — **146**
3.2.2   Plato's Criticism of Democracy — **146**
3.2.3   Wonder (*thaumazein*) is the Beginning of Philosophy
          (*philosophiā*) — **148**
3.3   Science — **149**
3.4   Summary — **150**
3.5   Law — **151**
3.6   Politics — **152**
3.7   The Arts — **155**
3.8   The Art of Discovering Good Things — **156**
    Conclusion — **159**

Part III **The Prophets and Soteriology** — **161**

Chapter 6
**A Genealogy of Prophetic Salvation: Isaiah, Second Isaiah, and
Jeremiah** — **163**
    Introduction — **163**
1   From the Book of Isaiah — **163**
1.1   The Call of Isaiah — **163**
1.2   Early Messianic Prophecies — **165**
1.3   David's Scion — **166**
1.4   Those Who Received Instruction — **167**
1.5   Second Isaiah's Suffering Servant — **168**
2   From the Book of Jeremiah — **172**
2.1   Jeremiah and the Deuteronomistic Historian — **172**
2.2   False Prophets — **174**
2.3   Messiah — **175**
2.4   Sacrifices — **176**
2.5   The New Covenant — **178**

Chapter 7
The Prophets and Deuteronomism: The Book of Jeremiah —— 181
1   Questions about Authenticity —— 181
2   True and False Prophets —— 183
3   An Examination of Thiel's Theory about the Deuteronomistic
         Historian's Redactional Intentions —— 186
3.1   The Theology of Thiel's Deuteronomistic Historian —— 187
3.2   Ideas and Expressions Unique to the Deuteronomistic Historian
         (Other than those Cited by Thiel) —— 190
3.3   Ideas Unique to Jeremiah —— 190
4   Interpretation of the "New Covenant" Prophecy: The First Point of
         Debate —— 192
5   Interpretation of the "New Covenant" Prophecy: The Second Point of
         Debate —— 196
6   The Prophetic Content of Jeremiah's Authentic Texts —— 198
7   A Comparison of the Ideas of the Deuteronomistic Historian and
         Jeremiah —— 201
8   Revisiting Questions about Authenticity: The Task of Philosophical
         Interpretation —— 205

Part IV **Old Testament Studies in Japan —— 209**

Chapter 8
Old Testament Studies in Japan: A Retrospect and Prospects —— 211
   Introduction —— 211
1   A Retrospect —— 211
1.1   A Brief History of the Society for Old Testament Study in Japan and
         the Japanese Biblical Institute —— 211
1.2   Brief Overview of International Research Achievements —— 213
1.3   Brief Overview of Domestic Research Achievements —— 221
2   Prospects —— 224
2.1   Old Testament Studies in Japan: Reflections and Prospects —— 224
2.2   Looking to the Future of the Society for Old Testament Study in
         Japan —— 225
         2.2.1 —— 226
         2.2.2 —— 226
         2.2.3 —— 226
         2.2.4 —— 227
         2.2.5 —— 228
         2.2.6 —— 228

2.2.7 ── **228**
2.2.8 ── **229**
2.2.9 ── **229**
Conclusion ── **230**

Subject Index ── 231

Author Index ── 241

Ancient Sources Index ── 244

Preface

This book includes seven chapters from my Japanese monograph *Kyūyaku Seisho to Tetsugaku: Gendai no Toi no Naka no Isshinkyō* (The Old Testament and Philosophy: Monotheism in the Context of Contemporary Challenges) (Tokyo: Iwanami Shoten, 2008) and an additional chapter on "Old Testament Studies in Japan," which is based on a paper presented elsewhere. It has been reconceived with overseas readers in mind. The following is an overview of the contents.

Part I The Old Testament and Philosophy

Chapter 1 discusses the story of Abraham's sacrifice of Isaac, his beloved son. How should we understand the unethicality of God, who commands filicide, and Abraham, who obeys? In the history of interpretation, this question has been raised more frequently in the interpretative attempts of philosophers who do not presume faith than in historical and theological research. Through a critical survey of leading interpretations from Kant and Kierkegaard to Levinas and Derrida, this chapter constructs my own philosophical interpretation and a new philological proposal based especially on hints from Kitarō Nishida's interpretation of the Abraham story.

Chapter 2 attempts to reveal the philosophical significance and characteristics of various Old Testament texts that appear at first glance to be non-philosophical. My considerations converge on "suffering" thought, which is at the heart of the Old and New Testaments, and I explain its philosophical significance by following the thread of Socrates' and Aristotle's philosophical analyses of suffering and sacrifice.

Based on the first two chapters, Chapter 3 then presents a range of philosophical criticisms concerning prophetic understandings of God that are considered to be the source of monotheism, and it explores the possibility of responses based on modern philosophy and theology.

Part II Old Testament Thought and the Modern World

Part I focused on Old Testament monotheism, while also considering issues relating to its different aspects and contemporary significance. Yet, of course, monotheism is not the only concept being challenged today. In the course of explaining doubts about the Old Testament on the part of thinkers such as Qohelet, Schoenberg, and Jung, Chapter 4 explores the possibility of responding to a wide range of acute issues concerning contemporary understandings of God, such as questions concerning a personal God, salvation history, and the maldistribution of suffering.

Chapter 5 applies the potency of such responses from the Old Testament to the specific problem of contemporary Japan's ethical collapse and regeneration. There I develop my considerations of the contemporary range of Hebraic and Christian ethics based on solutions to ethical problems as proposed from Plato to Locke, and while taking postmodern ethical criticism into account.

Part III The Prophets and Soteriology

In Part III, I consciously focus in particular on the complementary relationship between philosophical and historical interpretation, and I explore how we can arrive at a philosophical interpretation based upon historical textual criticism, source criticism, and redaction history.

Focusing mainly on my published Japanese translations, textual criticism, and exegeses of the books of Isaiah and Jeremiah (Iwanami Shoten, 1997, 2002), Chapter 6 discusses philosophical prospects concerning determinations of historical meaning and their limitations, as well as the genealogy of soteriological understandings that emerge beyond this.

Chapter 7 focuses on the book of Jeremiah and the problem of Deuteronomism, which is one of the greatest points of debate in modern Old Testament scholarship, and seeks to open up the possibility of a new philosophical interpretation by supplementing and developing Thiel's redaction-historical research with philosophical considerations.

This concludes the discussions in this book that probe various possibilities for a philosophical interpretation of the Old Testament.

Part IV Old Testament Studies in Japan

Part IV is a supplementary essay. It, too, refers to research by Japanese who have attempted philosophical interpretations of the Old Testament, but its aim is to give non-Japanese readers an overview of the diverse range of Old Testament studies in Japan spanning approximately a century. In Chapter 8, for the sake of non-Japanese readers, I have revised my memorial lecture titled "Old Testament Studies in Japan: A Retrospect and Prospects," which I delivered as president of the Society for Old Testament Study upon its eighty-eighth anniversary. The original contributions made by Japanese researchers have not been sufficiently introduced to researchers elsewhere because of the language barrier. While focusing on research that is accessible to non-Japanese readers, I offer a retrospect of the history of Old Testament studies in Japan and outline prospects for the future. It is my hope that this might be used as a foundation for constructing a new international network.

The above is an outline of the four parts and eight chapters of this book. The three points that I especially hope to communicate through this book could perhaps be summed up as follows.

(1) Constrained by theological and historical-critical methods, Western biblical studies have tended toward either faith-based apologetics or value-free philology. Research that would explore values and be free from a particular faith is possible only through philosophical methods. In this book, I call for the use of these methods, consciously apply them to the interpretation of several texts, and search for new possibilities for Old Testament readings.

(2) Based on this approach, it is possible, for example, to weave new thoughts about the mystery of the sacrifice of Isaac story or solutions to problems concerning Jeremiah and the Deuteronomistic Historian and to offer proposals to contemporary conflicts among monotheistic faiths or to postmodern ethical criticisms. Today there is a need for Old Testament research that deliberately takes a step in these directions.

(3) In that event, perhaps the investigations in this book, in which I have sought out the underpinnings of Eastern and Western thought while adopting Kitarō Nishida's philosophy of the self-identity of absolute contradiction, together with the supplementary essay surveying the history and prospects of Old Testament studies in Japan can raise new questions from the East in relation to Western biblical studies and the spirit of the times. Though my considerations here have only scratched the surface, I aim through this book to foster exchanges between East and West and to call for that possibility.

In the humanities it is common for Japanese researchers to study at Western universities and to write and publish doctoral dissertations there, but they rarely then go on to present their publications in a European language. In addition to my many teaching and research activities in Japan, however, I have worked toward exchanges with foreign researchers and toward publishing my work internationally. Translating Japanese works that have the potential to make an international contribution and publishing them in European languages is essential for the accountability of researchers from this island nation in the Far East. This has long been my ideal. The outcome has been the publication of my German dissertation, *Die Tritojesajanische Sammlung (Jes 56 – 66) redaktionsgeschichtlich untersucht* (BZAW 175; de Gruyter, 1989), followed by two of my Japanese works translated into English: *Transcendency and Symbols in the Old*

Testament (BZAW 275; de Gruyter, 1999) and *A Comparative Study of the Origins of Ethical Thought: Hellenism and Hebraism* (Rowman & Littlefield, 2005). The work of translation is not something I can do on the side, but a task that requires the full energies of skilled professionals. As with the previous translated books, I am deeply delighted to have benefited from the collaborative efforts of two dear friends who produced this English translation. Associate Professor J. Randall Short translated the book. Professor Judy Wakabayashi proofread and edited the entire translation, and her translation of an earlier article served as the basis of Chapter 7. I wish to offer my deep gratitude for their capable and conscientious work.

I am deeply gratified to have this book published together with the above-mentioned volumes in the prestigious BZAW series. In particular, I wish to express here my wholehearted appreciation to Prof. John Barton (Oxford), Prof. Reinhard G. Kratz (Göttingen), Prof. Choon-Leong Seow (Princeton), and Prof. Markus Witte (Frankfurt) for reviewing and accepting my manuscript for publication, and to Dr. Albrecht Döhnert (de Gruyter/Berlin) and his editorial staff for guiding this project to publication.

Finally, I wish to note that, as with my previous two works in English, this translation has been published with the support of a Grant-in-Aid for Publication of Scientific Research Results from the Japan Society for the Promotion of Science (JSPS KAKENHI Grant Number 246001). In the midst of economic circumstances that allow little optimism, it is an honor to be able to use Japanese taxpayers' money for the purpose of international cultural exchange. It is my strong desire that this book might make some small contribution to that goal. I express my sincere and heartfelt gratitude to everyone who has made this possible.

Komoro, Summer 2013
Seizō Sekine

Explanatory Notes

1. Old Testament quotations from Isaiah and Jeremiah are translations of the author's original Japanese translations, which are based on *Biblia Hebraica Stuttgartensia*, edited by K. Elliger and W. Rudolph (Stuttgart: Deutsche Bibelstiftung, 1997). English quotations from other biblical texts, unless noted otherwise, are from the New Revised Standard Version of the Bible, copyright © 1989, by the Division of Christian Education of the National Council of the Churches of Christ in the U.S.A.
2. The *ketiv* reflects the original consonantal text, whereas the *qere* readings are based on Masoretic corrections and newly suggested readings dating to the seventh to fourteenth centuries.
3. For text-critical purposes, I have referred to various ancient versions. The Septuagint is the Greek version dating to the third to second centuries BCE; the Targum is the Aramaic version dating to the second and following centuries CE; and the Vulgate is the Latin version completed by Jerome around the same time.
4. For Hebrew and Greek readings, I have adopted a simple transliteration system for the sake of readers who do not read the original languages.
5. Modern Bible versions that I have consulted are as given on the Abbreviations page below.
6. Bracketed sections in biblical quotations are the author's.
7. Italics by the author are so noted.
8. When readily available, English translations of the German and French works quoted here have been used. All translations from Japanese works are by J. Randall Short.
9. Japanese names are written in Western order, with the surname last.

Abbreviations

Abbreviations for Hebrew Bible / Old Testament Books

Gen	Genesis
Exod	Exodus
Lev	Leviticus
Num	Numbers
Deut	Deuteronomy
Josh	Joshua
Judg	Judges
Ruth	Ruth
1Sam	1 Samuel
2Sam	2 Samuel
1Kgs	1 Kings
2Kgs	2 Kings
1Chr	1 Chronicles
2Chr	2 Chronicles
Ezra	Ezra
Neh	Nehemiah
Esth	Esther
Job	Job
Ps	Psalms
Prov	Proverbs
Eccl	Ecclesiastes
Song	Song of Solomon
Isa	Isaiah
Jer	Jeremiah
Lam	Lamentations
Ezek	Ezekiel
Dan	Daniel
Hos	Hosea
Joel	Joel
Amos	Amos
Obad	Obadiah
Jonah	Jonah
Mic	Micah
Nah	Nahum
Hab	Habakkuk
Zeph	Zephaniah

Hag   Haggai
Zech   Zechariah
Mal   Malachi

Abbreviations for New Testament Books

Matt   Matthew
Mark   Mark
Luke   Luke
John   John
Acts   Acts of the Apostles
Rom   Romans
1Cor   1 Corinthians
2Cor   2 Corinthians
Gal   Galatians
Eph   Ephesians
Phil   Philippians
Col   Colossians
1Thess 1 Thessalonians
2Thess 2 Thessalonians
1Tim   1 Timothy
2Tim   2 Timothy
Titus   Titus
Phlm   Philemon
Heb   Hebrews
Jas   James
1Pet   1 Peter
2Pet   2 Peter
1John   1 John
2John   2 John
3John   3 John
Jude   Jude
Rev   Revelation

Abbreviations for Bible Versions

BBE   The Bible in Basic English (1949/64)
DRB   French Version Darby, 1885

EIN   Einheitsübersetzung (1980) (German)
ELB   Revidierte Elberfelder (1993) (German)
ELO   Unrevidierte Elberfelder (1905) (German)
KJV   King James Version (1611/1769)
LSG   Louis Segond Version (1910) (French)
LUT   Revidierte Lutherbibel (1984) (German)
NAB   The New American Bible (1995)
NEG   Nouvelle Edition Geneve (1979) (French)
NKJ   The New King James Version (1982)
NRS   The New Revised Standard Version (1989)
RWB   Revised 1833 Webster Update (1995) (English)
SCH   Schlachter Version (1951) (German)
TEV   Today's English Version (1976)

Ancient Versions

MT   Masoretic Text
LXX Septuagint

Introduction Philosophical and Historical Interpretations

When we read the Old Testament from an academic perspective, what hermeneutical approach do we adopt? Today, there are two broadly competing views that seem to be facing a transitional period. In this introduction I wish to lay the ground for the discussion in the following chapters by giving a rough overview of several basic points related to the theory and practice of these two approaches.

Historical Interpretation

Most of the texts in the Old Testament have undergone a complicated transmission process. So the first task is to ascertain the original form of the Old Testament text. In doing so, scholars attempt to determine the original text—that is, the original Hebrew text—through comparisons between Hebrew manuscripts and each ancient version and through analyses of phonology, meter, morphology, lexemes, syntax, literary techniques, structure, and the like. This is the work of *text criticism*.

Next, through an examination of each original text's subject, style, and so on, it is necessary to determine each unit and examine its special characteristics within the larger context of interconnected textual composites. That is the stage of *source criticism*.

The above research pertains to textual transmission. Scholars assume, however, that many biblical texts underwent a long stage of oral tradition before they were fixed as written texts. It is the work of *tradition-historical* research to explain each stage of oral tradition and consider historical factors, original speech intentions, and other aspects that factored into each stage.

Next, *redaction-critical* research examines the tradition history of texts once they have been written down, usually after a long history of oral tradition. The main task of redaction history is to trace the history of the original text from its initial composition as a written text through the transmission process where supplementary glosses and other additions are made, right up to the final form in which it has been handed down to us today.

Form criticism takes the view that ancient authors and editors used and composed literary forms that were transmitted within the particular life-settings (*Sitz im Leben*) of the communities in which they lived. To demonstrate the validity of their perspective, form critics must comparatively read texts from as diverse a range as possible, gather the forms that share similarities, and determine the life-settings that can be assumed to have evoked these forms.

Whether or not one recognizes the validity of form criticism, certainly the authors and editors of the original text, as well as its transmitters and falsifiers, implicitly and explicitly assumed some sort of intellectual history and thought environment. Scholars generally label the environment that determined their thinking as "tradition," and so it is also the task of *tradition-historical* research to investigate the intellectual environment that constituted these traditions and to consider how the biblical text was established, based on research into particular terminological contexts and the like.

The ultimate aim of historical interpretation is to arrive at an *interpretation as the determination of the original text's historical meaning* by effectively integrating the various hermeneutical methodologies. This is the traditional method employed in modern biblical interpretation, and today it retains its standing as an influential hermeneutical approach.[1]

Examples of Historical Interpretation

How, then, do scholars carry out this type of historical interpretation in actual practice? I shall give a very brief glimpse into this approach by considering how scholars might interpret the Old Testament's "Decalogue of Moses."

The Decalogue appears in Exodus 20 and Deuteronomy 5 in nearly parallel form. The form of the original text can be surmised by comparing the two and investigating the connections to a number of commandments that occur in the prophets in fragmentary form, as well as variations in the Greek and Latin versions (*text criticism*).

Furthermore, the Decalogue has been inserted into the text in a way that breaks the surrounding narrative relating the exodus from Egypt and the wilderness wanderings. Therefore, these ten commandments can be viewed as a cohesive literary unit (*source criticism*).

The sixth, seventh, and eighth commandments—the prohibitions against murder, adultery, and theft—are referred to in different orders in the prophetical

---

1 For more details, see Hermann Barth and Odil Hannes Steck, *Exegese des Alten Testaments: Leitfaden der Methodik* (Neukirchen-Vluyn: Neukirchener Verlag, 1971); Hermann Barth and Odil Hannes Steck, *Kyūyaku Seisho Shakugi Nyūmon: Sono Hōhō to Jissai* (Introduction to Old Testament Exegesis: Methodology and Application) (trans. Tetsuo Yamaga; Tokyo: The Board of Publications The United Church of Christ in Japan, 1984); also see Georg Fohrer, *Exegese des Alten Testaments: Einführung in die Methodik* (Heidelberg: Quelle & Meyer, 1973).

texts of Hosea 4:2 and Jeremiah 7:9. The transmission process within which the ten commandments were collected can be variously surmised through a comparison with these texts (*tradition history*).

The most prominent difference between the accounts of the Decalogue in the books of Exodus and Deuteronomy is found in the passage that provides the basis of the fourth commandment concerning the Sabbath. The Exodus account commands Sabbath observance as an imitation of God's rest after his work of creation, while the account in Deuteronomy commands Sabbath observance in order to give slaves a rest. In these texts, we can detect the particular intentions of each editor (*redaction history*).

The literary form of the Decalogue is fundamentally that of a legal text. It does not take the form of casuistic law, which is determined case by case, but rather that of apodictic law, which issues universal commands. Its life-setting can be provisionally viewed as that of the law court (*form criticism*).

Because *tradition history* needs to treat each commandment separately, let us focus here on the sixth commandment, "You shall not murder." The original Hebrew term for "murder," *ratsach*, does not refer to all kinds of killing. It is thought to be a special word that does not cover three types of killing in particular. That is, it seems that there are no instances in the Old Testament where *ratsach* is used to refer to killing in war, in the case of the death penalty, or with reference to the slaughter of animals.[2]

We can hence understand the meaning of the sixth commandment as prohibiting the murder of innocent Israelites, while permitting the three exceptions noted above. In this way, we can arrive at an *interpretation based on determination of the text's historical meaning*—the ultimate task of historical interpretation.

Philosophical Interpretation

There is another hermeneutical approach, however, and this has gained attention in recent years by raising fundamental questions and doubts about the course of *historical hermeneutics*. This alternative approach is *philosophical hermeneutics*, whose chief aim lies in the fusion of horizons and in interpretive conflict. With this approach, some interpreters consider it impossible from the outset

---

2 A. Jepsen, "Du sollst nicht töten! Was ist das?" *ELKZ* 13 (1959): 384 f. Although the above view represents the prevailing theory until now, in my personal view *ratsach* occurs once in a text where it applies to the death penalty—in Num 35:30. This would undermine Jepsen's theory. See Seizō Sekine, *Rinri no Tansaku: Seisho kara no Apurōchi* (The Quest for Ethics: An Approach from the Bible) (Tokyo: Chuko Shinsho, 2002), 113.

to determine the objective, historical meaning of the original text by adopting general methods. They disdain the hermeneutical experience of having the text "assault" the interpreter, an experience inherent in the view that it is possible to determine the objective meaning, and they regard this as a mere pipe dream based on a crude analogy with the natural sciences. Instead, they argue that interpreters inevitably bring their own fixed, subjective preconceptions to the text, and they view the work of interpretation as nothing other than a process of conflict, dialogue, or fusion between the horizon of the interpreter and that of the text. Therefore it is first necessary to make each interpreter's subjective horizon self-consciously clear. Then, whenever the interpreter pursues the process of clashing with the text, he or she must aim for an *interpretation based on the determination of philosophical meaning that is intertwined with the interpreter's own thought.* Enquiries along these lines have frequently been neglected in traditional biblical studies, but ever since H. G. Gadamer modern interpreters have come under pressure to adopt aggressively the theories and practices of this hermeneutical approach.[3]

Examples of Philosophical Interpretation

What does philosophical interpretation look like? I shall take as an example the sixth commandment, already mentioned above.

First, if the interpreter is a fundamentalist, he might adhere to the narrow meaning of *ratsach* and, in particular, emphasize that killing in wartime is permitted. For instance, a fundamentalist might approve of the slaughter of Palestinians by the Israeli army in wartime and even find an endorsement in this commandment.

If, however, the interpreter is a *Jew* who takes into account the essence of thought that runs throughout the Old Testament, it is unlikely that he or she will adhere solely to the sense of the sixth commandment as derived from historical interpretation—that is, as meaning that one must not murder an "Israelite." This is because the Old Testament is not monochromatic. Rather, its thought gradually matures over time, and its originally narrow nationalism develops into a broad universalism (especially in the sixth-century writings of the prophet

---

3 Hans-Georg Gadamer, *Wahrheit und Methode: Grundzüge einer philosophischen Hermeneutik* (Tübingen: Mohr, 1960), 263 ff.; Paul Ricœur, *Finitude et culpabilité. II. La symbolique du mal* (Paris: Aubier, 1960), 11–17; Paul. Ricœur, *Rikūru Seisho Kaishaku-gaku* (Ricœur Biblical Hermeneutics) (trans. Hiroshi Kume and Kei Sasaki; Tokyo: Jordan, 1996); Seizō Sekine, *Transcendency and Symbols in the Old Testament: A Genealogy of the Hermeneutical Experiences* (trans. Judy Wakabayashi; Berlin: Walter de Gruyter, 1999), see Introduction.

Second Isaiah during the Babylonian exile). If readers reconsider the sixth commandment on the basis of this culmination of the entire Old Testament, they will consider it appropriate to understand the commandment in the broad sense, namely, that one must not kill people in general.

If the interpreter is a *Christian* who takes the New Testament into account, he or she will no doubt recall Jesus' interpretation of the sixth commandment in Matthew 5. We can understand Jesus to be asserting that merely becoming angry at others or viewing them with contempt is the same sin as murder, whether or not one actually commits murder. In this view, whether or not one commits the act depends upon one's environment and personal propensities. And if we take the view that ethics are fundamentally and ultimately concerned with the good and evil in one's heart and feelings, we are bound to interpret the sixth commandment broadly as meaning that one must not hold any feelings whatsoever that might possibly lead to murder.

Furthermore, if we sincerely pursue this as *modern people with a holistic view of contemporary politics and economics*, the range of collective responsibility in contemporary society encompasses the whole world. This may lead us to conclude that we cannot remain ignorant of, or indifferent to, those around the world who are starving or who are victims of natural disasters, environmental pollution, war, or societal structures, simply because they do not fall within our own sphere of activities. To do so would to become already complicit in their murder. Furthermore, it is possible to interpret the sixth commandment as implying not only that we should come to the physical and emotional aid of such people, but that we should also work to transform society so as to prevent people from leading disadvantaged lives. A philosophical interpretation could possibly be taken to that extent.

While taking each person's thought horizons into consideration, philosophical interpretations bear the task of seeking a wide range of possibilities for each interpretation.

The Relationship between the Two Approaches and the Task at Hand

These two hermeneutical directions are not necessarily opposed to one another. Rather, they stand in a complementary relationship. Without incorporating the fruits of objective, historical hermeneutics as much as possible, philosophical hermeneutics might fall into dogma and bias through arbitrary eisegesis. On the other hand, without adding philosophical hermeneutics and scrutinizing the subjective horizon of the interpreter, there is a risk that historical hermeneutics might lack ideological reflexivity and accountability concerning the significance of the research. Modern interpreters face the necessary task of comprehensively inquiring into specific ways through which these two hermeneutical approaches can strike a mutually beneficial balance. The days when scholars could remain holed up in their ivory towers and simply follow their intellectual curiosity while neglecting the world around them under the dignified name of Weberian "asceticism" are coming to an end. We live in a complex yet fascinating era.

While I acknowledge this hermeneutical situation in today's world, the primary task of this book is consciously to pursue possibilities for a philosophical interpretation of the Old Testament. This is especially needed today because historical hermeneutics have been overwhelmingly dominant in Old Testament studies and there is poor understanding of philosophical hermeneutics. This implies, then, an integrative approach—not one that ignores historical hermeneutics, but one that also emphasizes philosophical hermeneutics.

Monotheism in the Context of Contemporary Challenges

When interpreters approach the biblical text in this way, they can no longer ignore various problematic circumstances, such as the following examples.

How should we understand the seemingly irrational, supra-ethical acts of the God of Old Testament monotheism? Can we settle matters simply by asserting that religion transcends ethics? Do the ancient ethics of the Old Testament have any bearing on contemporary ethics? To start with, does our contemporary age of autonomous humanism even need God as an authority figure? Consider the experiences of modern people who have witnessed tragedies such as the massive slaughter of innocent peoples through war or terrorism, and the experiences of those who have achieved material well-being through scientific developments that exclude God. Have not these experiences justly declared the death of God?

At the very least, the religious form consisting of monotheism is being subjected to criticism today as conflicts increase among exclusive monotheistic religions. Doubts are being raised about the monotheistic concepts of the Old Testament prophets, who are the source of monotheism. Today we find ourselves in religious circumstances and, by extension, philosophical and intellectual circumstances where we are under pressure to reconsider these ideas and reconstruct monotheism. Furthermore, monotheism's concept of a personal God is being challenged and shaken by philosophy's logic of topos. New questions are also being raised about the philosophical range of atonement thought, which is at the center of Hebraism and Christianity. And it is not only concepts pertaining to the one God or transcendence or ethics that are being challenged and shaken. The very manner of questioning these concepts—namely, the interpretive methodology discussed above—is itself being questioned and challenged.

While I take as broad a view as possible of these contemporary challenges and interconnected ideas, my primary task in this book lies in philosophically and thoroughly raising these questions anew, with the Old Testament, which is my field of expertise, as my reference point.

In the process, I am afraid it was necessary to question and challenge some of my esteemed colleagues. Of course, it has not been my intention to be unnecessarily polemical. While collaboratively highlighting the host of issues forced on us by our current scholarly situation, which is in a transitional period as we undergo a paradigm shift, I simply wish to approach the truth of these matters while playing catch ball, not dodge ball. And if I occasionally throw a wild pitch, I hope my readers will not regard that as deliberate, but will instead magnanimously catch my true intent. Some chapters of the book were originally delivered in the form of lectures at academic society meetings and elsewhere. They were presented within the framework and shared perspective of collaborative settings, so in order to reflect their significance within those contexts I have not removed all references to these settings. I hope that readers will pardon this indulgence and enjoy these chapters according to the flow of each particular context.

What new insights will the Old Testament reveal when we proceed in the direction of philosophical interpretation, whether collaboratively or in an isolated fashion, alone and without aid? I invite readers to embark on a journey in which they share my desire to interpret a variety of Old Testament texts and explore the philosophical range of monotheism in the context of contemporary challenges.

Chapter 1 Philosophical Interpretations of the Sacrifice of Isaac: Inquiring into the True Significance of the Akedah

Introduction

Allow me to begin my reflections in this chapter with personal memories concerning the story of Abraham's sacrifice of Isaac as recounted in Genesis 22:1–19.[1] Following convention, I shall refer to this account as "the Akedah" (the Hebrew for "binding"). When reading this story, I often recall the print of Rembrandt's "Sacrifice of Isaac" that my late father, Masao, who devoted his life to Old Testament studies and Christian evangelism, hung in his study. Though it was an eerie painting to me as a child, as I grew and came to understand its meaning, I could not accept that I might have been killed for the sake of my father's faith. I eventually left home to pursue Old Testament studies in Munich. Whenever I viewed the original of this painting during visits to the Alte Pinakothek, which was diagonally across from my dormitory, I was left dissatisfied. People should view it from Isaac's perspective, I thought. Looking back, however, I realize that since I am my father's third-born son there would in fact have been no obligation or right for me to have been offered up in the firstborn sacrifice. My father might have hung this painting as a memorial to his firstborn son, whom he lost shortly after birth in the midst of hardships while dedicating himself to evangelism. I did not have the opportunity to confirm this while my

---

1 This chapter is a compilation of my invitational lecture titled "Philosophical Interpretations of the Sacrifice of Isaac" (July 18, 2007) at the Nineteenth Congress of the International Organization for the Study of the Old Testament (IOSOT) at the University of Ljubljana in Slovenia (July 15–20, 2007) and my president's address titled "Inquiring into the True Significance of the Akedah: Collaboration between Old Testament Studies and Philosophy" at a meeting of the Society for Old Testament Study in Japan on November 3, 2012, at the University of Tokyo. I wish to thank my colleagues for the active question and answer session at each lecture. Already I have been able to incorporate some insights from these sessions into the present chapter. The former lecture was published in *Congress Volume Ljubljana 2007* (ed. André Lemaire; Vetus Testamentum, Supplements 133; Leiden: Brill, 2010), 339–66, but this has been significantly revised on the basis of the latter talk. During the time between these two lectures, I surveyed forty-two ancient to contemporary interpretations of the Akedah in a 334-page Japanese anthology titled *Aburahamu no Isaku Kenkyō Monogatari: Akedaa Ansorojii* (The Story of Abraham's Sacrifice of Isaac: Akedah Anthology) (Tokyo: The Board of Publications, The United Church of Christ in Japan, 2012). My revisions in the latter half of this chapter are largely based on my survey and examination of the Akedah's interpretative history.

father was alive, but that is what I now think. Whatever the case, the story of this father who almost committed filicide is, for a son, terrifying.

Yet it seems that there is a general abundance of interpretations lavishly praising Abraham, who was on the verge of killing his son, without considering Isaac's plight. The prime example is Sören Kierkegaard's *Fear and Trembling*. I would like to begin my interpretation of this baffling text, which is so tied up with my own personal memories, by considering whether his interpretation hits upon the nub of the text.

1 An Evaluation of Kierkegaard's Interpretation

1.1 Kierkegaard's Interpretation

Let us briefly review the interpretation of the Akedah in *Fear and Trembling*.[2]

Kierkegaard praises Abraham as a "knight of faith" in that "even after he sacrificed his own will he held on to it firmly," "he was a man who hoped for the impossible," and "he was a man who believed God." Someone who merely relinquishes the finite for the infinite is a "knight of infinite resignation," but someone who, after relinquishing it, is able to make the "double movement" of regaining what he has lost through the "strength of the absurd" is a "knight of faith."[3] Kierkegaard indirectly accepts Kant's categorical imperative.[4] (1) He states that while the ethical is universal, it may lead to a "teleological suspension."[5] That is, from the standpoint of a higher religious objective, there are situations in which the ethical temporarily ceases to apply, such as when the ethically reprehensible act of killing a child becomes, under exceptional circumstances, religiously acceptable as a sacrificing of that child to God—that is Abraham's "paradox of faith." (2) Kierkegaard expresses this as an "absolute duty to God" and says that "in this tie of obligation the individual relates himself

---

2 Søren Kierkegaard, *Fear and Trembling* (trans. Alastair Hannay; London: Penguin Books, 1985 [first published in 1843]). [Translator's note: Whereas in the original version of this chapter the author generally gives his own Japanese translations of quotations, this English translation draws on published English works when readily available or unless otherwise noted. Citations of original non-English works are given in parentheses for certain works below. English quotations of other non-English works are my translations.]

3 Ibid., 65 ff.

4 Søren Kierkegaard, *Osore to Ononoki, Kirukegōru Chosaku-shū Dai 5-kan* (Fear and Trembling, Vol. 5 of Kierkegaard's Collected Works) (trans. Keizaburō Masuda; Tokyo: Hakusuisha, 1962), from the translator's commentary on p. 364.

5 Kierkegaard, *Fear and Trembling*, 83 ff.

absolutely, as the single individual, to the absolute" and "relinquishes the universal."[6] This is a "lonely path," so (3) Abraham cannot be held ethically accountable for not divulging his intentions to Isaac and others.[7] Rather, it is silence and secrecy that make a man truly great, and Abraham must be praised because he lived out this kind of faith that is "the ultimate passion in man."

The above is a bare-bones view of the portrayal of Abraham in *Fear and Trembling*.

1.2 Westermann's Critique

From the perspective of Old Testament studies, a commentary by Claus Westermann has cast doubt on Kierkegaard's interpretation.[8] Kierkegaard was unaware of the problem of source layers, and so of course he could not even imagine literary-critical and redaction-critical problems arising from secondary additions and the like. Based among other reasons on the view that verses 15–18, which praise Abraham, are an addition from a later period, Westermann argues, however, as follows:

> It is a misunderstanding of the narrative to hear it as the song of praise of a person ... It seems to me ... that when one refers the praise to Abraham (Kierkegaard), one has not understood the narrative ... The narrative looks not to the praise of a creature, but to the praise of God [who saw the suffering].[9]

If we restrict ourselves to the original text, problems such as this arise in Kierkegaard's interpretation. Yet is Westermann's alternative conclusion satisfactory? Is praise of God the aim of this text?

---

6 Ibid., 96 ff.
7 Ibid., 109 ff.
8 Claus Westermann, *Genesis 12–36* (trans. John J. Scullion; Minneapolis: Fortress Press, 1995); translation of *Genesis 12–36* (Neukirchen: Neukirchener Verlag, 1981).
9 Ibid., 365 (1981, p. 447). The bracketed phrase "who saw the suffering" does not appear in the original commentary. I have based this on Tetsuo Yamaga's translation of Westermann's KBB commentary (an abbreviated version of his BK commentary) in *Sōseki*, 1 (Genesis, Vol. 1) (Tokyo: Kyo Bun Kwan, 1993), 371–72.

1.3 Questions for Westermann

Let us reconsider now the God depicted in this text. Here, God is a god who commands bloody filicide (v. 2). Even if we suppose, with Kierkegaard, that God transcends the ethical and may require whatsoever he wishes, it is a contradictory god who on the one hand commands not to kill (Exod 20:13, etc.) and on the other commands filicide. What is more, perhaps God gave this command to test Abraham's obedience (vv. 1, 12), and perhaps it stemmed from God's jealousy of Isaac (Exod 34:14; Deut 4:24; 6:15; etc.). Furthermore, if it was "God's plan from the beginning" that nothing happen to the child, as Westermann claims,[10] and if Abraham believed all along that he would not lose Isaac, as Kierkegaard says,[11] this is tantamount to Abraham seeing through this test by God from the outset. Although Westermann calls God the "God who saw the suffering," this is only natural because it was God himself who gave the suffering in the first place, so it is not clear why he merits praise for taking away the suffering at the appropriate moment.

From this perspective, it seems there is no need to agree with Westermann's conclusion. Instead, we must confront the text with our candid questions on its portrayal of God and then listen to the text's response. If, then, we wish to understand the history of interpretation on this issue, above and beyond theological works that presuppose Christian faith (including those of historical-critical Old Testament scholars), we can find sustained interest in these questions in statements by philosophers who do not presuppose faith. That is why examining "philosophical interpretations of the sacrifice of Isaac" is the focus of this chapter. In fact, besides Kierkegaard, the concept of God in the Akedah has stimulated the thinking of Kant and many other modern philosophers down to the present day. Below, let us take a critical look at several leading interpretations.[12]

---

10 Westermann, *Genesis 12–36*, 361 (1981, p. 442).

11 Kierkegaard, *Fear and Trembling*, 65.

12 The following two essays that deal with how modern philosophers have approached this text differently from historical-critical biblical scholars also merit special attention: Marianus Bieber, "Religiöser Wahn oder Urerfahrung des Glaubens? Die Deutung des Abraham-Opfers im neuzeitlichen Denken," *Una Sancta* 51/4 (1996) 316–28; and Xavier Tilliette, "Bible et Philosophie: le sacrifice d'Abraham," *Gregorianum* 77/1 (1996) 133–46. Both essays refer to Kant and Kierkegaard. Bieber's essay also introduces the works of L. Kolakowski and F. W. J. Schelling, while Tilliette's essay introduces those of L. Schestow, R. Maritain, and G. Lequier. Also see, for instance, Jürgen Ebach, "*Theo*dizee: Fragen gegen die Antworten. Anmerkungen zur biblischen Erzählung von der "Bindung Isaaks" (I.Mose 22)," in *Philosophische Orientierung. Festschrift zum 65. Geburtstag von Will Oelmüller* (eds. F. Hermanni and V. Steenblock; München: W. Fink Verlag, 1995), 215–39; Hartmut Rosenau, "Die Erzählung von Abrahams Opfer (Gen 22) und ihre Deu-

2 Interpretations by Kant, Buber, Levinas, Derrida, and Miyamoto, and a Critical Summary

2.1 Kant's Interpretation

In his 1798 *Der Streit der Fakultäten* ("The Contest of the Faculties"), Immanuel Kant refers to the Akedah and declares it impossible that a god who makes a demand such as this, which violates moral law, could be the true God. Kant makes the interesting statement that Abraham should have replied as follows:

> The fact that I should not kill my good son is absolutely certain. But that you who appear to me are God, I am not certain and can never become certain.[13]

Though perhaps obvious when viewed in the light of Kant's categorical imperative, surely the first half of the reply that Kant desires of Abraham was not "absolutely certain" within the ancient religio-cultural context that governed the author's composition of this narrative.[14] It is likely that through influences from the Moloch cult the tradition of firstborn sacrifice also existed in Israel (Exod 22:28 is from the JE source, the traditional core of which is thought to date back to the thirteenth to twelfth centuries BCE) and that the understanding that God requires ethical practice and religious faith rather than this sort of cultic sacrifice was not expressed until the latter half of the eighth century BCE, through the prophet

---

tung bei Kant, Kierkegaard und Schelling," *Neue Zeitschrift für Systematische Theologie und Religionsphilosophie* 27 (1985) 251–61.

13 Immanuel Kant, *Der Streit der Fakultäten* (Philosophische Bibliothek 252; Hamburg: Meiner, 1959 [first published 1798]), 62.

14 In modern biblical scholarship the author has generally been identified as the Elohist. See, for instance, Hermann Gunkel, *Genesis* (9. Aufl.; Göttingen: Vandenhoeck & Ruprecht, 1977), 236–42; Gerhard von Rad, *Genesis: A Commentary* (trans. John H. Marks; Old Testament Library; rev. ed.; Philadelphia: Westminster Press, 1972), 238 (*Genesis* [Das Alte Testament Deutsch; Göttingen: Vandenhoeck & Ruprecht, 1981 (11. aufl.)], 189); and more recently, Ludwig Schmidt, "Weisheit und Geschichte beim Elohisten," in *"Jedes Ding hat seine Zeit ...": Studien zur israelitischen und altorientalischen Weisheit. Diethelm Michel zum 65. Geburtstag* (eds. A. Diesel et al.; BZAW 241; Berlin: W. de Gruyter, 1996), 209–25. In recent years, however, the consensus has been shaken. Georg Steins (*Die "Bindung Isaaks" im Kanon [Gen 22]. Grundlagen und Programm einer kanonisch-intertextuellen Lektüre* [Herder: Freiburg, 1999]), for example, counts it as one of the latest texts in the Pentateuch, not as a product of Israel's earliest period. Heinz-Dieter Neef (*Die Prüfung Abrahams: Eine exegetisch-theologische Studie zu Gen 22,1–19* [Arbeiten zur Theologie, Bd. 90; Stuttgart: Calwer Verlag, 1998], viii, 1–102, esp. 10–15) also concludes that it is not Elohistic but was composed after the Jehovist and before the Deuteronomist. At the earliest, therefore, Neef dates it to the late 7th century BCE.

Micah. Therefore the move toward replacing firstborn sacrifice with animal sacrifice—which is the position of the biblical law as it has been handed down to us—would have begun in the seventh to sixth centuries BCE (Exod 13:12–13 is JE; Exod 34:19–20 is also JE; Num 3:44 ff. is P). If the author of the Akedah was the Elohist of the early eighth century BCE, he might well have viewed Abraham's obedience to God's demand that he sacrifice his firstborn as his natural response to the law. Even if we follow many recent scholars and date it to the seventh to sixth centuries BCE,[15] it is reasonable to assume that the custom of firstborn sacrifice remained a common practice. Because any author would have been constrained by his own historical-traditional context, for interpreters to criticize and attempt to modify this point based on modern and foreign conceptual categories, as did Kant, is to overstep their bounds.[16]

But what about Kant's latter point?[17] This cannot necessarily be dismissed as nothing more than a foreign, philosophical understanding of the transcendent that ignores the Bible's tradition history. If we resituate this problem in the biblical context, it accords with the following suggestion by Martin Buber.

2.2 Buber's Interpretation

In his essay "On the Suspension of the Ethical,"[18] Martin Buber does not cite Kant, but he criticizes Kierkegaard as follows:

> He does not take into consideration the fact that the problematics of the decision of faith is preceded by the problematics of the hearing itself. Who is it whose voice one hears? For Kierkegaard it is self-evident because of the Christian tradition in which he grew up that he who demands the sacrifice is none other than God. But for the Bible, at least for the Old Testament, it is not without further question self-evident. Indeed a certain "instigation"

---

15 See, for example, Neef, *Die Prüfung Abrahams* (also see others in the above note).
16 It is possible to defend Kant on the grounds that, although he was probably aware of this point, in the end he was speaking from the perspective of philosophical thought as a professor in the philosophy department. Whatever the case, the text of Genesis 22 itself does not present firstborn sacrifice as something that is unproblematic for humans. Rather, verses 12 ff. reach a conclusion that denies the need for firstborn sacrifice. I shall discuss this point further below.
17 Kant further explains his view as follows: "Even if God truly speaks to man, he can never *know* that it is God who speaks to him. It is utterly impossible that man should understand the Infinite through his senses, distinguish him from sensory beings, and thereby *know* him" (Kant, *Der Streit der Fakultäten*, 62; italics in original).
18 Martin Buber, *Eclipse of God: Studies in the Relation between Religion and Philosophy* (New York: Harper & Row, 1952), 113–20; translation of *Gottesfinsternis. Betrachtungen zur Beziehung zwischen Religion und Philosophie* (Zürich: Manesse Verlag, 1953), 138–44.

to a forbidden action is even ascribed in one place to God (2 Samuel 24:1) and in another to Satan (1 Chronicles 21:1).[19]

According to Buber, "Moloch imitates the voice of God." Of course, Abraham, as God's chosen one, "could not confuse with another the voice which once bade him leave his homeland and which he at that time recognized as the voice of God."[20] It is possible, however, that "you and I," who are not exceptional figures like Abraham, might confuse the voice of the true God with the voice of Moloch commanding unethical filicide. We must know that God demands of ordinary people such as ourselves not unethical sacrifices but the ethical requirement only "to do justice, and to love kindness, and to walk humbly with your God" (Mic 6:8). "Where, therefore, the 'suspension' of the ethical is concerned, the question of questions which takes precedence over every other is: Are you really addressed by the Absolute or by one of his apes?"[21] Buber's contention in his 1953 *Eclipse of God* was that today is an age in which "[false absolutes] pierce unhindered through the level of the ethical and demand of you 'the sacrifice'."[22]

2.3 Levinas's Interpretation

About a decade after Buber, in the mid-1960s, Emmanuel Levinas presented his critique of Kierkegaard on the same theme in two essays.[23] Here is the crux of his critique from the second essay:

> Ethics as consciousness of a responsibility [*responsabilité*] toward others ... far from losing you in generality, singularizes you, poses you as a unique individual, as *I*. Kierkegaard seems not to have experienced that, since he wants to transcend the ethical stage, which to him is the stage of generality. In his evocation of Abraham, he describes the encounter with God at the point where subjectivity rises to the level of the religious, that is to say, above ethics.
>
> But one could think the opposite: Abraham's attentiveness to the voice that led him back to the ethical order, in forbidding him to perform a human sacrifice, is the highest point in the drama. That he obeyed the first voice [commanding sacrifice] is astonishing: that he had sufficient distance with respect to that obedience to hear the second voice [forbidding sacrifice]—that is the essential.

---

19 Buber, *Eclipse of God*, 117–18 (1953, pp. 141–42).
20 Ibid., 118 (1953, p. 142).
21 Ibid., 118–19 (1953, pp. 142–43).
22 Ibid., 120 (1953, p. 144).
23 "Kierkegaard: Existence and Ethics" and "A Propos of 'Kierkegaard vivant,'" in Emmanuel Levinas, *Proper Names* (trans. Michael B. Smith; Stanford, Calif.: Stanford Univ. Press, 1996); translation of *Noms propres* ([Montpellier]: Fata Morgana, 1976).

Moreover, why does Kierkegaard never speak of the dialogue in which Abraham intercedes for Sodom and Gomorrah on behalf of the just who may be present there? Here, in Abraham, the precondition of any possible triumph of life over death is formulated.[24]

2.4 Derrida's Interpretation

Jacques Derrida is the only philosopher since Kierkegaard to publish his reflections on the Akedah in a monograph. The somewhat strange title of this 1992 work—"Donner la mort"[25]—carries a dual meaning. First, Abraham "gives death" to Isaac, in the sense that he sets out to kill his son. In the second sense, Abraham gives Isaac's death to God as a sacrifice.

Derrida discusses the meanings of *donner* ("give") and *don* ("gift," "donation") in Chapter 1 of "Donner la mort," but he explains them in even more detail in *Donner le temps: 1, Fausse monnaie*.[26] According to him there, *don*, or gift, is nothing other than an experience of impossibility. For example, suppose that A gives a gift to B. If it is truly a gift, A must not expect anything in return, and B must not feel indebted to reciprocate. Otherwise, it ceases to be a "gift" and becomes a circle of exchange or reciprocity (Derrida calls this *économie*). In fact, there is an aporia in the concept of "gift"—if either A or B perceives it as a "gift," it ceases to be just that. If so, points out Derrida, a gift, strictly speaking, is an impossibility because it cannot appear as a gift.[27]

Following Levinas, Derrida understands *responsabilité* as ability to respond,[28] and so he pays close attention to Abraham's response of "Here I am" to God's call of "Abraham!" in the Akedah.[29] Derrida then attempts to reconsider Kierkegaard's interpretation of the Akedah as the paradox of responsibility. The paradox of responsibility refers to the dilemma between the responsibility of responding to God, who is uniquely and absolutely "wholly other," and the responsibility of responding to other "others."

---

24 Ibid., 76–77.
25 Jacques Derrida, *The Gift of Death* (trans. David Wills; Chicago: University of Chicago Press, 1995); translation of "Donner la mort" in *L'éthique du don* (ed. Jean-Michel Rabaté and Michael Wetzel; Paris: Métailié-Transition, 1992).
26 Jacques Derrida, *Donner le temps. 1, Fausse monnaie* ([Paris]: Galilée, 1991). In English, see Jacques Derrida, *Given Time. I, Counterfeit Money* (trans. Peggy Kamuf; Chicago: University of Chicago Press, 1992).
27 Derrida, *Donner le temps. 1, Fausse monnaie*, 17 ff.
28 Derrida, *The Gift of Death*, 3 (1992, p. 17).
29 Ibid., 71 (1992, p. 102).

Like Kierkegaard, Derrida focuses on Abraham's "secret."[30] He must make the decision on his own. Upon uttering language, one loses solitariness. If so, the decision must be reached without words, in the silence of one's secret closet. Derrida agrees with Kierkegaard that the bearing of absolute responsibility for such an act must then imply that one bears no responsibility to act or respond to others.

The contradiction between absolute responsibility and general ethical responsibility reaches its climax in the act of "giving death to Isaac."[31] Giving to the "wholly other" is fulfilled as "sacrifice" in an unethical act of hating one's beloved (Luke 14:26).

Derrida, however, considers Kierkegaard's "teleological suspension of the ethical" more generally within what Kierkegaard calls the religious stage. "Every other (one) is every (bit) other" (*tout autre est tout autre*).[32] The God Yahweh is not the only one who is uniquely and absolutely "wholly other." Isaac, Sarah, and Eliezer, too, are each unique and absolute others. Whoever the other, therefore, upon entering into a relationship with that other, a person is required to sacrifice all other others and respond to the calling of that unique and absolute other.

> As soon as I enter into a relation with the other, with the gaze, look, request, love, command, or call of the other, I know that I can respond only by sacrificing ethics, that is, by sacrificing whatever obliges me to also respond ... to all the others. I offer a gift of death, I betray ... Day and night, at every instant, on all the Mount Moriahs of this world, I am doing that, raising my knife over what I love and must love, over those to whom I owe absolute fidelity, incommensurably.[33]

2.5 Miyamoto's Interpretation

Hisao Miyamoto's "The Suffering of Abraham and the Horizon of the Other—From Bleached Narrative to *Hayatological* (Hebraic Ontology) Symbiosis" (2006) is the most meticulously and thoroughly argued work in recent years to present a philosophical interpretation of the Akedah with an eye to Kierkegaard and others.[34] Al-

---

30 Ibid., 58 ff. (1992, pp. 85 ff.).
31 Ibid., 65 ff. (1992, pp. 95 ff.).
32 Ibid., 68, 82 ff. (1992, pp. 97–98, 114 ff.).
33 Ibid., 68 (1992, p. 98); see Tetsuya Takahashi, *Derida: Datsu Kōchiku* ("Derrida: Deconstruction") (Tokyo: Kōdansha, 1998), 236.
34 Hisao Miyamoto, "Aburahamu no Junan to Tasha no Chihei: Hyōhaku no Monogatari kara Hayatorogia (Heburai-teki Sonzairon) teki Kyōsei e" (The Suffering of Abraham and the Horizon of the Other: From Bleached Narrative to *Hayatological* [Hebraic Ontology] Symbiosis), in *Junan no Imi: Aburahamu, Iesu, Pauro* (The Meaning of Suffering: Abraham, Jesus, and Paul) (eds.

though his work covers a wide range of issues (such as the distinction between *syntagme diachronique* and *paradigme synchronique*, the proposal and application of narratological interpretation, and the proposal of a Hebraic ontology), I shall limit my comments here to two of Miyamoto's newly proposed readings that relate to the subject of this chapter, interpretations of the Akedah.

Miyamoto sees two possible translations for the Hebrew preposition *le* in the latter half of verse 2: (1) "offer [Isaac] *as* a burnt offering," following most translations; or (2) "lift up [Isaac] on the mountain *in order to* offer a burnt offering." The first reading means accepting the unbearable fate of killing Abraham's beloved son, resulting in the revocation of God's promise (prosperity of the tribe).[35] This leads to absolutization of religious existence, as in Kierkegaard, and disregard of the ethical, as Levinas points out. The second reading, however, leads to privatization of God's blessing through Abraham and to a tribe-conquering narrative identity. Standing at the narrow path between religious absoluteness and self-absolutization, Abraham and the reader are at a loss and in agony. Miyamoto calls the dismantling and breaking down of one's identity "differentiation." For both Abraham and the reader, this agony forces the question of whether to cling to one's former self, and it becomes an opportunity to face self-differentiation.

According to Miyamoto, this self-differentiation can be seen in the strangely long and dispassionate depiction of Abraham's actions during the silent three-day journey in verses 3–4a. That is, if we interpret the significance of these three days of silence based on the viewpoint that Abraham and Isaac are physically a composite character portrayed as one flesh, the dual meaning of Derrida's *donner la mort*—i.e., (1) Abraham "gives death to Isaac" and (2) he "gives that death to God"—can be differentiated even further and taken to imply that (3) "Abraham gives death to himself." Miyamoto suggests that Abraham "like Moses asked God to kill him (Num 11:15)." This, argues Miyamoto, is "a third way to surpass the absolute aporia of the death of Isaac, his beloved son, and betrayal toward God."[36]

What Miyamoto means is as follows: "After killing Isaac, inasmuch as his own life would have become meaningless, he would not want to live any longer."[37] Furthermore, Abraham's death would be "the dissolution of his identi-

---

Hisao Miyamoto, Takashi Onuki, and Takashi Yamamoto; Tokyo: Tokyo University Press, 2006), 81–162.

35 On the view that this represents not only the revocation of the promise from God's side, but its revocation from humanity's side as well, see Konrad Schmid, "Die Rückgabe der Verheißungsgabe," in *Gott und Mensch im Dialog: Festschrift für Otto Kaiser zum 80. Geburtstag* (ed. Markus Witte; BZAW 345; Berlin: W. de Gruyter, 2004), 271–300.

36 Miyamoto, "Aburahamu no Junan to Tasha no Chihei," 114.

37 Ibid.

ty/self, which could be described as the body of Abraham deeply attached to Isaac," and it would simultaneously mean the dissolution of his own flesh and blood, "the entity of Isaac that was God's blessing in bodily form and privately appropriated by the tribe." "In the end, Abraham's death necessarily encompasses Isaac's death. When we consider this ... we cannot help but be struck with something akin to a feeling of awe over the profundity of Abraham's silent agony during his three-day journey."[38] Readers, too, while overcome by a presentiment of their own selves' dissolution, face the third day.

Miyamoto understands Abraham's statement to the young men that the two of them would return (v. 5) as Abraham's "final struggle" against the present threat of self-dissolution.[39] By the time of verse 8's *Elohim yir'e-lo hasse le-'ola beni*, however, Abraham has resolved to accept self-dissolution, and he makes a statement meaning "My son, God will provide me, Abraham [therefore including Isaac, his own flesh], as a sacrificial holocaust."[40] This is the first point of the new reading presented in Miyamoto's essay.

Miyamoto's other new reading relates to verses 12, 15–18. Having formally designated as "kenosis" (self-emptying) "the root dissolution" that happened to Abraham in the course of the struggle leading up to the slaying of Isaac, Miyamoto argues that it is the language of verse 12, where Isaac is called 'boy' instead of 'son,' that "indirectly indicates the depth of Abraham's kenosis by taking up a blade to cut off his own private ownership (my *son*), and Isaac's autonomization (boy) which results from that."[41] Furthermore, "Isaac ... is no longer the *son* of Abraham's flesh and blood; he is a purged *boy* of a different character. And now through Abraham, who is now newly born, and Isaac, who has been given once again, is told a narrative of reconciliation with a future other and of reciprocal blessing."[42] Miyamoto then takes verses 15–18, which are typically treated as a later addition, as original to the narrative and argues that "verse 18's 'and by your offspring shall all the nations of the earth gain blessing for themselves' can be understood as a differentiated expression that opens up a horizon of symbiosis."[43]

---

38 Ibid., 115.
39 Ibid.
40 Ibid., 116.
41 Ibid., 117.
42 Ibid., 118.
43 Ibid., 112.

2.6 Critical Summary

Here we have traced philosophers' interpretations of the Akedah, beginning with Kant and continuing through Kierkegaard, Buber, Levinas, Derrida, and Miyamoto. They candidly argue God's irrationality, Abraham's unethical compliance, and related issues in this narrative that theological interpretations tend to leave unquestioned. What can we gather from this discussion? While heeding their mutual criticisms, I shall contribute my own and attempt to draw these views together.

First, we notice that all interpreters since Kierkegaard use him as a springboard for discussion. Among these, Levinas is in all likelihood criticizing Kierkegaard based on a lapse of memory. Levinas argued that whereas Kierkegaard holds to a "teleological suspension of the ethical" for the sake of religious sacrifice, the point of the narrative is instead to lead "him back to the ethical order, in forbidding him to perform a human sacrifice." "Teleological Suspension of the Ethical" is a section heading in Kierkegaard's work, and this theme is widely known, but for Kierkegaard it does not all end with a "teleological suspension" that gives up by sacrificing the things of the world. Kierkegaard concludes by praising Abraham not as a "knight of resignation" but as a "knight of faith" who believed, on the strength of the absurd, that he would regain the sacrifice he relinquished.

In fact, if we reread Kierkegaard carefully, we see that his and Levinas's conclusions lead in the same direction. We must ask, however, whether these conclusions are appropriate interpretations of the text. Kierkegaard points to v. 8 as the decisive verse in this text.[44] He argues that Abraham's response to Isaac—"God himself will provide the lamb for a burnt offering ['ola], my son"—is evidence that Abraham continued to hold this kind of hope from faith. If so, however, it would mean that Abraham sees through it all, knowing that God will stop him when he raises his knife and that God will provide a lamb in Isaac's place. The entire story becomes a transparent ape act. One recalls von Rad's justifiable critique of Delitzsch, an Old Testament scholar who presented a similar interpretation based on his detection of an "intuitive hope" in verse 8: "It is given with 'tender love,' to be sure, but not with 'intuitive hope' (Del.), which would deprive the narrative of some of its most important substance."[45] In other words, the meaning of the "test" (v. 1) in this story should be Abraham's tempering through hopeless suffering. If Abraham entertains even a superficial hope

---

44 Kierkegaard, *Fear and Trembling*, 139–40. Levinas does not cite the text in his two short essays.
45 Von Rad, *Genesis*, 241 (1981, p. 191).

that Isaac will be restored to him, it is not a true test. This is a problem that remains with this interpretation.

Of course, Kierkegaard does not state that verse 8 is an effusion of manifest hope, but he skillfully argues that it is the necessary and exquisite response—impossible in any other form—of one who knows "agony," "angst," and "silence."[46] In this case, however, if Abraham somehow believed that Isaac would not be killed, then to put it in Derrida's terms, in the instant of giving, an exchange would recur in which the true gift that had severed the calculated economy is recouped back into a cycle of calculated economy. One cannot help but recall Derrida's penetrating way of putting it, though not directed at Kierkegaard: "It is given back to [Abraham] because he renounced calculation. Demystifiers of this superior or sovereign calculation that consists in no more calculating might say that he played his cards well."[47]

I cannot agree, therefore, with the thrust of the interpretations by Kierkegaard, Levinas, and Delitzsch, who see hope for recovery of the gift, receiving back the sacrifice, and reinstatement of the ethical. How about Derrida? Derrida has discussed the Akedah from more perspectives than any other philosopher since Kierkegaard, and he correctly points out the problem with Levinas's critique of Kierkegaard. If other people are also infinite others, maintains Derrida, it ought to be difficult to distinguish completely between one's relationship with God and one's relationship with another person. But Levinas draws too complete a distinction between the two because, for him, ethics is so deeply steeped in religion. At this point Derrida presents his proposition introduced above that "every other (one) is every (bit) other," and he replaces God in the Akedah with one of "every other (one)." Generally speaking, he says, this one other requires that I respond to none of every other one, except for him, and that I forsake them all. Therefore, Derrida proceeds to argue, Abraham, who follows God's command and raises his knife to slay Isaac on a mountain in Moriah, is in fact ourselves when we follow the demands of one other. This is an adaptation typical of Derrida, who professes "radical atheism" (though with the qualification that he "carries the memory of God").[48] We must, however, conclude that as an interpretation of the Akedah, whose subject is the preeminently religious problem between God and Abraham, it is an overly expansive interpretation that misses the vital point by turning the problem into one of ethical interpersonal relations.

---

46 Kierkegaard, *Fear and Trembling*, 137, 139.
47 Derrida, *The Gift of Death*, 97 (1992, pp. 132–33).
48 Takahashi, *Derida* ("Derrida"), 223.

It was Buber, rather, who correctly approached the problem of religion and ethics. He also criticized Kierkegaard for failing to address the question of whether a religion that commands the unethical is conveying the true voice of God.[49] The more religious a "sinful man," the more eager he will be to offer to God religious sacrifices that run contrary to interpersonal ethics in order to atone "for his sins."[50] The question is, is this valid?

This question has a broad contemporary scope. Buber's answer was as follows. Abraham was an exceptional figure and in a different class from Kierkegaard or any modern "you and I." God no longer gives us commands like that of the Akedah. On the contrary, ever since the prophet Micah, God commands only ethical acts.

In my view, however, Buber's argument must be challenged from several directions. First, on what basis does he distinguish so clearly between Abraham and us? If God's command to Abraham has nothing to do with us, does it mean that the author simply wrote a biography of a great hero? At the very least, it would seem that even Buber does not have the right to prohibit the interpretation of readers who take this question as directed at them. In the case of Kierkegaard, most likely prior to his interpretation of this text he sensed God's command to offer up Regina. Just because religious people sensitively perceive a conflict with ethics, they cannot jump to the conclusion that it is a deception by Moloch. Furthermore, Buber argues as if people offer sacrifices solely to atone for their sins. Yet other fundamental reasons for offering sacrifices should not be ruled out, such as when one wishes to offer God one's most prized possession or when one wishes to return a gift to the divine giver out of recognition that all of one's possessions are gifts from God. It seems that Buber's view of the significance of sacrifice is too narrow and that he is not free from the prejudice that a Christian sense of guilt leads to excessive sacrifice. In view of the above, I think that Buber's critique of Kierkegaard does not necessarily hit the mark either.

Let me refer back to the interpretation by Miyamoto, who has attempted a dynamic reading of this text, which he has formulated as "a narrative of reconciliation with a future other and of reciprocal blessing" through Abraham's kenosis.[51] I agree with many of Miyamoto's ideas, but here I must focus on interpretive issues. He presented two new interpretive proposals. Let us start by considering the second one.

---

49 Buber, *Eclipse of God*, 118 (1953, p. 142).
50 Buber, *Gottesfinsternis*, 162.
51 Miyamoto, "Aburahamu no Junan to Tasha no Chihei," 118.

Miyamoto argues that we should read the words of Yahweh's angel in verse 12, where he calls Isaac "the boy" instead of "your son," as evidence that Abraham has severed his own private ownership and that Isaac has become autonomous. Yet it is very common in Biblical Hebrew for "son" (*ben*) and "boy" (*na'ar*) to occur alternately (e. g., see Judg 13:5, 7, 24; 1Sam 2:21; 17:55, 58; 2Sam 13:32; Prov 7:7; Hos 11:1). It is a bit too fanciful, therefore, to detect any intentional significance in this shift. In the same verse 12, in fact, immediately after God says "Do not lay your hand on the boy [*na'ar*]," he alternates again and says "since you have not withheld your son [*ben*], your only son." In addition, Abraham already calls Isaac *na'ar* in Gen 22:5, before matters come to a head.

Nevertheless, Miyamoto continues by treating verses 15–18, which are typically regarded as a later addition, as original to the narrative, and he argues that "verse 18's 'and by your offspring shall all the nations of the earth gain blessing for themselves' can be understood as a differentiated expression that opens up a horizon of symbiosis."[52] It appears, however, that the preceding verse 17—"I will make your offspring as numerous as the stars of heaven ... And your offspring shall possess the gate of their enemies"—speaks of conquest of the other, rather than "reconciliation with the other," and has as its chief concern "prosperity of one's (the tribe's) identity."[53] Furthermore, v. 16's "your son [*ben*], your only son" repeats the language of verse 12 and thereby undermines Miyamoto's conclusion that the text reflects a shift of interest from "the 'son' of Abraham's flesh and blood" to "a purged 'boy' of a different character."

Miyamoto also forces the mysterious conclusion in verse 19, which makes no reference to Isaac, to fit his interpretive formulation. He states, "If Isaac did not return to Beer-sheba with Abraham but went in a separate direction, we can read from this—together with the severance of flesh and blood relations between father and son through Abraham's kenosis—the emergence of a new relationship of otherness for the two; a horizon of otherness that transcends the tribe is opened."[54] Instead it is highly probable that this shows only that the story of Abraham concentrates on Abraham and that Isaac is merely a supporting character in it.

This point is of no small significance. Isaac plays no more than a supporting role in this narrative. Therefore, we should not focus excessively on matters such as his character or rights and thereby read a different meaning into this narrative, which concentrates on the binary relationship between Abraham and God.[55]

---

52 Ibid., 112.
53 Ibid., 116.
54 Ibid., 119.
55 Recently, while referring to the psychoanalyst J. Lacan, who interpreted the Abraham narrative by linking Abraham to ancient patriarchy, Jean-Daniel Causse has argued that Genesis 22

Let us return, now, to Miyamoto's first proposal. He reads into verse 8 Abraham's anticipation of his own death. Indeed, this would seem an excellent interpretation. If we can understand it in this way, the irrationality of the narrative dissipates, and instead the "profundity of Abraham's agony"[56] is cast in even greater relief. The question, however, hinges on whether it is appropriate to understand the narrative this way. Again, the context does not appear to support this position.

Firstly, as Miyamoto himself recognizes, the standard translation of verse 8 is "God himself will provide [*yir'e*] the lamb for a burnt offering, my son." Here the "lamb" refers to the "ram" caught in a thicket in verse 13 and, the author proceeds to explain, this is why this place is called "Yahweh will provide [*yir'e*]." Nowhere does it seem that the author intends to identify Abraham as "the lamb." Secondly, and even more pointedly, in the climax in verse 10 Abraham "took the knife to kill" not himself, but Isaac.

Of course, Miyamoto is saying that Abraham's slaying of Isaac would mean, in terms of "corporate personality," the slaying of Abraham himself, who is of one flesh with his son. This is why Miyamoto maintains that Abraham's "self-dissolution privately appropriates God's blessing and is dissolution of 'the effort of existence' which strives for prosperity of one's (the tribe's) identity. It is the root of identity, therefore, and it is nothing other than dissolution that extends to dissolution of himself and Isaac, his own flesh."[57]

H. W. Robinson's "corporate personality"[58] refers to ancient ways of thinking in which the individual and the group are fluidly and symbiotically connected. It includes both the aspect of the individual as individual and the aspect of the individual as a member of the group. It seems, however, that Miyamoto has emphasized only the latter aspect, largely overlooking the former. Although Miyamoto only emphasizes their union as "one flesh," Abraham and Isaac are of course also two separate individuals. Unless one ignores this point, Abraham's killing of Isaac should remain an ethical stumbling block.

---

is particularly marked by its functioning as a narrative directed toward opening the child's future through ceremoniously offering up an archaic figure, rather than as a narrative in which Abraham demonstrates his patriarchal authority ("Le jour où Abraham céda sur sa foi. Lecture psycho-anthropologique de Genèse 22," *Études Théologiques et Religieuses* 76/4 [2001] 563–73). For another essay that concentrates on the figure of Isaac—i.e., on the trauma that he suffered through the Akedah, with reference to interpretations up to early midrashic texts—see Murray J. Kohn, "The Trauma of Isaac," *Jewish Biblical Quarterly* 20/2 (1991–1992): 96–104.

56 Miyamoto, "Aburahamu no Junan to Tasha no Chihei," 115.

57 Ibid., 116.

58 H. Wheeler Robinson, *Corporate Personality in Ancient Israel* (Philadelphia: Fortress Press, 1964).

Let us return to the beginning of our argument. If Miyamoto's excellent proposal is beset with interpretive weaknesses such as those mentioned above, then we must conclude that this narrative's unethical irrationality, which has attracted the attention of modern philosophers since Kant, remains unsolved. Derrida wanders in the wrong direction when he reads this religious narrative as a problem of ethics of otherness. And if the criticisms by Buber and Levinas in response to Kierkegaard, who tends to absolutize religious faith, are inadequate, must we return to Kierkegaard after all? Even setting aside the question of the merits of Westermann's argument against reading the account as praise of Abraham, we were forced to conclude that Kierkegaard's emphasis on the hope of the knight of faith misses the vital point of this narrative which, from the outset, is presented as a test.

Now that we have traced the line of philosophical interpretations that have in some way problematized God's unreasonableness and Abraham's unethicality and attempted to solve this issue from various directions, must we give up at this point and agree with Kant that God's command and Abraham's response were both wrong, thereby exerting our own violence on the text in order to rework the narrative into something more palatable to our tastes?

In my view, there remains one other path for a philosophical interpretation. It is the path suggested by Kitarō Nishida, a leading philosopher of modern Japan, who was most likely inspired by Hegel. Their philosophical review of the concept of God should carry inescapable weight with everyone who discusses religion in a form that does not conflict with post-Enlightenment rationality. Regrettably, however, this appears to have been neglected in Old Testament interpretation. While keeping the results of Old Testament scholarship in mind, I wish to devote the rest of this chapter to pursuing this possibility of a philosophical interpretation, a new possibility that has been unattainable within traditional interpretation.

3 Examining the Theory that Treats Verses 15 – 19 as a Later Accretion

3.1 Translation of Verses 15 – 19 and Notes

First, let us read the conclusion to the Akedah.

15 The angel of Yahweh once again called Abraham from heaven, 16 and he said, "I swear upon myself—this is the oracle of Yahweh. Because you have done this thing,[59] and you

---

[59] Notice the correspondence to "these things" in verse 1.

have not withheld your son, your only son,[60] 17 Truly, I will bless you abundantly, and I will abundantly increase your descendants like the stars of heaven and like the sand on the seashore. And your descendants shall possess the gate of their enemies. 18 All nations of the earth shall be blessed by your descendants. That is your reward for listening to and following my voice."[61] 19 And Abraham returned to his young servants. They arose and went together[62] to Beer-sheba.[63] Abraham lived in Beer-sheba.

3.2 Grounds for Treating Verses 15–19 as a Later Accretion

Verses 15 to 19 have been treated by many influential commentators such as Westermann, introduced above, as a later addition to the text. Previously, I also simply thought that these verses spoke of nationalistic retribution in contrast to the psychologically-interested and stoic text up to verse 14, and so I thought the latter verses did not originally belong to the text. Upon conducting a detailed examination of the theory that regards verses 15 to 19 as a later accretion, however, I have come to the conclusion that this view is not necessarily compelling. Because von Rad's grounds for treating all the verses in 15–19 as a later accretion (160–61)[64] overlap with Westermann's grounds for treating verses 15 to 18 as an accretion (169),[65] I shall sum them up and briefly consider each reason in turn. (The grounds offered by recent scholars such as Moberly, Veijola,

---

60 The Samaritan Pentateuch, Septuagint, Peshitta, and Vulgate add *mimmeni* after *yechidekha*. It thus means the same as verse 12's "you have not withheld your son, your only son, from me." Though BHS proposes this reading in its notes, it is more likely that these passages were not harmonized in the original text. From a text-critical perspective, therefore, it is difficult to dismiss the Masoretic reading that is reflected in BHS, so I have adopted it for my own translation.
61 Though it is standard to translate 'eqeb 'asher as "because," I have distinguished it from ki, which indicates a reason (see vv. 12 and 16).
62 The term *yachdav* is used in verses 6 and 8 to indicate that Abraham and Isaac went "together," but for some reason Isaac does not appear in verse 19.
63 An oasis in southern Palestine. The name means "seven springs" (Gen 21:28 ff.) or "spring of oath" (Gen 21:31). Abraham originally lived here (Gen 21:25 ff.), and according to a different tradition, Isaac also lived and built an altar here (Gen 26:23 ff.).
64 Von Rad, *Genesis*, 237–38 (1981, pp. 192–93). Here and below, numbers in parentheses following names of interpreters are page numbers in my anthology, *Aburahamu no Isaku Kenkyō Monogatari* (The Story of Abraham's Sacrifice of Isaac), which I introduced in note 1. I have included them here for the convenience of readers who understand Japanese. For the majority of readers who do not understand Japanese, I have cited original works in the notes. For an English introduction of my anthology, see the following blog post by J. Randall Short, an American Old Testament scholar who is proficient in Japanese and is the translator of this volume: <http://www.japanesebiblicalstudies.com/2012/10/09/an-anthology-of-akedah-stories-in-japanese/>.
65 Westermann, *Genesis 12–36*, 363 (1981, p. 445).

and Ruppert for attributing these to a redactor in the Josianic period are very similar.[66] Wenham, on the other hand, is against treating them as a later accretion, for reasons that I shall discuss below.)

(1) The story's internal structure comes to a completion in verse 14. Also, from the perspective of the cultic purposes that the narrative serves, it is fitting for it to conclude with a theophany, an offering of sacrifice, and the naming of a holy place. (2) The original narrative is an ancient cultic legend. The accretion, however, is different in that it aims to establish a connection to the promise motif that runs through and connects the Abraham story in chapters 12 onward. (3) The style of the accretion praises Abraham enthusiastically, to the point of being excessive. The style of the original text is quite different in that it is extremely restrained. (4) In no other similar scenes does God say "I swear upon myself." (5) From a stylistic point of view, it is quite odd for God to speak of his own words as "this is the oracle of Yahweh." (6) To say that Abraham's descendants "shall possess the gate of their enemies" does not match fundamental aspects of the promise in the Abraham story (12:1– 3, 7; 13:14 – 16; 15:7, 18; 24:7; 26:3, 4, 24).

3.3 Examining the Theory that Treats Verses 15 – 19 as a Later Accretion

Having established the primary grounds of the accretion theory, I now wish to examine each of these reasons critically.

Let us first look at (1). Under his topic "Temptation," Von Rad himself (156) says that although temptations (or tests) can be traced back to divination in cultic settings (Exod 15:25b; 2Kgs 8:31– 32), the form they take in the Akedah and similar historical settings wherein Israel and individuals are subjected to temptation or testing "is to be understood as a suppression of the ritual and an exit from the cultic realm."[67] We must conclude, then, that it is logically inconsistent to argue that cultic purposes are prominently evident in this text.

Concerning (2), I would point out again that it is inappropriate to treat the original narrative as "cultic legend." Furthermore, the original narrative already presupposes the motif of promise found throughout the Abraham story. "These

---

66 R. Walter L. Moberly, "The Earliest Commentary on the Akedah," *Vetus Testamentum* 38 (1988): 302– 23; Timo Veijola, "Das Opfer des Abraham: Paradigma des Glaubens aus dem nachexilischen Zeitalter," *Zeitschrift für Theologie und Kirche* 85 (1988): 129 – 64; Lothar Ruppert, *Genesis. Ein kritischer und theologischer Kommentar, 11:27– 25:18* (Forschung zur Bibel; Würzburg: Echter Verlag, 2002), 514 ff.
67 Von Rad, *Genesis*, 234 – 35 (1981, p. 190).

things" in verse 1's "After these things[68] came to pass[69]" relate to the story of the covenant with Abraham in chapters 12 onward—namely, to God's promise and his fulfillment of the promise in Isaac. That is precisely why it is a "test" for Abraham to offer "your only son, whom you love." If this is true, we must conclude that the account in verses 1 to 14 and the account in verses 15 to 19 both relate to the promise motif.

Assessment of style along the lines of (3) is quite subjective. On the contrary, it is also possible to regard the style as brilliantly expressing the contrast between restrained emotions before Abraham passes the test and the relief that comes afterward.

(4) is von Rad's assertion, but Westermann points out that this expression occurs in Exodus 32:13: "Remember Abraham, Isaac, and Israel, your servants, how you swore to them by your own self, saying to them, 'I will multiply your descendants like the stars of heaven, and all this land that I have promised I will give to your descendants, and they shall inherit it forever'" (NRSV; also see Gen 15).

As is well known, the expression in (5) occurs frequently in the prophets, and it is not unusual to see third-person and first-person forms mixed together (Isa 1:24; 3:15; 14:22, 23; etc.). Von Rad dates the accretion to the period immediately following the Elohist (160),[70] and Westermann supposes that it belongs to a period that begins with the prophets and presupposes Deuteronomistic theology (169).[71] It would not have been at all unusual for an author who was a contemporary of the prophets, or perhaps who came a little afterward, to speak this way.

As evidence for (6), von Rad cites passages related to the promise motif surrounding the Akedah. Upon closer examination, however, we find that "fundamental aspects" related to "shall possess the gate of their enemies" are not necessarily absent. For example, the God who says "the one who curses you I will curse" in 12:3 indicates enmity against Abraham's enemies, and 12:7 ("Yahweh appeared to Abram, and said, 'To your offspring I will give this land'") is a statement that must presuppose conflict with the native inhabitants. More specific is the narrative in 15:18–21: "On that day Yahweh made a covenant with Abram,

---

68 The term *dabar* can mean both "things" and "words." Also see verse 16.

69 In general Hebrew usage, a temporal particle following *wayehi* indicates a new pericope (Wilhelm Gesenius=E. Kautzsch, *Hebräische Grammatik* [New York: G. Olms, 1995], 111 g), thus typically resulting in, for instance, "After these things God tested Abraham" (NRSV). Translated literally, however, it becomes "When it became [the time] after these things," so I have emphasized this nuance in my translation.

70 Von Rad, *Genesis* (1981), 192.

71 Westermann, *Genesis 12–36*, 363–64 (1981, p. 445).

saying, 'To your descendants I give this land, from the river of Egypt to the great river, the river Euphrates, the land of the Kenites, the Kenizzites, the Kadmonites, the Hittites, the Perizzites, the Rephaim, the Amorites, the Canaanites, the Girgashites, and the Jebusites.'" Specifically, it can only mean that Abram "shall possess the gate" of these various "enemies" and take away the land of the native inhabitants. Chapter 14 appears to be indifferent to matters concerning Abraham's self-defense and property, but we can gather that in fact he lived in the midst of battles. In short, 22:17's statement "shall possess the gate of their enemies" is not necessarily dissimilar to the fundamental aspects of the promise running throughout the Abraham story. Furthermore, whereas (6) asserts that 22:15 ff. is an accretion because it is different from the promise motif in other passages in the Abraham story, (2) says it is an accretion because it has the same aim as the promise motif elsewhere. These are contradictory reasons.

Based on the above examination, we must conclude that each of the primary grounds for the accretion theory is weak. On the other hand, are there any positive reasons for viewing verses 15 ff. as authentic? In fact, research in recent years has found at least a few strong reasons.[72]

First, without the promise concerning the propagation and prosperity of Abraham's descendants through Isaac in verses 15 ff., the Abraham story would come to an end having emphasized more strongly the promise to Hagar and Ishmael (21:18). This would create a significant problem, as the covenant promise that Isaac, the rightful heir, would be a king of nations (17:16 – 19) would be left unresolved.

Second, in view of the internal structure of the Akedah, the narrative would be incomplete without reference to the "reward" (v. 18) in verses 15 onward. The trials that Noah and Job encountered are representative cases in the Old Testament, and these stories find their resolution with Noah and Job being rewarded after their trials (Gen 9:1 – 17; Job 42:10 – 17).

The third reason, though less conclusive, lies in the fact that there is correspondence in God's speech at the beginning of the Abraham story, in chapter 12, and at the end, in chapter 22. The story begins with "go" (*lekh lekha*) to "the land" (*'erets*) that God will "show" you (12:1; 22:2), and one expects it to end with the result of his going, namely, "all" (*kol*) the nations of the earth being

---

72 See Gordon Wenham, *Genesis 16 – 50*, Vol. 2 (Word Biblical Commentary 2; Dallas, Tex.: Word, 1994), 101 – 3, 111, which I did not include above. Also see John van Seters, *Abraham in History and Tradition* (New Haven, Conn.: Yale University Press, 1975), 239; George W. Coats, "Abraham's Sacrifice of Faith: A Form-Critical Study of Genesis 22," *Interpretation* 27 (1973): 389 – 400; T. Desmond Alexander, "Genesis 22 and the Covenant of Circumcision," *Journal for the Study of the Old Testament* 25 (1983): 17 – 22.

"blessed" (*barakh*) through Abraham and his descendants (12:3; 22:18). Without verses 15 ff., however, it seems that this expectation would be left unresolved.

3.4 The Theory that Treats Verse 19 as a Later Accretion

Hence none of the six grounds of the theory that regards verses 15 ff. as an accretion are necessarily persuasive, and it seems more reasonable to treat them as original to the narrative. I do, however, regard verse 19 as an accretion. Westermann (169) comments that "verse 19 should be read as the immediate continuation of verse 14a ... Abraham returns to Isaac and his servant, and they return together to Beersheba."[73] However, this is not accurate. There is no mention of Isaac in verse 19. "Abraham" alone "returned to his young servants"—Isaac's whereabouts are unclear (Westermann notes that "together" [*yachdav*] refers to Abraham, Isaac, the young servants, and the donkey, but we must conclude that the strangeness of the third-person, masculine, singular verb "returned" [*wayyashob*] remains[74]). Up until verse 14, however, the story is about God, Abraham, and Isaac, and one would not expect the original author to forget any one of these three chief characters. That is so even if the main focus of the original narrative was Abraham's obedience and God's blessing (Wenham, 195).[75] It also appears that Miyamoto's theory (295) reads a bit too much into verse 19, at which point in the narrative any reference to Isaac has disappeared, when he says, "If Isaac did not return to Beer-sheba with Abraham but went in a separate direction, we can read from this—together with the severance of flesh and blood relations between father and son ... —the emergence of a new relationship of otherness for the two."[76] Additionally, there is no reference to Beer-sheba in the original narrative. The nearest mention of it is in 21:31–34. In the light of this, it is most logical to understand 22:19 as a redactional verse by an editor who placed the Akedah after 21:31–34 and as a somewhat careless redaction that forgets to mention Isaac.

In sum, if the Akedah contains any later accretion, it is only verse 19. As I have concluded above, we cannot identify any accretions among verses 15–18 because the grounds for treating any of these verses as an accretion are weak and, conversely, there are strong reasons for regarding them as original to the narrative. Later,

---

73 Westermann, *Genesis 12–36*, 364 (1981, p. 446).
74 Westermann, BK, I/2, 446.
75 Wenham, *Genesis 16–50*, 112.
76 Miyamoto, "Aburahamu no Junan to Tasha no Chihei," 119.

while drawing on other considerations, I shall return to a consideration of how this conclusion relates to the interpretation of the Akedah as a whole.

4 A Reconstruction of the Dialogue among God, Abraham, and Isaac, and their States of Mind

4.1 Silence or Dialogue

Surveying the history of interpretation and reading the text anew presents us with one more point of controversy to reconsider. This is the question of whether or not we should understand that a profound silence prevailed among God, Abraham, and Isaac throughout the ordeal. Under the influence of Kierkegaard, who, as noted above, emphasized the silence, influential scholars such as Jacob[77] and von Rad (158)[78] have traditionally taken the position that a silence literally prevailed among them. Among those who have taken this position, Auerbach's emphasis on this point, based on stylistic considerations drawn from a comparison with Homeric literature, has also been influential (216).[79] In the history of interpretation of the Akedah, the ancient reconstruction by Josephus of the dialogue among the three figures certainly merits attention for its rich imagination (39 – 42). While deeply interested in the contents of the dialogue that Josephus has them speak, I expressed in an earlier work my apprehensions that Josephus' reconstructed dialogue is far removed from the actual speech in the Akedah (Sekine, 317).[80] Upon a careful re-reading of the text, however, I became aware that the author of the Akedah does not necessarily presume that silence prevailed among the three. On the contrary, the author assumes that there was dialogue, but he omits it as a narrative technique for the sake of moving the story along. For instance, let us consider the following passage while paying special attention to the underlined phrases.

---

77 Benno Jacob, *Das Erste Buch der Tora—Genesis* (Berlin: Schocken Verlag, 1934), 496; cited in von Rad, *Genesis*, 236 (1981, p. 191).
78 Von Rad, *Genesis*, 235 – 36 (1981, p. 191).
79 Erich Auerbach, *Mimesis: The Representation of Reality in Western Literature* (trans. Willard R. Trask; Princeton, N.J.: Princeton University Press, 1953), 7 – 8; translation of *Mimesis: dargestellte Wirklichkeit in der abendländischen Literatur* (Bern: Francke Verlag, 1946; 7. Aufl. 1982), 13.
80 Seizō Sekine, *Kyūyaku Seisho to Tetsugaku: Gendai no Toi no Naka no Isshinkyō* (The Old Testament and Philosophy: Monotheism in the Context of Modern Challenges) (Tokyo: Iwanami Shoten, 2008), 26.

4.2 Translation of Verses 2–4 and Verse 9 with Notes

2 [God] said, "Take your son, your only son, whom you love[81]—Isaac—and go[82] to the land of Moriah.[83] And there, on one of the mountains <u>that I tell you</u>,[84] offer him as a burnt offering."[85] 3 Abraham woke early the next morning. Then he placed a saddle on his donkey, and he took two of his young servants[86] with him, and also his son Isaac. He split the wood for the burnt offering, arose, and set out towards <u>the place that God told him</u>. 4 On the third day, Abraham lifted his eyes. Then he saw the <u>place</u> far off in the distance.

9 And they arrived at the <u>place</u> <u>that God told him</u>.

4.3 When Was Abraham "Told" about "the Place"?

The verb *'amar* (to say) is used in the imperfect form in verse 2 and in the perfect form in verses 3 and 9. *Maqom* (place) occurs repeatedly in verses 3, 4, and 9. Any mention of where and how God "told" Abraham about the "place," however, is omitted in the narrative. Furthermore, based on the correspondence between the

---

81 The perfect form of verbs that express a state rather than an action often carries a present meaning. See Paul Joüon, *Grammaire de l'hébreu biblique* (Rome: Institut biblique pontifical, 1923), 112a.

82 For other occurrences of *lekh-lekha*, an expression that carries emphasis, see Gen 12:1; also Gen 21:16.

83 The Hebrew *hammoriyya* is rendered in Symmachus' Greek version as *tēs optasias*, indicating that he read the Hebrew as *hammar'e* (the vision; the Vulgate also follows this tradition). The Syriac Peshitta has *mwry'*, leading us to surmise that the translator read it as *ha'emori* (the Amorites). Regarding other renderings, see the notes in BHS. There is a strong possibility, though, that the Masoretic Text simply refers to a place name.

Moriah appears in two Old Testament texts: this passage and 2Chron 3:1. The latter refers to the mountain where Solomon constructed the Jerusalem temple, but Gen 22:3 appears to have in mind a wasteland where one cannot even find firewood. Among the ancient versions, the Vulgate renders it as "land of vision," the Peshitta as "land of the Amorites," and the Septuagint as "the high land." None of these appear to have any connection with the Jerusalem temple. It is best, therefore, to view these as the same name referring to different locations.

84 It is customary to translate this as "command" or "show," but I prefer to render the original term *'amar* more transparently here as "tell."

85 *'ola* in Hebrew. In the ancient Israelite cult this was the most important offering. None of the meat was eaten; instead, it was consumed by fire. Before the meat was burnt, the blood was drained and poured around the sides of the altar. The fat was then burnt and offered up as smoke (Lev 3:2, 16). Normally, this offering was made in the morning and evening, using a sheep and a goat. Several of each were offered up, depending on the holiday. Bulls were also commonly offered on the altar by the priest (Num 28; 29).

86 The Hebrew term *na'ar* basically means "boy."

'amar perfects in verses 3 and 9, and also on the supposition that Abraham already knows the "place" in verse 4, we can infer that God had already "told" Abraham about the "place" after he told him to sacrifice Isaac on the day before he set off. (The circumstances during this period might be a bit more complicated. It might seem that "Moriah" was inserted into the narrative from 2 Chronicles 3:1 and that, at that stage, "the place" pointed vaguely to "Moriah" or perhaps to a certain "place" that could be viewed from "Moriah" [von Rad, 156]. If we read the narrative closely, however, it is unlikely that this interpretation is valid.) Similarly, we might presume that in all likelihood Abraham took the donkey and the two young servants after having received instructions from God concerning them as well, but the narrative omits any mention of this (Wenham, 189).[87] If that is the case, we should be somewhat freer from the assumption that only silence prevailed among the three, as well as from unnecessary constraints against reconstructing their dialogue on the basis that it does not match the circumstances simply because their dialogue is not recorded in the narrative.

4.4 Toward Understanding the Characters' States of Mind

The word order in verse 3 appears to be problematic. Should he not have "split the wood for the burnt offering" before "he placed a saddle ... and he took"? Should the text not mention "Isaac" before it mentions the "servants"? Is this reflecting Abraham's stunned heart after he heard God's cruel command? Or does it intimate the state of mind of a father who wishes to postpone the painful act of offering "Isaac" as "a burnt offering" (Wenham, 188)?[88] We should notice here this author's adeptness at depicting the characters' states of mind through his depictions of their actions (von Rad, 157).[89] Therefore it should be appropriate for the interpreter to take up the task of consciously revealing the states of mind suggested in this way.

As noted above, Josephus has gone to considerable lengths in leaving us with a gem of a dialogue as a possibility of the specific dialogue that might have taken place among God, Abraham, and Isaac. If there had been such a dialogue, the irrationality of this story might have been resolved to a considerable extent. In that sense, Josephus' proposed dialogue is richly persuasive. Of course, it does not seem that the Akedah was written in a way that suggests

---

87 Wenham, *Genesis 16–50*, 106.
88 Ibid., 105.
89 Von Rad, *Genesis*, 235–36 (1981, p. 191).

that they spoke together at such length. Rather, it depicts them acting in silence while considering each other's feelings. At the very least, however, the narrative encourages us to inquire into their feelings that underpin the story and to use our imaginations to reveal the characters' states of mind. We must acknowledge that Josephus' interpretation is richly suggestive for that purpose.

So far two points have emerged that ought to inform our interpretive approach as we read the text anew: a) verses 15–18 are not a later accretion, but an authentic part of the original Akedah; and b) it is appropriate to use our imaginations concerning the implied thoughts and feelings in the omitted dialogue. From this perspective, I wish to reflect now upon the speech, and especially the thoughts, of Isaac, Abraham, and God, the central characters in the Akedah.

5 Isaac's Feelings

5.1 The Father's Love

I wish to turn now to the task of offering an exposition of Isaac's state of mind as suggested by the depiction of his actions. That Isaac was deeply loved by his father Abraham can be discerned from the simple yet subtle portrayal of these actions:

> 6 Abraham took the wood for the burnt offering, he placed it on his son Isaac's back, he took in his hand the fire and the knife, and so the two of them went on together.

As the commentators point out, the father takes in his own hand the things he fears could harm his child and has the child carry only the wood. In this, we can see "Abraham's attentive love for the child" (von Rad, 157).[90] This love is explicitly mentioned in God's words in the introduction—"your only son, whom you love" (v. 2)—and it fills in the background of the story here and in verse 7's "my father … I am here, my son," a simple exchange that overflows with "deep affection between father and child" (Arimasa Mori, 231).[91] This love is assumed throughout this tragedy.

---

[90] Von Rad, *Genesis*, 235 (1981, p. 191).
[91] Arimasa Mori, *Aburahamu no Shōgai* (The Life of Abraham) (Tokyo: The Board of Publications, The United Church of Christ in Japan, 2004), 101.

5.2 Translation of Verses 7–8 with Notes

In the Akedah, Isaac speaks only in verse 7.

> 7 Isaac said to his father Abraham, "My father." He replied, "I am here, my son."[92] [Isaac] said, "Here are the fire and the wood.[93] But where is the lamb for a burnt offering?" 8 Abraham replied, "God will find for himself the lamb for a burnt offering, my son." And so the two of them went on together.

5.3 Isaac's Self-sacrifice

Interpreters have come to various conclusions concerning Isaac's age. Wenham (192) thinks he is in his teens,[94] Luther (86) thinks he is 21,[95] Josephus (40)[96] and Uchimura (102)[97] think he is 25, while the Midrash Rabbah (52) says he is 37.[98] None of these views are based on conclusive evidence.

If readers imagine Isaac as a sweet little boy, they will imagine him innocently asking his father where the lamb is and then naively being persuaded by his father's reply. This creates the heart-breaking and pitiful image of Isaac then taking his father's hand without any concerns for himself and walking to his death.

On the other hand, if Isaac was a fully mature adult, a different picture emerges. During the journey, Isaac finally broke the profound silence to ask the question he could no longer contain. Upon hearing his father's agony-filled reply, he determined not to trouble his father any more. As readers, our hearts are stirred even more at the image of a sacrificial son as Isaac falls silent again and prepares for his death in dutiful obedience to his father and to God.

---

92 The same form as the question and answer between God and Abraham at the end of verse 1 is repeated here.

93 The interjection *hinne* (behold), which is the same term as *hinneni* in verses 1 and 7 without the suffix, is used here.

94 Wenham, *Genesis 16–50*, 109.

95 Martin Luther, *D. Martin Luthers Werke: kritische Gesamtausgabe* (Weimarer Ausgabe), Bd. 43 (Weimar: H. Böhlaus Nachfolger; Graz: Akademische Druck- und Verlagsanstalt, 1964), 201.

96 Josephus, *Jewish Antiquities* (Book I), in *The Works of Josephus* (trans. William Whiston; Peabody, Mass.: Hendrickson, 1987), 1.227. The below quotations from *Jewish Antiquities* are taken from this volume, which incorporates the Loeb references.

97 Kanzō Uchimura, "Isaku no Kenkyō" (The Sacrifice of Isaac), in *Uchimura Kanzō Zenshū* (Collected Works of Kanzō Uchimura), 16 Volumes (Tokyo: Iwanami Shoten, 1928), 110.

98 Moshe Aryeh Mirkin, ed., *Midrash Rabbah, Bereshit Rabbah, Seder Vayera* (Yavneh, Tel Aviv: 1956–1967), 260.

5.4 Why Did Isaac Not Run Away?

Verse 9, from which we get the title "Akedah," reads as follows.

> 9 And they arrived at the place that God told him. Abraham built the altar there. Then he arranged the wood. Then he bound Isaac his son.[99] Then he placed him on the altar, on top of the wood.[100]

Here we find ourselves with a simple yet important question. Why did Isaac not run away? Why did he not resist? Whether Isaac was in his teens, twenties, or thirties, there is no doubt that he was stronger and more agile than his father, who was more than 100 years old (Gen 17:17; 21:3). The only way to explain why Isaac allowed himself to be easily bound by his father and to be placed upon the wood is to understand that it was because he was prepared to become the sacrifice. Furthermore, as we saw in 4.3, there is a strong possibility that the characters did not proceed in utter silence except for the dialogue given in the story, but that the narrator omitted a number of dialogues. If so, we cannot rule out the possibility that the sort of explanation and acceptance that Josephus reconstructs between this father and son, who trusted each other deeply, did not take place.

The father says, "I suppose he thinks thee worthy to get clear of this world neither by disease, neither by war ... but so that he will receive thy soul with prayers and holy offices of religion, and will place thee near to himself." And the child replies, "That [I was] not worthy to be born at first, if [I] should reject the determination of God and of [my] father, and should not resign [my]self up readily to both their pleasures" (Josephus, 41).[101]

Even if they did not outwardly speak together in this way, the philosopher Arimasa Mori is correct in pointing out that the love and trust that "can be communicated through the simple words" of "my father" and "my son" "were displayed here in the most beautiful and most natural way" in the face of this "violent tragedy" (231–32). There is no doubt that Isaac accepted the situation and was prepared. And it is precisely for this reason, we must understand, that he did not run away or resist, but instead "went immediately to the altar to be sacrificed" (Josephus, 41).[102]

---

99 'aqad in Hebrew. The nominative 'aqeda refers to the "binding [of Isaac]" and has come to be used as the name of this narrative in Genesis 22 (see the introduction to this chapter).
100 Verse 6 might be translated literally as "he placed [the wood] on Isaac," and this verse as "he placed [Isaac] ... on the wood." The two form an opposite pair.
101 Josephus, *Jewish Antiquities*, 1.230–32.
102 Ibid., 1.232.

In the concise narrative of the Akedah, references to Isaac are few. Furthermore, there are very few words spoken by him. In between the lines, however, it is fitting to imagine—rather, we are encouraged to imagine—words such as these that might have been spoken, or at least the presence of such feelings.

6 Abraham's Feelings

6.1 In His Relationship with Isaac

How about the father, Abraham? First, we can well imagine the elderly father's feelings in his relationship with Isaac. This father is put in a predicament wherein, suddenly, by his own hands he must take the life of his "only son, whom [he] love[s]," and who had appeared to have a rich future ahead of him. How must this elderly father have felt to watch this "boy" who, without a doubt, could very easily have broken free and run from his aged and weakened father? How did he feel to watch this "son" who refused to do so even though he could? Here was his delicate, clever, and patient "only son," who sensed his father's duty to the absolute God he had encountered, who would not allow himself to trouble his father with any more questions. How did Abraham feel to see this son lying there on the wood, having given himself to be bound by his elderly father while clenching his teeth in readiness or perhaps shaking with fear? It is difficult to imagine this scene without shedding a tear.

6.2 Abraham's Logic and Conviction: With Reference to Josephus

Yet, perhaps it runs counter to the intentions of this author, who calmly narrates events, to bring too much emotion into the reading of this narrative. How did Abraham convince himself, and if there was any dialogue between them, how did he also convince Isaac and go on to act in this way? Perhaps we are meant to concentrate cool-headedly on the logic that led to this conviction.

Here, too, Josephus presents a plausible line of logic. He does so by having Abraham speak in a highly persuasive manner. The passage is rather long, but I wish to quote Josephus here.

> God ... has thought fit now to require this testimony of honor to himself, on account of the favors he hath conferred on me.

Accordingly thou, my son, wilt now die, not in any common way of going out of the world, but sent to God, the Father of all men, beforehand, by thy own father, in the nature of a sacrifice.

I suppose [God] thinks thee worthy to get clear of this world neither by disease, neither by war ... but so that he will receive thy soul with prayers and holy offices of religion, and will place thee near to himself.[103]

6.3 Abraham's Statement: Returning to the Akedah

Again, however, perhaps we must guard against reading too much into the text. The Akedah does not directly and explicitly present Abraham's feelings for his child as Josephus depicts them. What, then, does the Akedah itself have Abraham say? Let us return now to the text of the Akedah and approach Abraham's true feelings and intentions from another angle.

In the Akedah, Abraham speaks in verses 1, 5, 7, 8, and 11, whereas Isaac speaks only in verse 7. In verses 1, 7, and 11, however, it is just Abraham's brief response to God or Isaac of "hinneni" (here I am), and the remaining verses 5 and 8 have problematic statements on which interpretations are divided. Firstly, verses 4 and 5:

4 On the third day, Abraham lifted his eyes. He saw the place far off in the distance. 5 So Abraham said to his young servants, "You stay here with the donkey. I and this boy[104] will go there, worship, and return to you."

Secondly, Abraham's reply to Isaac's question discussed above:

8 Abraham replied, "God will find for himself the lamb for a burnt offering, my son." And so the two of them went on together.

6.4 The True Meaning of Abraham's Statement

We cannot be certain whether Kierkegaard and many other interpreters are correct in imagining that a profound silence reigned over the three-day journey, or whether the dialogue was omitted because of the author's style, as it was in verse 3.

---

103 Ibid., 1.229–31.
104 The same Hebrew word translated as "young servants" (*na'ar*) in verses 3 and 5a is used here to refer to Isaac.

Whatever the case, "three days" is a typical length of time spent preparing for important matters (Gen 31:22; 40:20; 42:18; Exod 3:18; 5:3; 19:11 [2x], 16; etc.). Here it serves to increase the severity of the trial and especially to increase Abraham's torment (Calvin I, 565; Wenham, 189).[105] And not only that. As Nahmanides pointed out long ago (70)[106] and von Rad has pointed out more recently (157),[107] it gives assurance that Abraham is not rashly killing his son in a momentary fit of anger (by contrast, in the Quran's narrative [81], Abraham shares the instructions he received in a dream and, with that, holds Isaac down to sacrifice him).[108] Why does Abraham speak of Isaac as "this boy" in verse 5, though Isaac is repeatedly referred to as "son" in verses 2, 3, and 6? Could it be a subtle hint that, in his heart, Abraham has already established some distance in his private parental relationship with Isaac and that he is coming to acknowledge Isaac as an independent personality who belongs to God? (Miyamoto [290] overlooks verse 5, but he holds to an interpretation along these lines concerning "the boy" in verse 12.[109])

Whatever the case, the statement in verse 5 that, after "worship[ing]," both Abraham and Isaac would "return" together presents a problem that must be addressed. After worshiping, Isaac will no longer be alive, so it should be only Abraham who "returns" to them. Why does the text make this statement?

We can think of four possible interpretations of Abraham's statement: (1) he says this in order not to alarm the servants; (2) he says it to avoid interference from the servants, who might view his actions as murder and try to stop him; (3) Abraham held firmly to his faith-based hope that God's promise of a multitude of descendants through Isaac (Gen 12; 15; 17) would not be broken; and (4) Abraham could not bring himself to imagine killing Isaac out of obedience to God's command (Wenham, 190–91).[110]

Setting aside for the moment the question of which interpretation is most appropriate, we will consider the meaning of Abraham's response in verse 8 that "God will find for himself the lamb for a burnt offering." Inasmuch as this is his reply to Isaac's question in verse 7, a blunt response should have been "The burnt offering will be you." Why did Abraham not respond in this

---

105 John Calvin, *Commentaries on the First Book of Moses Called Genesis*, Vol. I (trans. John King; Grand Rapids, Mich.: Wm. B. Eerdmans Publishing Company, 1847), 565; Wenham, *Genesis 16–50*, 106–7.

106 Moses Nahmanides, *Mikra 'ot Gedolot "Haketer"; Genesis pt. 1* (ed. M. Cohen; Ramat-Gan, Israel: Bar-Ilan University, 1997), 195.

107 Von Rad, *Genesis* (1981), 190–1.

108 Qur'an 37:95–113.

109 Miyamoto, "Aburahamu no Junan to Tasha no Chihei," 112.

110 See Wenham, *Genesis 16–50*, 107.

way? If we substitute "Isaac" for "the servants," it seems possible to offer the same explanations in (1) to (4) above.

Here we may recall the philosopher Kierkegaard's interpretation wherein he detects a praiseworthy faith in Abraham, "the knight of faith" who believed that Isaac would be returned to him (117).[111] This would lead us toward the third interpretive option noted above. Without referring to Kierkegaard, the Old Testament scholar von Rad (158) argues against this view and criticizes Delitzsch, who detected "intuitive hope" in both verses 5 and 8. We must not forget von Rad's point that this view "would deprive the narrative of some of its most important substance."[112] In this narrative whose topic is introduced at the beginning as a "test," if Abraham clings to a half-hearted hope and attempts to avoid his hopeless torment, the test does not function as a test. This is the difficult problem that would arise. In fact, these are "not the words of [a praiseworthy] faith, but rather sinful words. At this stage, Abraham presumes it impossible for the promised child he has grasped in his own hands to be taken from him again. He retains the vestiges of indulgent thinking whereby he does not truly confront the severity of God's command" (Sekine, 326).[113] In other words, it appears that we cannot dismiss the fourth line of interpretation.

How should we understand this? Let us consider the text once again. The term "worship" (*hishtachava*) in verse 5 and the phrase "God will find the lamb [*se*]" in verse 8 merit our particular attention. Although God commanded Abraham to "offer him [Isaac] as a burnt offering [*ha'alehu le'ola*]" (v. 2), it seems that Abraham interprets this loosely according to his own personal needs. If so, the following possibility emerges as a fifth interpretation. Because Abraham believes it impossible for God to break his promise as in (3), he is confused by God's new command that contradicts that promise. Although Abraham does not necessarily intend willfully to disobey God's command, it is possible that he cannot yet imagine killing Isaac, as in (4). Furthermore, this does not exclude the possibility that his words imply consideration and precautions concerning the servants or Isaac, as in (1) and (2). It is as if Abraham is groping for a way to understand with some consistency this contradiction that comes from God, and he is testing the possibility that he need not take God's command literally. Is it not possible that Abraham's statements in verse 5 that the two of them would "worship and return" and in verse 8 that "God will find for himself the lamb for a burnt offering" are expressions of his worries in the midst of such

111 Kierkegaard, *Fear and Trembling*, 139.
112 Von Rad, *Genesis*, 236 (1981, p. 191).
113 Sekine, *Kyūyaku Seisho to Tetsugaku*, 37.

confusion? Inasmuch as it is difficult to dismiss interpretations (1) to (4) as contextually inappropriate, this fifth interpretation comprehensively allows for the possibility of each of these and is thus highly plausible.

6.5 Faith and Unbelief

If we view the narrative in this way, we must recognize that although Abraham wavers between faith and unbelief, the ultimate source of his wavering lies in none other than God himself, who sends contradictory messages by promising the propagation and prosperity of Abraham's descendants and then commanding the annihilation of those descendants. The interpretations from philosophy (Kierkegaard) and Old Testament studies (von Rad) have stood opposed to each other, but it should become apparent that this opposition can be traced back to none other than the contradiction that comes from God himself. If so, are we not forced to confront this contradiction head-on? Now that I have identified the locus of this fundamental problem, I wish to set it aside momentarily and return to it in Part 7.

6.6 Contradictory Views of the Talkative Abraham

Here I wish to add two further points concerning the image of Abraham that emerges from the Akedah.

First, it is notable that Abraham is not at all talkative in the Akedah, in which he gives only two "ambiguous" (von Rad, 157)[114] and painful responses apart from his three *hinneni*'s. In the Abraham story beginning in Genesis 12, however, we could say that Abraham is quite talkative, and normally he converses with God about matters on which he does not agree (many view Gen 18:23 ff. as a later accretion, but see also 15:2, 8; 17:18). Why does Abraham not argue with God here despite the fact that God has given a command breaking his promise? Though a simple question, it is undoubtedly an essential one to ask.

One answer is that it is simply because God's command has hit a sore spot in Abraham's heart (Sekine, 326).[115] This command ripped through Abraham's heart and exposed the fact that he so greatly "loved" his "only son, Isaac," who was a blessing from God, that he appropriated the gift for himself personally, while his

---

114 Von Rad, *Genesis*, 236 (1981, p. 191).
115 Sekine, *Kyūyaku Seisho to Tetsugaku*, 37.

heart became distant from the giver. Again Josephus' insight hits the mark here when he says "all creatures that live enjoy their life by his providence, and the kindness he bestows on them," and so "Abraham thought that it was not right to disobey God in any thing" (39).[116] Through this "test," Abraham newly "understands the gift of promise as a pure gift" (von Rad, 163),[117] and so he does not permit himself any protests. Instead, he sets out on his journey in silence.

6.7 The One Who is Weak and the One Who Fears God

Second, however, we must note that, rather than being Kierkegaard's "knight of faith" or a monstrous giant of faith, Abraham is merely a man with many human weaknesses.

In the story leading up to the Akedah, Abraham had offered his wife's chastity for the sake of self-preservation (Gen 12:11ff.; 20), and he had involved the slave-girl Hagar because he did not fully believe God's promise (Gen 16). Furthermore, he is unable to protect their son Ishmael when the child becomes the source of discord in the home; he abandons him by casting him out into the desert with no water (Gen 21:9ff.; there is no evidence in the text to support Rabbi David Polish's view that Abraham offered Isaac as atonement for this [Arieti, 117]). Also, after setting out on the journey of trial in the Akedah, in verses 5 and 8 Abraham is not yet able to submit fully to God's command. And one cannot entirely dismiss the possibility that the string of verbs in verses 9–10 depicts Abraham's hesitation, as if he pauses after each action out of hope that an angel will break in and stop him. Following verse 9, which was discussed in 5.4, verse 10 declares:

> 10 Then Abraham reached out his hand. Then he took the knife, and he started to slaughter his son.

The commentators have pointed out the author's skillful style here in verses 9–10 (von Rad, 157; Wenham, 192).[118] Since verse 4, the tempo of the narrative has slowed, and the narrative has become marked by a style that causes the reader to feel the solemnity of the journey. Finally, in verses 9–10 there is an almost unnatural string of verbs composed in a way that heightens the reader's unease. The string of eight verbs—"[T]hey arrived [*bo'*] at the place," "built [*bana*] the altar," "arranged ['*arakh*] the wood," "bound ['*aqad*] Isaac," "placed [*sim*] him on ... top of the wood,"

---

116 Josephus, *Jewish Antiquities*, 1.225.
117 Von Rad, *Genesis*, 239 (1981, p. 194).
118 Von Rad, *Genesis*, 236 (1981, p. 191); Wenham, *Genesis 16–50*, 109; etc.

"reached [*shalach*] out his hand," "took [*laqach*] the knife," "started to slaughter [*shachat*]"—is a "postponement of the critical moment" and, at the same time, "may also hint at Abraham's reluctance to come to the point" (Wenham, 192).[119] Furthermore, it appears to be a reflection of Abraham's repeated hope and disappointment. That is, it seems that with each action Abraham hopes to be stopped by God, who would "find for himself the lamb for a burnt offering," or to have an angel intervene, but each time he looks around these hopes are dashed.

The image of Abraham here corresponds to that in the rest of the Abraham story. Here, too, the narrative lays bare Abraham's calculating weakness. At the end of his hesitations the moment of truth arrives, and Abraham no longer has hope of escape. "At that moment, something happened in Abraham, and he accepted God's command without qualification. With brave determination there ... Abraham raised his knife to slay Isaac. And though he raised his knife to slay Isaac, this was undoubtedly an act of kenosis in which he slew his former sinful self (Miyamoto).[120] Instead, at that moment, Abraham once again—or perhaps for the first time—was given the life of one who truly 'fears God' (v. 12)" (Sekine, 327).[121] As such, it must be possible to detect here a dynamic mixture of hesitation and decisiveness.

7 God's Self-Denial

7.1 Doubts about "God"

In contrast to these acts of self-denial by Isaac and Abraham, is God resting in comfortable self-affirmation high up in heaven, from whence he "tests" the loyalty of humans down on earth?

When we have secret doubts about references to God in Scripture, we tend to suppress them because we think it impious to voice such doubts about the text. Ultimately, however, this is a shallow understanding of "God" and nothing more than a superficial relationship with him. Even Job, when he said "Yahweh gives, Yahweh takes away, Yahweh's name be blessed" (Job 1:21), is still wearing the mask of piety and merely smoothing things over. Did he not encounter the true God later in his straight-talking dialogue with God? Furthermore, we know that God in the book of Job and God in the Akedah are, in the end, merely how the authors understood

---

119 Wenham, *Genesis 16 – 50*, 109.
120 Miyamoto, "Aburahamu no Junan to Tasha no Chihei," 119.
121 Sekine, *Kyūyaku Seisho to Tetsugaku*, 38.

and depicted God. Is it not acceptable, then, to raise bold questions about this "God" and thereby elucidate the intentions of the author?

If we search for examples of this in the history of interpretation, again we find that Judaism's Rabbis (concerning Rashi, see 57 ff. for Rashi;[122] concerning Maimonides, see 63 ff.[123]) and Christianity's systematic theologians (concerning Bonhoeffer, see 171 ff.;[124] concerning Barth, see 175 ff.[125]) are weak at this point. There is a taboo against raising doubts about the acts of God (among philosophers, too, in the Middle Ages tendencies toward theodicy, such as seen in Abelard, were firmly

---

122 Rashi (Rabbi Shlomoh ben Yitzchaqi), *Mikra 'ot Gedolot "Haketer"; Genesis pt. 1* (ed. Menachem Cohen; Ramat-Gan, Israel: Bar-Ilan University, 1997), 192–98. For instance, consider this discussion on pp. 60–61: "Rabbi Abba said, 'Abraham said to God, "Permit me to speak concerning [this] conversation." [He continued] "Yesterday, you said to me, 'Call Isaac your descendant.' Then you say again, 'Take up your son.' And now will you say, 'Do not lay a hand on the boy'?" said Abraham unhappily. Then God said to Abraham, "I have not neglected the covenant. I do not intend to change the words that have gone out of my mouth." "Because, although I said to you 'Take,' I do not intend to change the words that have gone out of my mouth. Therefore, I did not say 'Slaughter him!' Did I not say, 'Take him up'? I am the one who will raise him up and take him down."'"

123 Moses Maimonides, in *Doctor Perplexorum* (trans. R. Samuel Ibn Tibbon; ed. Yehuda Ibn Shmuel; Jerusalem: Mossad Harav Kook, 2000), 455–460. For instance, consider this discussion on pp. 64–65: "The meaning of a trial does not consist in a certain act being done in order to accomplish that particular act itself. Rather, it consists in that act's being a model for people to imitate and follow. Therefore, 'In order to know whether you love' does not mean that it is for God to know [of course, God already knows it], but it means "in order that you may know that I, the LORD, sanctify you" [Exod 31:13; NRSV]. In other words, it means that it is in order for the nations to know."

124 Dietrich Bonhoeffer, *Dietrich Bonhoeffer Werke*, Vol. 4 (ed. Martin Kuske and Ilse Tödt; Munich: Chr. Kaiser Verlag, 1989), 91–94. For instance, consider this discussion on pp. 173ff: "Abraham comes down from the mountain with Isaac just as he went up, but the whole situation has changed. Christ has stepped between father and son. Abraham had left all and followed Christ, and as he follows him he is allowed to go back and live in the world as he had done before. Outwardly the picture is unchanged, but the old is passed away, and behold all things are new. Everything has had to pass through Christ." Quotation from Dietrich Bonhoeffer, *The Cost of Discipleship* (London: SCM Press, 1948, 1959), 53.

125 Karl Barth, *Unterricht in der christlichen Religion, II: Die Lehre von Gott/Die Lehre vom Menschen 1924/1925* (ed. Hinrich Stoevesandt; Zürich: TVZ, 1990), 245, 249–252. For instance, consider this discussion on pp. 177ff: "There is no doubt in the 'seeing' (*videre*), and yet there is a chasm between God and man. Still, the fellowship between God and man must be depicted. This is God's providence (*providentia Dei*). This expression stems from Genesis 22:14. 'Yahweh Yir'e' (the LORD shall provide) is where Isaac's sacrifice was prevented for Abraham, and it was the place where, in the end, the path of God and the path of man met in this amazing way. 'The LORD shall provide' (*Dominus providevit*). This sentence signifies a double negation."

entrenched; see 73 ff.[126]). Within the tradition of Christianity it is not surprising that Old Testament scholarship has also hastily warded off such questions about God. For instance, Westermann criticizes the philosopher Kierkegaard and says that, in its entirety, the Akedah represents praise of God (170).[127] For Wenham, too, ultimately the main point of the Akedah is Abraham's obedience and God's blessings (195).[128] Even von Rad reaches this conclusion: "But in this way Yahweh tests faith and obedience! One further thing may be mentioned: in this test God confronts Abraham with the question whether he could give up God's gift of promise ... God therefore poses before Abraham the question whether he really understands the gift of promise as a pure gift" (163).[129]

The problem here, however, is that it is inconsistent and quite unseemly to ask someone to return a gift once it has been given. Yet even allowing for that possibility, the present case is different from asking someone to return a diamond gift. God's demand here is not for Abraham to return a diamond, but a child. In other words, is not this God recommending an unethical murder and, at the very least, committing the crime of soliciting murder?[130] In 6.4, above, I

---

126 Peter Abelard, *Peter Abelard's Ethics* (trans. D. E. Luscombe; Oxford: Clarendon Press, 1971), 30–32, 60. For instance, consider this discussion on pp. 74ff: "You will understand that it is not the execution of the act but only the intention behind the command that justifies God. That is because it was good for God to command that which was not good. The reason is not because God intended for Abraham to offer his son in sacrifice, nor was he commanding him to carry it out. Rather, it is because he intended, through this, to test the extreme limits of Abraham's obedience and the certainty of his faith and love, and for this to remain as an example for us."

127 Westermann, *Genesis 12–36*, 364–65 (1981, p. 447).

128 Wenham, *Genesis 16–50*, 112.

129 Von Rad, *Genesis*, 239 (1981, p. 194). It is not incorrect to characterize Isaac and Abraham as obedient to God, but if this means blind obedience to established authority, we "could very well object," together with Arimasa Mori (232–33). Rather, what is unmistakably important here is the hermeneutical experience of reading and understanding the dynamics of self-negation by Isaac and Abraham, who remain obedient to God even when he seems irrational.

130 This is a subtle matter. I do not side with the philosophers' ahistorical condemnations. For instance, Kant (94) rejects the unethicality of this God and argues that Abraham should have responded to God as follows: "The fact that I should not kill my good son is absolutely certain. But that you who appear to me are God, I am not certain and can never become certain" (Kant, *Der Streit der Fakultäten*, 62). Applying it to our day, Derrida (269) says this: "We can hardly imagine a father taking his son to be sacrificed on the top of the hill at Montmartre. If God didn't send a lamb as a substitute or an angel to hold back his arm, there would still be an upright prosecutor ... to accuse him of infanticide ... ; and if a psychiatrist ... were to declare that the father was [criminally] 'responsible' ... the criminal father would have no chance of getting away with it" (Derrida, *The Gift of Death*, 85 [1992, p. 82]). For Derrida, too, this act was simply a crime that ran counter to ethics. Yet we cannot forget that ancient Israelite law in fact commanded this as religiously desirable (Exod 22:28 [JE source from the seventh century BCE]). Gradually, however, Israel moved

pointed out that the source of Abraham's mysterious manner of speaking in verses 5 and 8 can be attributed especially to the self-contradiction of God, who breaks his promise. Beyond this, it should be acceptable to revisit the suggestion that the source of suffering for Abraham, who was being forced to commit the unethical act of filicide, traces back to the unethicality of God, who commanded it. Old Testament scholarship has simply dismissed the question of whether we can ultimately recognize as God an unethical God who has lapsed into self-contradiction in this way. Upon reading the Akedah, though, this is the final and, in fact, the most serious question that we must deliberately raise.

As far as I am aware, in the history of interpretation there have been only two philosophers who have frankly raised this crucial, almost unbearable question. One is Kant, and the other is Kitarō Nishida. Regrettably, as stated above, we must conclude that Kant ignored the ancient tradition-historical context and hastily criticized the Akedah from the standpoint of his ethics of the categorical imperative. (Of course, in the context of *Der Streit der Fakultäten*, Kant is consciously emphasizing criticism of theological statements from the perspective

---

in the direction of replacing sacrifice of the firstborn child with animal sacrifice (Exod 13:12–13 [JE]; also Exod 34:19–20 [JE], and Num 3:44 ff. [P source from the sixth to fifth centuries BCE]). Ultimately, among the texts that remain today there emerged an understanding on the part of the late eighth-century BCE prophet Micah (Mic 6:7–8) that an ethical God who loves justice seeks ethical practice and religious faith more than firstborn sacrifice or cultic offerings in general. Whether we view the author of the Akedah as the early eighth-century BCE Elohist or we date it as late as the exilic period along with recent scholars, the author lived in a traditional context that did not view firstborn sacrifice as absolute evil; at most, perhaps it was a period of transition toward viewing this as evil. It is undoubtedly a mistake to criticize and easily dismiss this story of firstborn sacrifice composed with such underlying presuppositions according to modern ethical judgments against filicide (I have not changed my views on this point that I discussed in *Kyūyaku Seisho no Shisō: 24 no Danshō* [Old Testament Thought: 24 Fragmentary Reflections] [Tokyo: Iwanami Shoten, 1998; Tokyo: Kodansha Gakujutsu Bunko, 2005], 62–64). What we must intentionally ask while seriously acknowledging these points is why firstborn sacrifice was widespread in the ancient world in the first place. A psychoanalyst such as Wellisch points to the Laius complex, that is, the father's fear of Oedipus, who killed his father and slept with his mother (Erich Wellisch, *Isaac and Oedipus: A Study in Biblical Psychology of the Sacrifice of Isaac, The Akedah* [London: Routledge & Kegan Paul, 1954], 76, 99; see Arieti, 244). But in the Akedah narrative, at least, the caring and love of both father and son overflow, as discussed above, so like Arieti (247), I cannot agree with Wellisch's explanation. Rather, it is the opposite case. Precisely because Isaac is his firstborn son whom he greatly cherishes and loves, Abraham's offering to God becomes a testimony of his love and faith toward God. We can surmise that this is how ancient readers understood the story. Having been prompted to offer up a religious sacrifice, Abraham suffered because of this act that ran counter to the ethical love and affection between parent and child. We must give consideration to Abraham's ethical suffering, and we are compelled to revisit the unethicality of God, who coldly imposed this suffering.

of philosophy, but for criticisms of Kant's overall rational religion, see the following, which were omitted in the above work: *Nishida Kitarō Zenshū, 10-kan* [Collected Works of Nishida Kitarō, Vol. 10], 373; and Yoshiharu Hakari, *Shūkyō Tetsugaku toshite no Kanto Tetsugaku* [Kantian Philosophy as Religious Philosophy], Chapter 7.) By contrast, Nishida, who possessed a rich knowledge of Buddhism as well as the Jewish and Christian traditions, has demonstrated an original and positive understanding of God in the Akedah from his deep and wide understanding of the root of religion in general.

7.2 Criticism from Philosophy of a Personal God, and its Outcome

Nishida begins with questions and doubts about the personal God of Christianity (see *Zenshū* Vol. 10, 315 ff.). He argues that a personal God who is relative to relative humans outside himself, who speaks to them, and who fluctuates between giving rewards and punishments for their actions is a relative absolute being who is relative to relative beings, a *contradictio in adjecto*. He is nothing more than a logically bankrupt God. On the other hand, a God who is not relative to any other being is a powerless God, and he is not God. As a logical necessity, therefore, the relationship between God and relative beings must be as follows. God must be relative to relative beings who exist within himself, not outside himself. However, God is an absolute being, and relative beings are a negation of that. Therefore, it must be that, through negation of himself, God causes relative beings to exist within himself and is relative to them. Some might call this an adaptation of Hegelian pantheism, but Nishida's originality lies in the point that it is panentheistic and not pantheistic. That is, the difference between them is the point that all things exist within God. Whatever the case, though Nishida does not refer to Hegel, if one probes the concept of God today based on the culmination of Hegelian philosophy,[131] the logical conclusion must be a God who is simultaneously absolute and relative and who is God of the self-identity of absolute contradiction. Furthermore, this does not end simply with logical matters. Rather, it touches upon the very nature of our religious experiences. Zen enlightenment involves grasping hold of this state. And because the atonement of the cross in Christianity means, from a Trinitarian perspective, that God negates himself by killing God himself and that God gives life to relative humans

---

131 Georg Wilhelm Friedrich Hegel, *Wissenschaft der Logik* (1812–1816), Kap 2, A–D; *Enzyklopaedie der philosophischen Wissenschaften* (1830), Kap. A a–d.

through this act, it is nothing more than one symbolic expression of the work of this God characterized by the self-identity of absolute contradiction.

7.3 Nishida's Understanding of the Akedah

Above, while drawing on Hegel at certain points, I have summarized in my own words the understanding of God in Nishida's philosophy, which rings with abstruseness. If this summary is correct, then based on the above, the meaning of Nishida's statements about the Akedah should be clear in and of itself. Consider this somewhat lengthy quote.

> It may sound extremely paradoxical, but the truly absolute God must be [diabolical] in a certain respect. Only as such is God both omniscient and omnipotent. Yahweh is a God who demanded Abraham to sacrifice his only son, Isaac [Kierkegaard, *Fear and Trembling*]. He demanded of Abraham the denial of his personhood itself. If God merely stands against evil and fights it, though he may conquer evil, he is a relative God. A God who is simply transcendent [and] supreme good is but an abstract notion. The absolute God must contain absolute negation in himself, and be able to descend to the most wicked; the God who saves the heinous is the truly absolute God.[132] (Nishida, 219–20)

In other words, a good God must also include within himself evil as his self-negation. A God who requests the murder of a child, a God who solicits murder, is a "diabolical" God who "descend[s] to the most wicked." Nishida says that precisely for this reason "the truly absolute God" is not the God who "merely judges" from his goodness on high, but the God who, from the depths of evil, "saves the heinous."

From this point, let us revisit the Akedah. Does Nishida mean that Abraham has fallen into "evil"? Nishida's intentions are not necessarily clear from his reference to the Akedah alone. In one other passage, Nishida says only this: "One early morning, when Abraham, taking [Isaac], departed for the land of Moriah, he faced God as a singular individual; he stood at the outer limit of being human" (Nishida, 222).[133]

---

132 Kitarō Nishida (trans. Michiko Yusa), "The Logic of *Topos* and the Religious Worldview (I)," *The Eastern Buddhist* 19:2 (1986): 24; translation of Kitarō Nishida, *Bashoteki Ronri to Shūkyō-teki Sekaikan* (Topological Logic and Religious Worldview) (*Nishida Kitarō Zenshū*, 11; Tokyo: Iwanami Shoten, 1949 [1946]), 321. [Translator's note: I have rendered *akumateki* as "diabolical" instead of "demonic," as Yusa renders it.]

133 Kitarō Nishida (trans. Michiko Yusa), "The Logic of Topos and the Religious Worldview (II)," *The Eastern Buddhist* 20:1 (1987): 95 (1949, p. 342). [Translator's note: I have corrected "Issac" to "Isaac."]

7.4 Abraham's Evil and God's Love

Let us return once more to the text of the Akedah and reconsider it with the above in mind. In the preceding section, we imagined various possibilities concerning Abraham's thoughts and feelings, and a number of things became clear. It was made evident that Abraham's heart had become somewhat distant from God, about whom he felt vaguely guilt-ridden, so he could only acknowledge the truth and silently follow God's command without protest (6.6). Yet even so, Abraham still wavered between faith, through which he believed in God's previous promise of the propagation and prosperity of his descendants, and unbelief, which made him unable to follow God's command entirely (6.5). Furthermore, he could not quite act decisively, because right until the very end he hoped for a favorable turn in his situation (6.7). This aspect of evil in Abraham, who was beset by human weaknesses, is dispassionately depicted here simply as it is.

The God who gives this "test" to determine whether Abraham could conquer such evil is not a God who is "self-contradicting," as von Rad suggests (163)[134] or as the conclusions of commentators noted in 7.1. would indicate. Rather, he is none other than a God with an "absolutely contradictory self-identity," as Nishida says (218 ff.).[135] We must conclude that God was able to draw near the sins of weakness and evil residing in Abraham's heart, save him from within, and truly become a God who could battle Abraham's fears and wipe his tears precisely because, through denying his own goodness, God himself descended into evil, even to the point of soliciting the sin of filicide. Only through this interpretation does God, as depicted by this author, avoid accusations of resting in transcendent self-affirmation high up in heaven and, on the contrary, appear as a being rich in the highest love because he dwells within humans on earth through self-negation (Sekine, 327).[136]

7.5 Summary

The exceedingly difficult question of whether we can ultimately acknowledge as God the God who breaks his promise and commands filicide in the Akedah can only be answered in the negative if one stops at an understanding of a good, personal God based on objective logic. We cannot acknowledge such a God as God.

---

134 Von Rad, *Genesis*, 239 (1981, p. 194).
135 Nishida, "The Logic of *Topos* and the Religious Worldview (I)," 25 (1949, p. 319 ff.).
136 Sekine, *Kyūyaku Seisho to Tetsugaku*, 38.

Ever since Hegel, however, philosophy has pierced through the darkness of this traditional concept of God. Contemporary religious faith and biblical interpretation must take this into consideration and not run counter to enlightenment rationality. Having probed the narrative philosophically along the line running from Hegel to Nishida, we have concluded that it is possible to answer in the affirmative the question of whether one can acknowledge the logic of a God who commands filicide. We have discovered here a consistently ethical God who himself temporarily descends into the evil of soliciting filicide and thereby saves Abraham, who had appropriated the gift for himself personally and had fallen into the sin of ingratitude toward the giver. We can acknowledge and come to terms with a God of this nature as truly the God of love.

Furthermore, when we interpret the narrative in this way, the three insights discussed below become newly apparent. Undoubtedly, these insights will testify more broadly to the appropriateness of this understanding of a self-negating God. (I wish to respond here to possible doubts about why I have not turned to Josephus concerning God even though I drew heavily from Josephus when reconstructing the feelings of Isaac and Abraham. This is because, if we follow Josephus and have God explain his intentions to Abraham in detail, an essential element of the narrative, namely, the "test," disappears. It is by hesitantly considering various thoughts about God's unknown intentions that a person's heart is kneaded and purified and that a test functions as a test. Therefore, while Josephus' brilliant reconstruction of the dialogue between Abraham and Isaac is valid, it is best to ignore his reconstruction of the dialogue between God and Abraham. This is why I have intentionally refrained from referring to Josephus in this section.)

7.6 Self-Negation within the Creator God

The first insight is the point concerning God's self-negation within creation. When Abraham says, "I raise my hand and swear toward Yahweh, God Most High, creator of heaven and earth," he presupposes creation faith (Gen 14:22). Creation is the creation of that which is other than God in the primordial place where only the absolute God existed (Gen 1:1–2). However, all of creation, including light, sky, sea, land, growing plants, sun, moon, stars, animals, and humans (Gen 1:3 ff.), consists of relative beings. And because relative beings are a negation of an absolute being, God created all things through self-negation in the place where only God existed. Therefore, we can conceive of the relationship between this God and all creation only in panentheistic and topo-logical terms. Of course, neither the Akedah nor the Old Testament in general logically reflect on this matter or bring any philosophical awareness concerning it. Nevertheless, as something that perceives the truth of religious representations, philosophical understandings of God should be fundamentally valid with respect to the representations under consideration. If so, the following point becomes apparent concerning God's command, which at first seems irrational. God is not an unethical God who is inconsistent and breaks his promise concerning the propagation and prosperity of Abraham's descendants when he commands the offering of Isaac. Rather, God gives the command for the purpose of kneading and purifying the awareness of humans (Ps 66:10; 139:23–24; Job 2:3, 10; Jas 1:2–4) as a "test" (or "trial") that brings anew to human consciousness the original truth that he possesses the right to give and take the lives of Abraham and Isaac, and, indeed, the lives of all that live. Is it ultimately going too far to say that this is not merely salvation within God's relationship with Abraham alone, or with Isaac alone, but that it also presents to all people, including the readers of the narrative, a God who urges reflection on the tendency to forget completely the original truth of the gift of creation?

7.7 Self-Negation within the Ethnic God

Another fresh insight that presents itself relates to the theory that regards verses 15 ff. as original to the narrative, as discussed above. At first glance, this passage seems to stop at an understanding of God who seeks nationalistic and materialistic retribution by giving a "reward" through military force in allowing Abraham's descendants to "possess the gate of their enemies." It would seem, then, that it drags this God down from the spiritual heights of the story up until verse 14 and comes to an incomplete and clumsy conclusion. As a result, Old Testament scholars have attempted to treat it as a later accretion. As we have already seen, however, all the evidence in support of this view is tenuous. Therefore, it is necessary to interpret its significance as an authentic part of the narrative. Here, too, its significance can be readily explained when we view it from the perspective of God's self-negation.

Because God must exist uniquely, absolutely, and universally, it is impossible for him to exist as the God of a single ethnic group, or as a multiply relative and individual God who competes with the gods of other ethnic groups. And yet this God of self-negation negates the universality of his own will and descends into particularity. He is a God who temporarily descends into becoming a particular ethnic God that causes Abraham's descendants to "possess the gate of their enemies" (v. 17), but also a God who moves beyond this and once again becomes a universal God who brings "blessing" to "all nations of the earth" (v. 18). In other words, we might call him a God with a self-identity of absolute contradiction of both particular and universal salvation. Of course, Nishida does not develop his argument this far, but to the extent that the God of philosophical self-negation is the ultimate form of a concept of absolute being at which we might arrive beyond our logical probing into the relationship between God and creation, we can discover an application concerning the problematic Akedah, and it becomes possible to grapple with this narrative that initially seems problematic. We might even say that it not only enables us simply to grapple with the narrative, but that perhaps we can detect here the Akedah author's ultimate intentions behind its composition. The author had his eyes fixed not only on Abraham's individual salvation, but also on the salvation of Israel and, furthermore, of "all nations of the earth." We might consider that herein lay the true significance of the Akedah.

Of course, this is a delicate matter. One might readily retort that it is an optimistic, Israel-centric story, and one that is intolerable for the nations whose gates will be possessed. One cannot completely dismiss the possibility that this text affirms brutalities of war that have occurred throughout history in the name of world peace. At least we cannot flatly state that the text does not promote a delusional "glorification of the situation of the pariah people," to use M. Weber's terms. We can point out the author's limitations here, and perhaps it is necessary to view this point suspiciously. It is more likely, however, that the text reflects a peaceful image of bloodless entry into city gates, because it entirely lacks depictions of the "enemy's" humiliating defeat, brutal deaths in battle, or nations reduced to rubble, such as those that are noticably present in prophecies of vengeance (e. g., Isa 47; Jer 50, 51; Nah 1). Therefore, we can and must recognize the unique foothold of this author who, despite living in the ancient world marked by conflicts in which only the strong survive, discovered God's self-negation by looking forward to the "blessing" of "all nations of the earth."

Whatever the case, in order for Old Testament scholarship that advocates objectivity to put a stop to ignoring needlessly the irrationality of a God who commands the sacrifice of Isaac and to plunging into subjective apologetics, and in order for this scholarship to dig deeper into the significance of a broader range of texts, it can and must benefit from philosophy in this way. Whatever the case, in order for Old Testament scholarship that advocates objectivity to put a stop to needlessly ignoring the irrationality of God depicted here and to plunging into subjective apologetics, and in order for this scholarship to dig deeper into the significance of a broader range of texts, it can and must benefit from philosophy in this way.

This ancient Israelite author must have experientially and intuitively felt some resistance to representing God simply as a supremely good God resting high up in heaven. God's greatness and depths that were experienced in reality also negated his own goodness, as well as his universality. Most likely they also temporarily negated his existence, so that he descended to the lowly level of humans, drew near to them, and caused them to exist. In other words, did not God exist especially in the place where he could save them? The climax of this sort of ancient Israelite understanding of God undoubtedly came to fruition in the Akedah. It is only the ruminations of contemporary philosophy that can analyze the true nature of these matters, not through intuition but through logic, while responding to the depths of such divine experience. Inasmuch as it enables us to determine the true nature of matters of which ancient authors could speak only intuitively, philosophy is meaningful for analyzing the Old Testament text, and it is indispensable for these purposes.

7.8 The Meaning of Self-Negation

At the conclusion of this series of considerations, one might still wonder why Isaac, Abraham, and even God reach the negativity of self-negation and why they must necessarily reach it. We can only conclude that it is because a relationship with the other opens up beyond self-negation, and at that point they reach the ultimate positivity of loving the other. Furthermore, it is because, having temporarily passed through the framework constituted by one's own people and the ethnic group with which one shares one's values, they are able to transcend this framework. That is, it is because *agape* as indiscriminate and divine live opens up beyond the restricted framework of *philia*. Ultimately, through the struggle in which God, Abraham, and Isaac staked their existences the Akedah depicted with tremendous tension and urgency how this *agape* might come about. It is precisely for this reason that this vital canonical text, which has continued to stir our hearts from ancient to contemporary times, only becomes clear when we think about it in this way.

7.9 Additional Comments on *Agape*: *Agape* in the Old and New Testaments

Nevertheless, some might argue that, unlike *eros* and *philia*, *agape* is a new form of love that Jesus discovered in the New Testament and that *agape* thinking cannot be found in the Old Testament. Certainly, this is what people generally tend to think. Whether this is actually true, however, is a point that I have questioned before. I have already written about this in several contexts,[137] so here I wish to note briefly only the main points.

When Jesus speaks his thought of love for enemies, he first quotes the Old Testament as a contrasting statement.

> You have heard that it was said, "You shall love your neighbor and hate your enemy." But I say to you, Love your enemies and pray for those who persecute you." (Matt 5:43–44; NRSV)

Commentators normally point out that the expression "hate your enemy" occurs nowhere in the Old Testament, but that "Love your enemies" underlies Leviticus 19:18 (see Matt 22:39).[138] In fact, though, we must notice the following statement that precedes this phrase in Leviticus.

> You shall not hate in your heart anyone of your kin; ... You shall not take vengeance or bear a grudge against any of your people ... (Lev 19:17–18; NRSV)

In other words, at issue here is an "enemy" in the broad sense, namely, among even "neighbors," one who has done bad things to "you," who is "hated" and against whom "grudges" are held and who would naturally be the target of "vengeance." In fact, the message of *agape*—Love that enemy—is already spoken in Leviticus 19:18.

Although hatred of enemies predominates throughout the Old Testament as a whole (for instance, Ps 139:21–23), through a careful reading of the text one recognizes that *agape* thought is not entirely unknown (in addition to the Leviticus text, see Prov 25:21–22; Isa 52:13–53:12; etc.[139]). The Akedah is included within this line of texts. One must not become bound up in a dogmatic schema of assuming that only Christianity knows of *agape*, thereby losing sight of the greatness of the Old Testament God, who descends to the evil level of sinners in enmity against him in order to save them and who temporarily abandons his own universality in order to bring blessing to a people in enmity against him.[140]

---

137 Sekine, *Kyūyaku Seisho no Shisō* (Old Testament Thought), 218–19.

138 Julius Schniewind, *Das Evangelium nach Matthäus* (NTD 2; Göttingen: Vandenhoeck & Ruprecht, 1968), 70 f.; Eduard Schweizer, *Das Evangelium nach Matthäus* (NTD 2; Göttingen: Vandenhoeck & Ruprecht, 1986), 80 f.

139 Regarding the interpretation of these texts, see Sekine, *Kyūyaku Seisho no Shisō*, 215 ff.

140 Elements of *agape* can ultimately be found in Aristotle's treatise on friendship in *Nicomachean Ethics*, though he calls it only *philia*. See Seizō Sekine, *A Comparative Study of the Origins of Ethical Thought: Hellenism and Hebraism* (trans. Judy Wakabayashi; Lanham, Md.: Rowman & Littlefield Publishers, 2005), chapters 3 and 10.

To reiterate, the thoughts of love for enemies and hate for enemies are inter-mixed throughout the Old Testament. In the Akedah, too, the statement that they "shall possess the gate of their enemies" is far from non-resistance or defeatism, as stated above, and it must be seen as a stage prior to arriving at pure *agape*. Yet we must not overlook the fact that, to the extent that one's attention is finally drawn to the "blessing" of "all nations of the earth," the text transcends hate toward the "enemy," which is characteristic of particularistic salvation, and that indiscriminate *agape* for "all nations of the earth," which is characteristic of universalistic salvation, is evident here at least in incipient form. We must re-consider the tradition that has overlooked this and has somewhat hastily buried verses 15 onward as a later accretion.

7.10 The Meaning of *be-har yahwe yera'e*

As further confirmation for the above considerations—this is the third insight that becomes apparent from the summary in 7.5—I wish to conclude this section with some additional comments on the translation and meaning of verse 14.

> 14 So Abraham named that place "Yahweh sees [*yahwe yir'e*[141]]." Today it is said, "On the mountain of Yahweh he shall be seen [*be-har yahwe yera'e*[142]]."

Because the Qal form of the verb *ra'a*, which here means "to see," is contrasted with the Niphal form, it is necessary to translate them literally as the active "Yah-weh sees [*yir'e*]" and the passive "is seen [*yera'e*]." (Apparently because of the difficulty in interpreting *ra'a* here as "to see," there has been a general tendency among traditional translations to follow the Peshitta and the Vulgate, and to par-aphrase both the active and passive forms as meaning "to provide" [for example, NAB, NRS, NEG, LSG, DRB, SCH, Japanese Colloquial Version, New Japanese Bible, New Interconfessional Translation, Masao Sekine version]). Nowadays, as far as I know, the pioneer von Rad and a handful of others are the only ones who translate the basic Hebrew meaning and forms literally. Yet while

---

141 According to BHS, some have proposed reading this as *yera'e* instead of *yir'e*, but there is no support in ancient versions or manuscripts. It would duplicate *yera'e* at the end of the verse, but that alone is an insufficient reason for adopting the reading. If one were to adopt any variant readings here, it would be preferable, rather, to read *yera'e* at the end of the verse as *yir'e* (see the Peshitta and the Vulgate).

142 Though there is a strong tendency to translate *yera'e* as "shall be provided," I prefer my translation here in order to reflect the contrast between *yir'e* and *yera'e*, the active and passive forms of *ra'a* (to see).

these might offer multiple interpretations concerning the object of "sees"—Abraham's obedience, the ram, that which truly benefits the man—they give no explanation of "shall be seen." In my interpretive view, however, it is possible to detect two or three meanings in Yahweh "shall be seen."

First, the text gives testimony that when Abraham, at the end of this great conflict, prepared himself to return to the giver that which he most cherished as a gift not of this world, it was then that God truly appeared immanently to him. Second, we can detect the following insight. People tend to forget the fundamental fact that a human life, which someone might love so dearly that he or she wishes to make it his or her own private possession, is a gift from the transcendental ground of existence that transcends humans. But someone who reaches this understanding through the work of God's descending into human sin can experience an inner fellowship with God of the most intimate kind. Third, we can detect here the pronouncement that God has been newly discovered not as a transcendent being who is "only good," as traditionally conceived, but as a truly immanent God who descends into extreme evil.

And that is not all. Is the subject of *yera'e* here only Yahweh? We are forced to consider the possibility that *yahwe yir'e* is being contrasted with *be-har yahwe yera'e*, and to consider the additional possibility that the implicit subject of the latter verb, a third-person masculine singular form, should not necessarily be limited to Yahweh.

What other possibilities besides Yahweh might we then consider as the hidden, implied subject? In a direct reading, there is a strong possibility that it is Abraham, who is regarded by God. Yet there are also other possibilities. Would it ultimately be an over-interpretation to view it as referring also to Isaac, who was approaching the bitter reality of death, and more generally to humans—indirectly referring to their self-negating obedience—and to the fact that "all nations of the earth shall be blessed by your [Abraham's] descendants" as a "reward" (v. 18)? If the true significance of the Akedah lies in verse 18, as we saw in 7.7, we cannot entirely exclude the possibility that verse 14, which concludes the first half of the Akedah, foreshadows what verse 18 brings into view and that it allows for the possibility of reading multiple meanings there.

Conclusion

A Retrospect of the Main Points Concerning "the True Significance of the Akedah"

My considerations in this chapter have extended over a wide range of issues. In conclusion, therefore, I wish to note once again the central points of my argument. After outlining the history of interpretation spanning well over two thousand years, and through approaching the text of the Akedah anew, I have identified two interpretive blind spots.

The first is the approach that regards verses 15 onward as a later accretion. Influential Old Testament scholars have made this claim, and in my own previous work I accepted this view. Upon a detailed examination, however, I concluded that all of the evidence supporting this view is tenuous. After reflecting carefully on the correspondences between the text leading up to verse 14, upon which modern commentators focus their attention, and verses 15 onward, I have concluded that it is valid to read the text up to verse 18, at least, as a single narrative and as the original text of the Akedah. This has been one fresh perspective.

One more blind spot in the history of interpretation has been the emphasis, notably on the part of Kierkegaard and many others, that silence prevailed throughout the story. Upon a detailed examination, it seems that this is an overstatement because frequent omission of dialogue is characteristic of this author's writing style. This author also made adept use of the technique of intimating the background thoughts and feelings of the characters by depicting their actions. It ought to be the interpreter's conscious task to expose the characters' thoughts and feelings that are at least hidden between the lines by reconstructing the dialogue that might have been omitted.

Through examining the history of interpretation of the Akedah, it became apparent that these two points have been blind spots in interpretation until now. Attending to these points has prompted us to a new reading of the Akedah.

First, how about the case of Isaac? We must start by noticing that a deep love between Isaac and Abraham imbues the simple yet subtle expressions. We might also simply ask why the "boy" Isaac, who thinks it suspicious that there is no animal for the "burnt offering" while he is being bound by his elderly father, does not break free and run. One can only answer that it was because Isaac chose to become the sacrifice himself out of love for his father and in accordance with his trust in God. It is not only fitting but also necessary to detect Isaac's thoughts and feelings of self-negation here.

Next, how about Abraham? Here a deep love for Isaac can be assumed. We cannot entirely exclude the possibility that the father clearly explained to his son

that, as Josephus imagined, "on account of the favors he hath conferred on me ...
[now God] will receive thy soul with prayers and holy offices of religion." It appears, though, that up until the point when he became convinced of what he
must do, the text of the Akedah depicts Abraham's thoughts and feelings as wavering somewhat more than Josephus depicts them. Why does Abraham, who in
other passages protests matters about which he cannot agree, obey silently
and without a single protest God's seemingly irrational command to offer up
his son? One answer is that it is because deep in his heart he accepted the cor-
rectness of God's command. That is, perhaps he was made painfully aware of his
own sin of holding selfishly onto Isaac, who had been a gift of miraculous
"favor," and of his tendency to forget God. Even so, Abraham clung to his wishful thinking that surely God would not break his promise of the propagation and
prosperity of his descendants, and so he gave ambiguous and elusive answers to
the servants and Isaac. Furthermore, it seems that until he reaches the moment
of decision to raise his knife he is expectantly looking for God to stop him. Having passed through the wavering of this human weakness, he finally dies to his
sinful self and resolutely raises his knife against the one he loves and against his
own self that clings to the one he loves. Through this self-negation, Abraham was
truly reborn as "one who fears God."

Here we have ruminated on the thoughts and feelings of Isaac and Abraham.
In each case, a key term has been "self-negation." By contrast, is God complacent and content in self-affirmation as he "tests" the loyalty of humans on
earth from high up in heaven? In the first place, is not a God who would
break his promise concerning the propagation and prosperity of descendants
and command the annihilation of those descendants inconsistent? Can we ultimately conclude that an unethical God commanding filicide is a righteous God?
In the end, it seems that the source of irrationality in this story is this irrationality on God's part. Based on an overview of more than two thousand years of
interpretive history, it seems that the religious traditions of Judaism and Christianity, as well as Old Testament scholarship, which stands in those traditions,
have avoided frank inquiries into this point. Rather, it has been philosophers
who have made such inquiries. After offering my critical considerations concerning the arguments by Kant, Kierkegaard, Buber, Levinas, Derrida, and Miyamoto,
as well as problems with these arguments, I have challenged the traditional concept of God from the philosophical perspective found in the criticism of a personal God from Hegel to Nishida. In doing so, I have taken up the challenge of reinterpreting the Akedah text while focusing on the true significance of its
concept of God that ultimately becomes apparent.

The first point to understand is that if one holds to a cursory understanding of
a personal God according to which God is simply relative to humans, this concept

of God falls into the self-contradiction of a relative absolute being who is relative to relative beings. On the other hand, one cannot call a God who is not relative to humans "God." Therefore, the logical conclusion must be that God is not relative to humans external to himself, but that he is relative to humans within himself. It is also the case that relativity is the negation of absoluteness. Therefore, we must view the relationship between God and humans in panentheistic terms. That is, the absolute being embraces within himself relative beings who negate himself, and he is relative to them. That is the meaning of atonement in the Old and New Testaments. This is because atonement points to the fact that God, whether through the servant of God or the son of God, negates his absoluteness and, by doing so, saves within himself relative beings who have fallen into sin.

As we saw in the case of Abraham, Abraham appropriated Isaac for himself personally and had fallen into the sinful tendency of forgetting God, who originally gave him Isaac. According to this concept of God, in order to save Abraham from his sin God descended into the evil of filicide, which negated his own goodness, and by doing so he prompted Abraham's healing from the selfish sin of clinging to the one to whom he had devoted his affections. Rather than being an unethical, self-affirming God, it becomes apparent that he is truly a self-negating God and a being who abounds in love.

Furthermore, when we reconsider the overall flow of the Abraham story, it seems to contain a general message urging Abraham and, by extension, the reader to return to the original truth that all creation is a gift from God.

Additionally, when we read as a single narrative the texts leading up to verse 14 and following verse 15, we can catch within this concept of God a certain glimpse of God, albeit in embryonic form. It is none other than a glimpse of a God who not only saves Abraham and Isaac but—while functioning as an ethnic God who temporarily negates his universality as an absolute being and causes Abraham's descendants to "possess the gate of their enemies"—is also a God of *agape*, abounding in indiscriminate love, and a universal God who envisions "blessing" for "all nations of the earth."

Finally, in the contrast between *yahwe yir'e* and *be-har yahwe yera'e*, there arose the possibility of multiple readings. First are the possibilities that Yahweh "sees" Abraham's obedience, the ram, and that which truly benefits the man. Secondly, though, are the possibilities that indirectly, on the mountain of Yahweh, the self-negating obedience of Abraham, Isaac, and humans in general, all of whom find themselves in difficult circumstances, "shall be seen," and the hope that "all nations of the earth shall be blessed by your [Abraham's] descendants" as a "reward" also "shall be seen."

I have given this chapter the somewhat exaggerated subtitle "Inquiring into the True Significance of the Akedah." If it is possible to speak of "the true significance of the Akedah," it is my present conclusion that it lies somewhere in this area.

Here I have summarized the main points of this chapter. Perhaps my journey of "inquiring into the true significance of the Akedah" will continue, and perhaps not. Perhaps von Rad's statement that "[t]here are many levels of meaning, and whoever thinks he has discovered virgin soil must discover at once that there are many more layers below that" (162)[143] is true, and perhaps not. I have outlined the history of interpretation spanning well over two thousand years and, with this as my touchstone, I have reconsidered my own interpretation. In this chapter, I have straightforwardly reported points where I have been forced to change direction, points that have not fundamentally changed, and ones that have become newly apparent. I shall leave it up to the reader to determine the merits of my arguments. Whatever the outcome, it is my modest desire that this chapter will prompt each reader's own "inquiry into the true significance of the Akedah" and that it will become a springboard for further considerations.

Prospects for Collaboration Between Old Testament Studies and Philosophy

In conclusion, I wish to bring together several issues raised at various points in my reflections above and consider whether there might be some prospects for collaboration between Old Testament studies and philosophy, as I suggested in the Introduction.

First, we should note that Old Testament philology, which advocates objective readings of the text, arrives at interpretations through operations that are to some degree subjective. Indeed, it is impossible for it to do otherwise. An example of this is the accretion theory concerning Genesis 22:15 ff. Because these verses appear to have taken the high level of stoic spirituality of the "test" in the narrative up to verse 14 and dragged it down to the mundane horizon of materialistic and nationalistic "reward," scholars assume that the text went through redactional stages. I would suggest that there is some subjective arbitrariness at work in how one determines the limits of the original text. When we consider the tenuous nature of each piece of evidence in support of the accretion theory, we are forced to reflect on this subjective arbitrariness within Old Testament scholarly interpretation (including on my own part).

Furthermore, Old Testament scholarship, which is one branch of Christian theology, somehow tends to be apologetic, especially concerning the concept

---

143 Von Rad, *Genesis*, 238.

of God. Scholars tend to become closed up in dialogue among "friends" who presuppose faith. They simplify the matter as obedience to God (Wenham) or praise of God (Westermann), for example, and though philosophers protest (Arimasa Mori)[144] and denounce (Kant), Old Testament scholars tend to overlook the unethicality and contradictions of this God. Moreover, Old Testament scholarship tends to run only to philological commentary, such as that which I have introduced throughout my notes, or to the dimension of historical speculation such as whether or not the author was the Elohist. Ultimately, however, I would suggest that it relates shallowly to this "God" and concludes without having reached deeper layers of the text and without having appreciated its true significance. I think these tendencies have been made apparent in the present study. The outcome is becoming unnecessarily closed to the wider range of meanings available in the Old Testament text and falling into paternalism toward a self-absorbed text. This point is facing sharp challenges from today's difficult intellectual and hermeneutical circumstances.

What, then, are we to do? Rather than stopping at value-freedom (*Wertfreiheit*) under the pretext of Weberian "asceticism," must not researchers responsibly explore and speak out concerning values? Certainly, unlike Old Testament philology, systematic theology speaks about values, but as we have seen in the interpretations of the Akedah by Bonhoeffer and Barth, it seems there is a tendency to become constrained by presuppositions that subjective Christian faith is self-evident. It is philosophy, after all, that opens the way for general consideration of objective values. In particular, apart from philosophy there is no other means of extensively exploring the limitations of the Judeo-Christian concept of a personal God, which falls into the logical contradiction of a relative absolute being, and, at the same time, of drawing comparisons with other religions and considering contemporary intellectual horizons.

On the other hand, things become too abstract through philosophy alone. It is also true that it is possible to walk speculatively alone and to fall into the trap of unnecessarily losing sight of the richness of symbolism filled with the riddles and metaphors of specific texts in the Old Testament and of the dynamics of decoding it. Kant's and Derrida's mistakes in ignoring the tradition-historical context of the Akedah[145] are examples of falling into this trap. Rather, we should not lose hope in the truth that the visceral power of the text can be revealed to us through the work of struggling with, and explaining, the concrete symbols that pull at our heartstrings.

---

144 See note 129.
145 See note 130.

Hence Old Testament scholarship and philosophy supplement one another, each making up for the other's deficiencies, and it is essential to construct a complementary relationship between them. Although more than half a century has passed since the philosophical-hermeneutical proposals of Gadamer and Ricœur, Old Testament scholarship still has a tendency to neglect the need for philosophy. In view of this situation, I have intentionally devoted space here to pursuing the possibility of philosophical interpretation. I wish to conclude these considerations, however, by noting that my ultimate intention is to construct a complementary relationship between the two.

Chapter 2 The Paradox of Suffering: Comparing Second Isaiah and Socrates

Introduction

If we have the Old Testament in mind when considering "the paradox of suffering," we might recall Max Weber's distinction between *Unheilstheodizee* and *Theodizee des Leidens* and his argument that the latter is "the only true and full-fledged theodicy."[1] In Japanese these two expressions have been rendered along the lines of "theodicy of calamity" and "theodicy of hardships,"[2] but it is more fitting to translate the latter as "theodicy of suffering." This is because Second Isaiah's theodicy is an apologetic centered on the unjust suffering of the righteous. In religious contexts the narrow sense of "suffering" does not simply refer to a general experience of hardships. Furthermore, its "paradox" points to the notion that suffering, which usually carries purely negative connotations, encompasses the possibility of some kind of positive transformation. *Theodizee des Leidens* can indeed be viewed as an example of that.

In the first half of this chapter, I consider the particulars surrounding Second Isaiah's theodicy of suffering. The argument could potentially develop in at least three directions. One would be a comparison of the many similar examples found in other Old Testament books such as Jeremiah and Job. A second direction might be a consideration of Jesus Christ's suffering on the cross, which became the center of New Testament Christianity while being implicitly and explicitly influenced by Second Isaiah. Here, however, I intentionally choose a third direction. I shall cast a comparative eye on the suffering of execution by Socrates, who appeared in Greece nearly contemporaneously with Second Isaiah in Israel, and on the explanation by his grandson-disciple Aristotle of the circumstances in which suffering is possible. The first two directions would result in comparing instances similar to and contiguous with Second Isaiah. By contrast, the third path results in a comparison with an apparently quite dissimilar and unrelated instance. This approach also includes the possibility of philosophical reflection on the essence of things typically lacking in Hebraic thought.

In Part 1, therefore, I explore examples in Hebraic thought of the religious paradox of the suffering of God's servant, and in Part 2 I follow the thread of Hel-

---

1 Max Weber, *Gesammelte Aufsätze zur Religionssoziologie III: Das Antike Judentum* (Tübingen: J. C. B. Mohr, 1920; 1971, 5. Aufl.), 384 ff.
2 Max Weber, *Kodai Yudaya-kyō II* (Ancient Judaism II) (trans. Yoshiaki Uchida; Tokyo: Misuzu Shobō, 1962), 472 ff.

lenic philosophical analyses to reflect on the universal significance of this suffering. This approach enables religion and philosophy to compensate for each other's deficiencies. The analyses in Parts 1 and 2 together call for a reflection in Part 3 that opens up additional prospects concerning the ultimate locus of the essence of the paradox of suffering.

1 Theodicy of Suffering in Israelite Religion

1.1 Suffering of the Righteous in the Book of Second Isaiah

In the prophetical writings of the Israelite prophet Second Isaiah (Isa 40–55), who is thought to have been active around 539 BCE, the year of liberation from Babylonian exile, there is a series of songs about a righteous person who died from unjust hardships. (The songs of God's servant are [1] Isa 42:1–4; [2] 49:1–6; [3] 50:4–9; [4] 52:13–53:12.) There are numerous theories about the identity of this righteous one. Although the songs are written in symbolically polysemous language that could connote the future messiah or the assembly of Israel, they should first be interpreted as pointing to Second Isaiah himself.[3] After liberation from exile, Second Isaiah urged the Israelite people to cross the wilderness, return to Zion, their homeland where Israel's God Yahweh dwelled, reconstruct the ruins of that homeland, and rebuild the temple that had been destroyed. Many of those in exile, however, were loath to relinquish the positions and possessions acquired in Babylon and to subject themselves to danger and hardships. We may presume that as a result they denounced and persecuted this prophet whose religious standpoint threatened their secular stability.

> I surrendered
> my back to those who struck;
> my cheeks to those who pulled out [my beard];
> from insult and spit
> I did not hide my face. (Isa 50:6)[4]

This passage portrays the persecution from Second Isaiah's viewpoint. The beard was a symbol of masculine strength, and it was humiliating to have it pulled out

---

3 For a critical glimpse of the history of research on this, see Seizō Sekine, *Transcendency and Symbols in the Old Testament: A Genealogy of the Hermeneutical Experiences* (Berlin: Walter de Gruyter, 1999), 341 ff.

4 Seizō Sekine, trans., *Izaya-sho* (Book of Isaiah) (Tokyo: Iwanami Shoten, 1997). All ensuing quotations from the book of Isaiah are also from this translation.

or shaved off (2Sam 10:4 – 5; Isa 7:20; etc.). The prophet's subjectively resolute response to persecution is expressed in this third servant song. Yet in the fourth song, which is thought to be that of a later disciple describing the prophet's state, the level of persecution escalates, indicating that the prophet suffered objectively wretched conditions.

> He was despised,
> forsaken by people,
> a person of suffering,
> one familiar with sickness.
> Despised as one from whom faces are turned,
> we regarded him not. (Isa 53:3)

"He" (Second Isaiah), who stirred up his people's rebellion the more he appealed for them to return from exile, was reduced to "a person of suffering" who was "forsaken by people," so that even "we" (the disciples around Second Isaiah) "regarded him not" and "despised" him. In this way, "He was oppressed, but ... he opened not his mouth" (Isa 53:7a), and in the end, "By oppressive justice, he was taken away ... he was cut off from the land of living ones" (Isa 53:8). What, then, is "justice" (*mishpaṭ*)? In general terms, it refers to God's governance that guides history, but here its concrete meaning becomes clear in the following verses:

> He was pierced for our infidelities,
> crushed for our iniquities.
> The punishment for the sake of our peace was upon him,
> by his bruises, we ourselves were healed.
> We all have wandered like sheep, each toward his own path.
> But Yahweh, regarding all our iniquities,
> made him to intercede. (Isa 53:5 – 6)

In short, this is substitutionary atonement. God's "justice" was concealed here.

1.2 Max Weber's Interpretation and its Merits

If a righteous person is to die a death of irrational suffering, God's history-guiding justice will not be established—hence the need for a theodicy that somehow vindicates God's righteousness. It is Max Weber who can be credited for reinterpreting these servant songs of Second Isaiah from a theodicean perspective and who introduced an important concept in Old Testament interpretation.[5]

Weber's interest in this topic lies in a comparison with the pre-exilic prophets. Problems of theodicy—namely, questioning whether the righteousness of a God who brings calamity after calamity upon his covenant people can ultimately be vindicated—also occur repeatedly in the pre-exilic prophets Amos, Hosea, Isaiah, and Jeremiah. Yet according to Weber, the answer was determined from the outset. A people who violate the covenant and commit sin are corporately responsible, and it is right for them to bear the punishment of God's wrath. Calamity, therefore, is not irrational. Rather, it establishes God's righteousness, because it is God's just punishment for the people's sin. Weber referred to this type of theodicy by the pre-exilic prophets as a "theodicy of calamity."

In contrast to this type of simple theodicy, Weber argued that the post-exilic prophet Second Isaiah "created the most thorough, no, the only true and full-fledged theodicy produced by ancient Judaism."[6] He called this "theodicy of suffering" and distinguished it from "theodicy of calamity." According to Weber, this theodicy leads to apotheoses of hardship, misery, poverty, self-abasement, ugliness, and the like. This embodies a reversal of the idea that the righteous assembly of Israel or a single righteous person will experience "unjust hardships" yet thereby bring universal salvation to all peoples. Weber argues that the intention of this "theodicy of suffering" was to vindicate God's justice, which on the surface appeared unjust, through "glorification of the situation of [Israel's current miserable condition as] the pariah people,"[7] thereby transforming the significance of the righteous one's irrational suffering from negative to positive.

Weber thus brilliantly expounded the uniqueness of Second Isaiah's theodicy of suffering in comparison with the pre-exilic prophets, but a number of questions remain about the interpretation of Second Isaiah.[8] Here I shall focus on two of these, merely noting the key points.

First, Weber goes much too far in reading the figure of corporate Israel into servant songs that originally depict the life and death of an individual. Second, he over-emphasizes "unjust hardships" and, by contrast, treats substitutionary atonement as secondary. As far as the first point is concerned, though we need not exclude comparisons to Israel, the songs first need to be explained as referring to the suffering of Second Isaiah the individual. Regarding the second point, which is particularly important in the context of this chapter on "the

---

5 Weber, *Das Antike Judentum*, 314 ff.
6 Ibid., 384.
7 Ibid., 392.
8 Sekine, *Transcendency and Symbols in the Old Testament*, 376 ff.

paradox of suffering," surely the negative value of suffering remains negative if we focus only on "unjust hardships." Even if we were to limit our focus to Weber's line of argumentation, we could not arrive at his positive conclusion about the "glorification" of the suffering of one who saves all peoples merely on the basis of the negative assessment that he experienced unjust hardships. It is only through investing this suffering with the positive significance of substitutionary atonement that the value of suffering is transformed from negative to positive and this servant is glorified.

Yet Weber might still have a valid point. Atonement thought can also be found in other parts of the Old Testament outside of Second Isaiah, so it cannot be the factor that makes "the only full-fledged theodicy" here "the only [one that is] full-fledged." Indeed, Weber cites the example of Moses (Exod 32:32), among others, and points out that atonement thought was generally known in the Old Testament.[9]

In my view, however, we should distinguish among three levels in Old Testament atonement thought. First are the animal sacrifices that atone for human sin, such as those in Leviticus and other books. Second are offers to die in the place of others by people such as Moses and Jeremiah (the offers are, however, rejected by God, so none die for others). Third is the suffering of Second Isaiah, the sole instance where a person actually "poured out his life to death" (Isa 53:12). Here atonement reaches a level unprecedented in the Old Testament, being actually accomplished through a person suffering death, not through animals or potential prayers. This alone is "the only full-fledged" atonement thought, and it is reasonable to regard this as the unparalleled factor that makes "the only full-fledged theodicy" "the only [one that is] full-fledged." For as Weber himself recognizes, Job experienced similarly "unjust hardships," which is Weber's distinguishing factor.

Finally, I might add that in the New Testament this atonement thought moves on to the ultimate level: it is the level of faith that the son of God—not animals or humans—poured out his life to death.

1.3 Despair in Life

Theodicy is symbiotically connected to anthropodicy. The reason is that when righteousness is restored to a righteous person who was regarded as unrighteous because he bore unjust hardships, God's justice, which appeared to tolerate in-

---

9 Weber, *Das Antike Judentum*, 389.

justice, is also vindicated. What I wish to reconsider here is the point at which this anthropodicy, which is simultaneously a theodicy, is established. Is it established during the righteous person's lifetime or after his death? In particular, when is it established in the righteous person's own self-awareness?

Second Isaiah's fourth servant song, though a problematic passage with many variant readings in ancient manuscripts and translations, reads as follows in its final strophe:

> 10b If you make his life an atonement offering,
> he shall see the days of his descendants last long.
> And Yahweh's will shall be accomplished in his hand.
>
> 11 After the tribulations of his life, he shall see.
> Through knowing, he shall be satisfied.
> My righteous servant shall make many righteous,
> he himself shall bear their sins. (Isa 53:10b–11)

The Latin Vulgate renders "you" in the first line of v. 10b as "he," and the Dead Sea manuscript and the Septuagint insert "light" after "he shall see" in the first line of v. 11. Generally speaking, the Septuagint differs considerably from the Masoretic Text in vv. 10 – 11, and the Peshitta, the Syriac version, also has one variant, but I shall not go into those here.[10]

If we first read this strophe according to the Masoretic Text, it means that when "you" (the Israelites) repentantly and self-consciously receive back the "life" that "he" (God's servant) "poured out ... to death" (v. 12) as "an atonement offering" for your own sin, then the servant shall see the prosperity of his "descendants" and "be satisfied" (52:13). It is not clear here whether the servant is resurrected, but some kind of life after death is assumed. And "Yahweh's will," which is substitutionary atonement, shall also "be accomplished" here. So in verse 11, after a life of "tribulations" filled with utter despair, the servant sees the "light" of hope for the first time, as the Dead Sea manuscript and the Septuagint correctly gloss, and he is "satisfied." Verse 11 concludes with the pronouncement that at that time "My righteous servant" shall, for the first time, self-awaredly assent to and accomplish the substitutionary atonement that "bear[s] their sins." The Vulgate's alternative reading at the beginning of verse 10b, then, anticipates the same meaning as that found in the conclusion of verse 11, but the Masoretic Text indicates that God's hidden "justice" (53:8), which consists of substitutionary atonement, shall be revealed in Israel's self-

---

10 Cf. Klaus Baltzer, *Deutero-Isaiah: A Commentary on Isaiah 40 – 55* (Fortress Press, 2001), 420 ff.

awareness followed by, and together with, the servant's self-awareness. Hence the Masoretic Text seems to depict the process of accomplishing atonement more clearly and with greater balance.

Whatever the case, the point I wish to make here is that it was after the servant's death that both Israel and the servant realized the redemptive significance of his death. During the servant's life, the people of Israel saw his wretched condition and disparaged it:

> We thought of him as
> beaten,
> struck by God, and afflicted. (Isa 53:4b)

As for the servant, he is described as follows:

> He was oppressed, but he himself endured,
> he did not open his mouth,
> like a lamb led to the slaughter,
> or like a ewe that stays silent before its shearers,
> he did not open his mouth. (Isa 53:7)

A "lamb" and a "ewe" are obedient, but they do not "know" (53:11) the meaning of being "slaughtered" and "sheared."

As for the atonement of Jesus Christ's cross, which represents the ultimate level of theodicy in the New Testament, we can presume that its redemptive significance was not revealed even to Jesus during his lifetime. Among the vast number of words and deeds from Jesus' lifetime that are transmitted in the Gospels, there is almost no mention of the redemptive significance of his giving himself up to death. (Depending on one's interpretation, one might consider Mark 10:45 and 14:24 and the parallel passages Matt 20:28 and 26:28, but these are insufficient in both number and meaning.) The oldest kerygma that clearly speaks about Jesus' atonement was proclaimed by Paul (1Cor 15:3–5; see also Rom 4:25), and it is thought to have been formulated by a primitive sect. Consider, too, Jesus' final cry on the cross, "My God, my God, why have you forsaken me?" (*Eli, Eli, lema sabachthani*) (Matt 27:46 par. Mark 15:34). If we read this straightforwardly—without assuming that the opening words connote the entirety of Psalm 22—we can only interpret it as a cry of desperation from Jesus as he lost sight of the meaning of his death and was abandoned by God.[11]

---

11 Masao Sekine and Susumu Itō, *Matai fukuin-sho kōgi* (Lectures on the Gospel of Matthew) (Shinchi Shobo, 1985), 559–62; Takashi Ōnuki, *Iesu to iu keiken* (An experience called Jesus) (Tokyo: Iwanami Shoten), 214–15.

In fact, to the extent that substitutionary atonement consists of bearing the punishment for the sin of another and atoning for this sin in his or her place, the punishment must be accompanied by a suffering sufficiently and completely proportional to the sin. If the meaning of the atonement is made known beforehand, being "beaten," "oppressed," and crucified would certainly be physically agonizing, but one could spiritually transcend the suffering by virtue of it being a deeply meaningful act by one chosen by God. It is precisely because one does not understand its meaning that the suffering is marked by despair and can become completely commensurate with the deepest sins of soul and body.

2 Egoism of Suffering in Greek Philosophy

2.1 The Execution of Socrates

In ancient Greece in the year 399 BCE, during the period when threads of atonement thought were being spun in Israel from Second Isaiah to Jesus, Socrates was tried in the court of Athens for "giving a corrupting influence to the youth, and not recognizing the gods that the state recognizes."[12]

According to Socrates' apologetic speech as related by Plato, Socrates merely engaged in philosophical dialogues with people in the streets of Athens in order to teach them the paradox of the knowledge of ignorance. From the outset he recognized the existence of the daimonion and that it referred to a god or a child of god; therefore, neither of the two charges against him were legitimate. Ever since Socrates' childhood, the daimonion had usually stopped him when he was about to do something wrong, but it did not do so even once in this trial. Hence he "could fully expect that this was good."[13] It was when the imprisoned Socrates held such hopes that his elderly friend Crito suggested that he escape from prison. In response, Socrates advocated a return to the "*logos*" whereby "That which we must value is not merely to live, but to live well."[14] According to that *logos*, even if he were to bear the injustice of an execution based on false charges, it would be neither good nor beauteous to respond in the form of yet

---

12 Plato, *Sokuratesu no benmei* (Apology of Socrates); *Sekai no meicho 6: Plato I* (Famous Writings of the World 6: Plato I) (trans. Michitarō Tanaka; Tokyo: Chuo Koronsha, 1978); John Burnet, *Platonis Opera*, 5 vols. (Oxford Classical Texts, 1900–1907), 24C.
13 Ibid., 40C.
14 Plato, *Kuriton* (Crito), 48B; *Sekai no meicho 6: Plato I* (Famous Writings of the World 6: Plato I).

another injustice—i.e., escaping from prison. Socrates argued that one ought not to do that which is not beauteous.

If this image of Socrates portrayed in Plato's early writings is historically accurate, it suggests that although Socrates consistently viewed his execution as unjust suffering, he accepted it in accordance with the *logos*. It also suggests that with hope in both the daimonion and the afterlife,[15] he calmly met his death "having good hope toward death."[16]

Commenting on the afterlife, Socrates says that death is either a deep sleep or a transition to another place. If it is the former, there could be nothing more pleasant. Even if it is the latter, surely that would be a blessing, because it would be a journey to meet good people from the past.[17]

There appears to be doubt as to whether Plato, in his middle writings, truly viewed his teacher's death as unjust suffering. For example, in his portrayal in the *Republic*[18] of youth manipulating philosophically weak arguments with the intention of overturning good traditions but ultimately drowning in a self-corrupted lifestyle, we find Plato's reflection on the potential dangers, at least, of philosophical dialogues originating with Socrates actually "giving a corrupting influence to the youth." There could also be a question of whether the "*daimonion*" (*to daimonion*), which are described philosophically with great care in the sense of "*daimōn*-like beings," are different from the distinctly mythical "gods that the state recognizes."[19] I shall not, however, delve into these points here. Instead, regardless of the extent to which Socrates and Plato viewed Socrates' execution as unjust suffering, I shall proceed to the grandson-disciple Aristotle's reflections on the general circumstances of suffering in a public speech where he, at least, treats it as unjust.

2.2 The Relationship between Love and Suffering in Aristotle

Aristotle does not in fact directly mention the suffering of Socrates. Yet in his contemplation on love, which is positioned as a summation of his virtue ethics

---

15 Plato, *Sokuratesu no benmei* (Apology of Socrates), 40Eff.
16 Ibid., 41C.
17 Ibid., 40Cff.
18 Plato, *Kokka* (Republic), 539Bff.; *Sekai no meicho 7: Plato II* (Famous Writings of the World 7: Plato II) (trans. Michitarō Tanaka; Tokyo: Chuo Koronsha, 1978).
19 Cf. Thomas C. Brickhouse and Nicholas D. Smith, *Socrates on Trial* (Princeton: Princeton University Press, 1989), 124 ff.

(*Nicomachean Ethics*, 819),[20] it seems that he is implicitly and explicitly attempting to elucidate the meaning of Socrates' unjust execution. At least he adds a lucid reflection concerning the fact that it is generally possible for the love of "good people" to end in suffering.

According to Aristotle, love has three objects: "the good, the pleasant, the useful."[21] Love of the latter two cannot be called proper love. They are nothing more than "egoism" (*philautos*)[22] that loves what is pleasurable and useful to oneself (ibid., 9:8).

> By contrast, love of ultimate quality is the love between good people, that is, people who are similar in virtue. I think that any among this kind of people share an equal desire for "the good of one's friend as long as they are good people" (ibid., 8:3).

There is room for interpretation regarding the referent of "the good of one's friend as long as they are good people." In view of how "reason" (*nūs*) is used, however, it is possible to understand this as follows: "Instead of using the other person as a body divorced from the spirit and as a means of pleasure and usefulness, this involves—while not excluding such a perspective on the body—respecting that person as an individual and as a free agent who assumes control through reason and is an autonomous purpose, and it also involves ensuring that this person can live according to reason."[23]

Now, "people criticize a person who loves himself above all others; they find this ugly, and they disdainfully call him an egoist."[24] Yet should egoism be criticized out of hand? Aristotle's answer is no. If "desire," following "the non-reasoning [*alogos*] part of the soul," covets "property, honor, or physical pleasure," such egoism culminates in ugly competition. It certainly deserves to be criticized. By contrast, when people "live according to reason [*logos*]," "have the ability to lead by their reason [*nūs*]," and "on their own generally attempt to obtain various things according to virtue," this kind of egoism, instead of being criticized, merits praise.

---

20 Aristotle, *Nikomakosu rinri-gaku* (Nicomachean Ethics) (trans. Saburō Takata; Tokyo: Iwanami Bunko, 1971, 1973); *Nikomakosu rinri-gaku* (Nicomachean Ethics) (trans. Shinrō Katō; Tokyo: Iwanami Shoten, 1973); *Aristotelis Ethica Nicomachea*, Recognovit brevique adnotatione critica instruxit I. (Bywater, Oxford Classical Texts, 1894).

21 Ibid., 8.2.

22 "Egoism" according to *Nikomakosu rinri-gaku* (Nicomachean Ethics) (trans. Katō), 308.

23 Seizō Sekine, *A Comparative Study of the Origins of Ethical Thought: Hellenism and Hebraism* (trans. Judy Wakabayashi; Lanham, Md.: Rowman & Littlefield Publishers, 2005), 248; also see Yasuo Iwata, *Arisutoteresu no rinri shisō* (Aristotle's Ethical Thought) (Tokyo: Iwanami Shoten, 1985), 298 ff.

24 *Nikomakosu rinri-gaku* (Nicomachean Ethics), 9.8.

After presenting this argument, Aristotle comments as follows about the ul-timate phase—i.e., the sacrificial death of such a praiseworthy egoist:

> Each person's reason chooses the best thing for himself, and a good person obeys the com-mands of reason ... Of course a good person does many things for friends and country, and if necessary, he will undeniably throw away his life for them. Indeed, he will not decline to abandon property, honor, and various good things for which people generally compete. How-ever, in that case, he would continue obtaining for himself the beauty of the act. After all, he will choose to enjoy pleasure intensely for a brief time rather than to enjoy pleasure luke-warmly for a long time; he will choose to live beautifully for a year rather than to live drably for many years; and he will choose one beautiful and great act rather than many trivial acts. As I think about it, this is the state among people who sacrifice their lives. This, therefore, is the reason they are choosing for themselves great beauty. (NE 9.8)

Socrates called out to his fellow Athenians: "Are you not ashamed that you have gotten caught up in your desire only to gain for yourself as much money as pos-sible? And that, though you care about reputation and status, you do not care about discretion and truth, nor do you care about or consider improving your soul as much as possible into that which is excellent and good?"[25] Socrates, who was persecuted and died for these very things, is the epitome of "a good person" who will "throw away his life" "for friends and country." In fact, "he [did] not decline to abandon property, honor, and various good things for which people generally compete"; as he himself testifies, he experienced "severe poverty" because he had "no leisure for performing public or private deeds."[26] Yet it can be assumed that he consistently chose for himself "great beauty" and that he went calmly to his execution.

2.3 Hope in Life

We can narrow the most important points concerning suffering, the subject of this chapter, down to the following four points:

(1) When viewed in the light of the values of everyday people, who highly value property, honor, and physical pleasure, the sacrificial death of a good person constitutes suffer-ing. Yet for someone who is indifferent to those values and instead strives to obtain the goodness and beauty associated with *logos* and *nūs*, it is simply a matter of choosing to attain what is truly beautiful to him.

---

25 Plato, *Sokuratesu no benmei* (Apology of Socrates), 29DE.
26 Ibid., 23BC.

(2) Ultimately, therefore, he is an egoist who loves and rewards himself, even if this is of a different dimension from egoism in the negative sense.

(3) Additionally, there is an unshakable trust in the value of the rational *logos* and *nūs*.

(4) While the above are ideas shared by Socrates and explained clearly by Aristotle, Socrates held the following view on death: whether it be a deep sleep or a transmigration to another place, death is filled with "good hope."

In sum, among the Greek philosophers Socratic suffering was regarded as nothing other than the achievement of egoism in a good sense. Once we view it in this light, a striking contrast to the Hebraic understanding of suffering seen in Part 1 becomes apparent. As far as the suffering of God's servant in ancient Israel and Christianity was concerned,

(1) There was no room for him to choose the good and the beautiful. The suffering was nothing but a miserable, ugly evil to be avoided if possible and a death of agony and despair.

(2) Yet by intentionally descending into this suffering for the sake of his people, he transcends egoism.

(3) For Second Isaiah and Jesus, trust in reason is not a question to be entertained. The only thing of value was a faith that clung to God, although his will was difficult to understand ("Eli, Eli" was an adherence to "my God" in the midst of despair).

(4) The afterlife in Hebraic thought is commonly depicted as a place of nothingness and despair, where communion with God is cut off (Ps 88:10–13; Eccl 9:10; etc.), and it would have been difficult to embrace hope in it.

In a nutshell, in Hebraic thought deaths of suffering ultimately ended in the absurdity of being cast down into a hopeless place through unjust attacks; in the sufferer's self-awareness during his lifetime such a death could not have been assigned anything other than a negative value. Only after the sufferer's death, to the extent that God's redemptive work was recognized in it, was there a faint possibility of transformation into something that could be assigned a positive value.

3 Suffering as the Starting Point of Liberation from Egoism

3.1 Abandonment of Egoism

As we have seen in our comparison thus far, within Greek philosophy both Socrates and Aristotle had trust in *logos*, and they were calculating and confident regarding the meaning of their own deaths, so that even suffering in a situation characterized by non-*logos* was acceptable. During their lifetimes they found positive value in suffering. By contrast, within Israelite religion both Second Isaiah and Jesus met their ends in despair, shaken by the meaninglessness of their own deaths on the occasion of their suffering. Yet was there truly nothing there but negative value?

That is not necessarily so. We could argue that here for the first time there occurs a reversal of the self-pursuit that consists of striving to "obtain for himself beauty" based on calculation and confidence. In other words, liberation from the egoism that people inherently and continuously pursue—in philosophy and re-lated areas this frequently becomes the work of reason;[27] in religion, it takes the form of the pursuit of self-enlightenment, salvation, and the like[28]—somehow occurs, and a horizon of *tariki* religion[29] that transcends philosophy or the path of enlightenment is opened for the first time. It does not lessen the suffering and disillusionment engendered by unjust suffering, but one would surely become conscious of this passive state when pressed into this path, even if it differs qual-itatively from an active path brimming with calculation and confidence.

God's servant—i.e., Second Isaiah—did not know the details of God's will, nor could he find "satisfaction" (Isa 52:13) in the midst of turmoil, but he "en-dured, he did not open his mouth, like a lamb led to the slaughter ... he did not open his mouth" (Isa 53:7), and he followed God obediently.

> "My Father, if it is possible, let this cup pass from me; yet not what I want but what you want." (Matt 26:39)

Though offered in the midst of anxiety over being unable to discern God's will clear-ly, Jesus' prayer in Gethsemane expresses the ultimate dynamism of conquering ego-ism by finally abandoning the self's desires and entrusting oneself to God.

3.2 Devotion

The German term *Hingabe*, which connotes this kind of self-abandonment, liter-ally means to throw (oneself) away. It refers to the "devotion" of suffering, but

---

27 Seiichi Yagi, *Shūkyō to wa nani ka: Gendai shisō kara shūkyō e* (What is religion: From modern thought to religion) (Kyoto: Hozo-kan, 1998), 198 ff.

28 Shojun Bando, "Jesus Christus und Amida. Zu Karl Barths Verständnis des Buddhismus vom Reinen Land," in *Gott in Japan: Anstöße zum Gespräch mit japanischen Philosophen, Theologen, Schriftstellern* (eds. Seiichi Yagi und Ulrich Luz; München: Kaiser, 1973), 77 ff.

29 *Tariki* religion is one whereby people are saved by an 'outside power' (that is, a power outside of oneself).

not only that. It is deeply interesting that it also refers to "conversion" to the religion opened up by that sufferer. Suffering brings about the conversions of those shaken by it and reproduces liberation from egoism.

My meaning is as follows. After some time of disaffection the disciples who had gathered around Second Isaiah wove together their teacher's prophetic collections when, with remorse, they learned the meaning of his atonement. And after Jesus' death, a primitive sect formed around the apostles who clung to faith in the atonement of the cross. In this way, a community of devotees was born in each instance. Admittedly, this looks suspiciously like a belated elegy on the part of those who had abandoned the sufferer or had tormented and killed him, or a Freudian "work of mourning"[30] to self-console victimizers indebted to the sufferer, or a fictional construct aimed at somehow turning the negativity of suffering into something positive. And perhaps we cannot erase doubts about why such a simple faith can have validity as a path of religious salvation.

Yet through devotion to their teacher—who was forced to abandon egoism, who atoned for their sins in their stead, and who died while praising the tranquility of abandoning the egoism of self-pursuit—and through faith in God's will for salvation as displayed in this act, did not they too become void and empty and experience transcendence over egoism? This is the only aspect in which easy religious practices where devotees rely upon the power of another, such as faith in the *nenbutsu* chant, are superior to difficult ascetic practices where people rely upon their own power, such as philosophical inquiry and ascetic practices of meditation. As Aristotle quite rightly said, philosophy is the egoist's path. And as Luther and the medieval Buddhist monk Shinran shrewdly observed, the ascetic path of pursuing self-enlightenment or mystical experiences also tends, in the end, to be beset by the dilemma of being unable to shake off the fetters of egoism, even though it can be regarded as "religious." By contrast, the believer who despairs over his or her own sins, abandons the powerless self, and clings to the atonement of the cross or the vows of Amida Buddha through prayer or *nenbutsu* will in due course realize that he or she has transcended egoism.

To the extent that Amida desired to sacrifice himself for the salvation of all beings, his 48 vows may be mentioned here as potential suffering in the broad sense. This merits correction of the Barthian understanding that the object of veneration in Jōdo Shinshū is merely the image of Amida Buddha.[31] As Shojun

---

30 Migaku Satō, *Higeki to fukuin: Genshi kirisuto-kyō ni okeru higeki-teki naru mono* (Tragedy and the Gospel: the tragic in primitive Christianity) (Tokyo: Shimizu Shoin, 2001), 115.
31 Karl Barth, *Die Kirchliche Dogmatik: Die Lehre vom Wort Gottes Prolegomena zur Kirchlichen Dogmatik*, Vol. I/2 (Zürich: Evangelischer Verlag, 1960), 374.

Bando correctly argues in rebuttal,[32] the object of veneration in Jōdo Shinshū is Namu Amida Buddha's name, rather than the image. Furthermore, that which is referred to as "Amida Buddha" is not a motionless object, but the actual occurrence of the desire to save all beings. "Namu" expresses the act of all beings devoting themselves (Selbsthingabe) to that desire. In that case, the whole phrase "Namu Amida Buddha" is not a material substance, but an event. This presumably refers to the same situation seen in the effective work of the Holy Spirit whereby "it is no longer I who live, but it is Christ who lives in me" (Gal 2:20) through faith in the atonement of Jesus Christ on the cross. In that case, I do not exercise faith; rather, the spirit of Christ lives in me and promotes faith. This is in line with the fact that all beings' call to Amida Buddha is actually a recitation of Amida Buddha's prior call to all beings.

When people devote themselves (Selbsthingabe) in response to the suffering caused by self-giving (Selbsthingabe) on the part of Christ or Amida Buddha, they discover that they have broken away from the thoughts of egoism attached to them.[33] Freeing oneself of self-interest is next to impossible for most people. Yet for those who simply devote themselves to suffering, it becomes possible to pull away from self-interest without special effort. If they have not devoted themselves in this way, however, it is exceedingly difficult to achieve this, no matter how great an effort they expend on ascetic practices or philosophy. By contrast, when they do devote themselves, they might find themselves already in a state of selflessness without having any intention of returning to such a state of selflessness. No longer then can be found the self that has not been liberated from self-interest; the self that has been engaged with other things; the self that, despite having accepted suffering, will not abandon calculations for obtaining the beauty of logos; or on the other hand, the troubled self that wavers while searching for salvation in another time and place; the self that complains of its impotence and lack of success after being unable to concentrate on learning the truth through meditation or after being lured by the things of this world and falling back into its old ways despite having once attained truth and enlightenment. In place of that self is none other than the peaceful self that has been purified by the Holy Spirit, or the original self that can be in a state of Nirvana. And who has experienced this peace of the Holy Spirit or the pure blessing of Nirvana more deeply than Christ and Amida Buddha, who suffered through self-devotion?

---

32 Bando, "Jesus Christus und Amida," 75 f.
33 Regarding here and below, see ibid., 78.

3.3 The Paradox of Suffering

"The paradox of suffering" boils down to this. For philosophers, who are scholars of rational inquiry, secular suffering is nothing more than an inconsequential episode from the non-rational world. Yet for religious people, no matter how severe the suffering, it can become an indispensable means to overcome self-saving egoism. It becomes a path that can open to charismatic and ordinary people alike a level of salvation that is closed to them by other methods.

Of course, when expectations or imitations of suffering occur in the further pursuit of meaning, one will likely be again pulled down by the device of the egoism of salvation, and when suffering fossilizes and is understood as a symbol of conferring meaning it loses its paradoxical power to break through egoism. In that sense, the paradox of suffering is singular and raw, and we are fundamentally blocked from consciously manipulating its life and death. As Tillich, among others, points out,[34] Christ's suffering and Amida Buddha's vows are therefore received into the subconscious depths of our existence; we cannot forcefully create a living and working era or society. For the same reason, due care must be taken so that the faith of suffering does not revert to imposing egoism in the name of evangelism, as has happened on innumerable occasions throughout history.

And finally, a Nietzschean censure that demands caution. The faith of suffering can become a shudder-inducing paradox fabricated to justify the ressentiment of the weak; it regards sinners, the sick, and the ignorant who lack wisdom as blissful; it turns all values upside down; and it can be eerily seductive.[35] In my view, from the outset Nietzsche's master morality takes into account only sinless nobles, the disease-free healthy, and noble people excelling in wisdom, and it has a strong tendency to abandon sinners, the sick, and the ignorant. By contrast, the true value of the faith of suffering lies particularly in its support for sinners and the sick, as well as slaves who are not superior in wisdom and *logos*, and in its declaration to them of forgiveness, healing, and acceptance.[36] Actual faith of suffering, however, often falls into attributing value to the sins of sinners, the sicknesses of the sick, and the ignorance of the ignorant. It is necessary to reflect, then, on the risk that the faith of suffering might merely end up as egoism's self-consolation.

---

34 Paul Tillich, "Wesen und Wandel des Glaubens" in *Gesammelte Werke*, Vol. VIII (Stuttgart: Evangelisches Verlagswerk, 1970), 140.
35 Friedrich Nietzsche, *Zur Genealogie der Moral*, in *Nietzsche Werke* VI-2 (Berlin: Walter de Gruyter, 1968), 271.
36 Sekine, *A Comparative Study of the Origins of Ethical Thought*, 239.

We must take great heed of the fact that the atoning events of Judaism and Christianity (and also the vows of Amida Buddha), as well as faith in them, are fraught with the possibility of devolving into this further paradox. These are unavoidable problems and levels that are essentially related to the themes of religion and violence[37] and to this modern age of frequent terrorism and wars based on religion. At this stage, it is necessary to complement the path of relying on the power of another (*tariki*) with the path of relying on one's own power (*jiriki*), through such means as philosophical meditation. Yet if we heed these concerns and return to "the paradox of suffering," which is the theme of this chapter, the following point must be emphasized. If the "paradox of suffering" fundamentally exists, we can manage somehow to speak of it only within the context of the faith of atoning sacrifice, which has a unique structure that "paradoxically" transforms "suffering"—which in and of itself has only a negative value—into a positive value as a religious symbol that transcends egoism.

In the spring of 2004 I taught an intensive lecture and seminar course at the University of Vienna while receiving daily news about the United States' Iraq War and the terrorist attacks in Madrid and Cologne. There I was blessed with the opportunity to read, together with European philosophy students who knew victims of war and terrorism among those close to them, the above-mentioned German essay by Shojun Bando that compares Protestantism and Amida Buddhism. That experience led me to reevaluate the contrasting examples of the sufferers Second Isaiah and Socrates, who made their appearances in Hebraic and Hellenistic thought, which are the two mainstreams of European intellectual history, within a new framework of religion, especially the *tariki* faith of atoning sacrifice, and philosophy, especially the *jiriki* egoism of self-inquiry. I pray for the repose of Shojun Bando, who met an untimely death that winter, and I wish to express my thanks to the students at the University of Vienna with whom I discussed *Hingabe*.

---

37 An earlier version of this chapter was originally included in *Bōryoku: Hakai to Chitsujo* (Violence: Destruction and Order) (Iwanami Kōza Shūkyō Dai-8 Kan; Tokyo: Iwanami Shoten, 2004).

Chapter 3 Reconstructing Old Testament Monotheism: A Dialogue between Old Testament Studies and Philosophy

Introduction

The reputation of monotheism has suffered of late. Since 9/11, in particular, its critics have tended to argue that monotheism has reached a "dead end" in the clash between the Christian and Muslim worlds.[1] In the course of giving genuine consideration to this criticism, let us deconstruct those concepts of "monotheism" that ought to be deconstructed. And if anything of revelatory power then remains, let us consider how it might be reconstructed.[2] That is the goal of this chapter: to examine this point critically while looking back at the Old Testament, which is regarded as the source of monotheism. The various types of Old Testament monotheism have already been discussed from many angles within the framework of Old Testament studies proper.[3] Here, therefore, I deliberately

---

[1] *Asahi Shimbun* (Morning Edition), December 31, 2003.

[2] I know of no explanation of "reconstruction" more precise than that of Jirô Watanabe, the supervising editor of *Seiyô Tetsugaku-shi Saikôchiku Shiron* (Tentative Treatises for a Reconstruction of the History of Western Philosophy) (Tokyo: Showado, 2007), a volume that far surpasses the present chapter on this topic. Watanabe describes reconstruction as a three-stage folding of intellectual work that comprises 'composition,' 'dismantlement,' and 'recomposition' of (1) uncertain intellectual givens regarded as self-evident; (2) testing of these through doubt, suspicion, and dismantling; and (3) the adventure of proposing truth concerning those matters that merit reconstruction." This, says Watanabe, is "the logical structure underlying the foundation of all reconstruction proposals" (ibid., 5). Though inadequate, the present chapter is an "adventure," if not a reckless attempt, that has the "logical structure" of such a "three-stage ... work." It is no more than a tentative treatise that I first presented in a keynote address at the Japan Society of Christian Studies with the intention of stimulating debate within that broader framework.

[3] For an overview of the research history, see note 16 below. The Japan Society of Christian Studies, to which I referred in the previous note, customarily holds the keynote address on the first day of its conference, followed by a symposium on the same theme the next day. In 2004, however, the symposium was cancelled due to a typhoon, so I lost the opportunity for debate, other than a question and answer time after the keynote address. The following year a symposium on "the Problem of Monotheism in the Old Testament," which I moderated, was held by the Society for Old Testament Study in Japan. On that occasion the following detailed presentations were given based on the framework of Old Testament studies proper, and these appear in *Kyûyaku-gaku Kenkyû* 3 (Old Testament Studies 3) (Society for Old Testament Study in Japan, 2006): Tetsuo Yamaga, "Kyûyaku Seisho wa Ikanaru Imi de Isshinkyô de atta no ka?" (In What Sense was the Old Testament Monotheistic?), 33–57; Akio Tsukimoto, "Kodai Isuraeru Isshinkyô" (Ancient Israel's Monotheism), 58–79; Kôichi Namiki, "Yudaya-kyô ni okeru

extend the framework to include philosophical viewpoints outside of Old Testament studies and attempt to propose a rough roadmap, while intentionally relating this topic to contemporary issues.

1 What is Problematic about Monotheism?

What is the problem with monotheism in the first place? An essay by Kazurô Mori summarizes the points at issue in contemporary Japanese discussions about monotheism,[4] so let us begin by reviewing these in order to confirm the loci of the problem.

According to Mori, monotheistic Jews and Christians both brim with self-confidence concerning their own "omnipotence" and "goodness" "by becoming the alter ego of the only absolute God."[5] Based on this confidence, Christians in particular worked toward developing scientific technology, colonizing new continents, and making the shift to capitalism. Though it was Hegel who upheld Christianity as the embodiment of absolute spirit, today the truth is found, rather, in Feuerbach, who criticized Hegel. Feuerbach maintained that "egoism is essentially monotheistic because it holds up only one thing—self—its purpose"[6] and that "Christianity spiritualized the egoism of Judaism and made it pure egoism."[7] Mori concurs that "because Christians (and Jews) are entirely devoted to divinely approved egoism, they have no self-awareness whatsoever that they are egoistic, and thus they are able to persist boldly and without limit in their sanctified egoism."[8] Mori calls this kind of believer an "ultra-egoist."

Isshinkyô no San Ruikei" (Three Types of Monotheism in Judaism), 80–98. I touch upon Tsukimoto's essay in note 48 below. In this chapter, however, it is Tsukimoto's older manuscript to which I primarily refer (see note 13). This warrants an apology in that Tsukimoto might not wish an essay he wrote more than a decade ago to be brought back to the table for discussion. At the time of my address, however, it was the leading work in Japanese on Old Testament monotheism. Additionally, I have chosen to retain both my general outline in the address and this contrasting essay as a record of how approaches in arguments concerning monotheism have changed considerably over the past decade or two.

4 Kazurô Mori, "Isshinkyô to Ryakudatsu-shugi" (Monotheism and the Ideology of Plundering), *Gakushikai Kaihô* (2004:1, No. 844), 136 ff.

5 Ibid., 138.

6 Ludwig Feuerbach, *Kirisuto-kyô no Honshitsu* (The Essence of Christianity) (trans. Shin'ichi Funayama; 9 vols.; Fukumura Shuppan, 1975), 215. I have, however, freely revised the translation.

7 Ibid., 223–4.

8 Mori, "Isshinkyô to Ryakudatsu-shugi" (Monotheism and the Ideology of Plundering), 139.

Mori cites the Puritans and their descendants as examples of such ultra-egoists. They crossed over to a new continent and plundered the American natives. As capitalists, he says, they exploited the lower classes. Not only did they become industrial leaders, but as the American economy evolved they also manipulated stocks and bonds as financial leaders, and they profited as a front for thugs. Because such ultra-egoists are unaware of their own egoism, they force all kinds of egoistic things on others in the name of justice or human rights. After the terrorist attacks in 2001, President Bush essentially said in his message that the world must choose whether it is on the side of civilization and good or on the side of barbarism and evil. Objectively, however, is it not he and the American nation who are on the side of barbarism and evil? And if Iraq is a "nation of thugs," does not America outdo it as a violent and plundering "nation of thugs"? Mori concludes his essay with these questions.

Mori's argument may be regarded as a typical example of contemporary arguments in which monotheism is implicitly or explicitly questioned and criticized and in which important points of debate are clearly laid out. We may also come across suggestions that we return to distinctly Japanese or Buddhist ways, such as can be seen in the dialogue between Hayao Kawai and Shin'ichi Nakazawa in the *Asahi Shimbun* on New Year's Eve, 2003. Nakazawa said that "At the time of the simultaneous terrorist attacks, many Japanese felt that monotheism, such as that of Christianity and Islam, has perhaps reached a dead end." Kawai responded that "We can see various moves based on the notion that in that case, perhaps Buddhism is the answer'."[9]

This phenomenon is not limited to Japan. It is evident in works such as Hick and Knitter's *The Myth of Christian Uniqueness: Toward a Pluralistic Theology of Religions*,[10] in which Christian theologians of religious pluralism reflect on and express regrets about Christianity's history of imperialistic plundering. For example, Knitter critically reconsiders the relationship between British imperialism and Christianity. Focusing on "Christic self-consciousness," Panikkar divides Christian history into five periods and comments especially on the period when the Christian empire was established through the Crusades from the 8th to the 16th century, as well as the ensuing period of foreign missions linked with colonial rule up to the 20th century. This book contains testimony after testimony of people telling how they realized that a richness of spiritual experience does in fact exist in other religions. Under these circumstances, how should

---

9 See note 1, above.
10 John Hick and Paul F. Knitter (eds), *The Myth of Christian Uniqueness: Toward a Pluralistic Theology of Religions* (Maryknoll, N.Y.: Orbis Books, 1987).

monotheism understand and position itself? Let us first examine the extent to which Mori's criticisms are applicable to the Old Testament.

2 Various Views of God in the Old Testament's Self-Understanding

2.1 The God Who Directs Israel's Wars

Can such an ideology of monotheism-driven plundering be found in the Old Testament? The provisional answer to such a straightforward question would be "yes." Although there are a number of subtle issues to be dealt with here, we must frankly acknowledge that the Old Testament is open to charges of this ideology of plundering. There are at least two reasons for this.

First is the period from the invasion of the plain of Palestine to its occupation by David. The Israelites repeatedly battled various groups of Canaanites, as well as Ammonites and Moabites who had already established kingdoms. When they were victorious, they viewed it as the result of the God Yahweh's guidance (Josh 10 – 11; Judg 5; etc.). On those occasions, as offerings to Yahweh, the victor of these Yahweh wars (Num 21:14; 1Sam 18:17), they annihilated towns and their inhabitants (Num 21:35; Deut 2:34; 3:3; Josh 10:20; etc.), property (Josh 6:24), and even animals (Deut 13:15), all in the name of the ban (*herem*). David's conquests through expanded military power and military strategy are what decided the invasion of Palestine. It extended to all of the arable regions in Palestine and as far as the Aramaean nations. And David did this in the name of Yahweh (2Sam 7; 23:5; etc.). At least from the perspective of the native inhabitants, we must say that the many battles to capture Canaan, ostensibly in the name of God, were horrifying massacres and plundering.

Second is the period of the prophets after establishment of the kingdom. There are no extant records of war in Israel during the Solomonic Period. Yet the reason is not so much that Israel had become a peaceful nation as that, after it occupied Palestine's important regions, defense became more important than plundering (1Kgs 10:26; 2Chron 11:5 – 12). It is also because small and weak Israel simply did not have the force to engage in war against Babylonia and Egypt, the two great empires surrounding Palestine. Nevertheless, it is also true that the prophets who prophesied peace in the last days often visualized Yahweh's brutal retaliation against their enemies, large and small. This is another dimension of the Old Testament ideology of plundering in God's name. Consider this passage:

I will sound the battle alarm against Rabbah of the Ammonites; it shall become a desolate mound, and its villages shall be burned with fire; then Israel shall dispossess those who dispossessed him. (Jer 49:2)

Prophecies such as this are too numerous to mention (in the book of Jeremiah alone, consider, for example, 46:10, 15–16, 25–26; 47:4, 6–7; 48:10, 12, 25–26, 42, 44; 49:5, 8, 15, 20–22, 27, 35–38; 50:9–16, 18, 21, 24–40; 51:1–2, 11, 20–24, 36, 55–58). Even if such prophecies were unrealistic, they were nevertheless visualized in the minds of the prophets, and they must surely be viewed as a potential ideology of plundering that was shared by more than a few Israelites.

Here I have cited two instances that confirm the existence of a monotheistic ideology of plundering in the Old Testament. As mentioned earlier, however, there are some subtle issues involved. Consider the following three general points about the ancient world. First, war was not simply a political and military event; it was also a religious matter directed by God. Second, nations existed in a brutal and violent world governed by the law of the jungle: eat or be eaten. Third, among the prophets, at least, there were also visions of an ideal peace among all nations that transcended cruel and inhumane wars and feuds (Isa 2:2–4 par. Mic 4:1–4). These are some of the subtleties that must be considered here. In other words, we must be especially careful not to simply dismiss this religious ideology of plundering out of a complacent "commonsense" that war is wrong. There is also something amiss when scholars such as L. Gilkey, a religious pluralist, prioritize modern Western values like liberty, justice, and equality, which differ from Old Testament values, and criticize the Old Testament from that perspective.[11] On the other hand, it is also true that many people today feel they can no longer accept these aspects of the Old Testament's religious ideology of plundering.

What, then, are we to do? We must not blithely smuggle in foreign values, but nor can we refrain from criticizing this aspect of the Old Testament. Herein lies a dilemma. To overcome this, it is imperative to find the correct principle of criticism. In fact, that principle is concealed within the Old Testament itself. With each passing age, the Old Testament sharply critiques and attempts to overcome this view of God characterized by an ideology of plundering. Let us turn now to examine this point.

---

11 Hick and Knitter, *Kirisuto-kyô no Zettai-sei o Koete* (Transcending the Absoluteness of Christianity), 98.

2.2 The God Who Uses Other Nations to Punish Israel's Sins

Rather than declaring that Yahweh directed Israel's battles and brought it victory, the prophet Isaiah, for example, corrected traditional views of God by prophesying that God would use the Assyrian Empire to punish Israel for its sins (Isa 5:26 ff.; 7:17 ff.). On the occasion of the Syro-Ephraimite War, Isaiah had nothing to do with plundering through military action. Instead, he calmly observed the situation and through his Immanuel prophecy advised King Ahaz to trust in Yahweh alone (Isa 7).

Jeremiah, too, is depicted as a prophet who viewed the Neo-Babylonian Empire as a punitive instrument of Yahweh's judgment on Israel's sins (Jer 21:8 ff.; 25:8 ff.). The book of Jeremiah reports that Jeremiah was persecuted as a traitor because he even urged Israel to surrender to its enemy Babylonia (Jer 21:9). This passage has a nuanced formulation because it has been edited by the Deuteronomistic Historian, but I prefer not to enter into a detailed philological discussion here.

Whatever the case, we could also mention others who belong to this line, such as the prophets Hosea and Micah, who called for the people to trust in Yahweh alone and to abandon their horses and chariots needed for war (Hos 1:7; Mic 5:9; also see Isa 30:16), as well as the Chronicler, who made the general declaration that the only legitimate war is one of self-defense based on trust in Yahweh alone (2Chron 20:1–30).

It is apparent, therefore, that "the Old Testament" is not monolithic. In it can be found not only understandings of a God characterized by an ideology of plundering, whereby God guides Israel to military victory, but also understandings of God as the one who instead guides other nations to victory and Israel to defeat for the sake of justice, or who calls on Israel to abandon all wars except those of self-defense.

2.3 The God Who Does Not Guide History

And that is not the full extent of it. Later there appeared an even more radical criticism of traditional views of God, to the effect that not only did God not direct Israel's wars, but it was even doubtful that God guided history. This was the issue that the nihilist Qohelet raised during the Hellenistic period.

Qohelet lived in a time when the segmented (*segmentär*) society of the Hellenistic period was in ruins. After the exilic period, segmented societal structures that had been based on the principle of collective responsibility among multiple egalitarian communities collapsed. There arose a situation in which unrighteous people who turned away from Yahweh and converted to pagan religions prospered economically, while righteous people who remained faithful were brought to ruin. This could not be explained by collective responsibility, and the view of God based on this principle—that of simple ethical retribution—faced a crisis. It was Qohelet who confronted this reality and insisted that the traditional understanding that God guides history according to retributive ethics was an utter lie.

> Moreover I saw under the sun that in the place of justice, wickedness was there, and in the place of righteousness, wickedness was there as well. I said in my heart, God will [fairly] judge the righteous and the wicked. (Eccl 3:16–17)

and, for example:

> ... there are righteous people who are treated according to the conduct of the wicked [that is, with misfortune],
> and there are wicked people who are treated according to the conduct of the righteous [that is, with fortune].
> I said that this also is vanity. (Eccl 8:14)

Such statements by Qohelet can be interpreted as expressions of doubt toward this God of retribution.

It is not the case, however, that Qohelet denied the very existence of God. It is true that he criticized the traditional understanding of God, but he must have taken pride in discovering a new understanding of God.

> I know that there is nothing better for them than to be happy and enjoy themselves as long as they live; moreover, it is God's gift that all should eat and drink and take pleasure in all their toil... God has done this. (Eccl 3:12–14; also 3:22; 5:18; 8:15; 9:7–9)

These words tell where Qohelet encountered a new God at the end of his quest for wisdom. The result of his quest was that he discovered God anew. Not as a great superintendent of history based on ethical retribution, but as a being whose workings were faintly perceptible only in such small joys in the daily life of individuals.

Elsewhere I have discussed additional problems with the book of Qohelet—its understanding of God is ultimately valid; the fact that the other appears nowhere in Qohelet; and the fact that he was unable to transcend egoism.[12] I shall not, however, go into these issues here. Suffice it to confirm that

---

12 Seizô Sekine, *Kyûyaku ni okeru Chôetsu to Shôchô: Kaishakugaku-teki Keiken no Keifu* (Tokyo: University of Tokyo Press, 1994), Chapter 2. This monograph has been published in English as *Transcendency and Symbols in the Old Testament: A Genealogy of the Hermeneutical Experiences* (trans. Judy Wakabayashi; Berlin: Walter de Gruyter, 1999).

such an understanding of God did exist as a third way of conceptualizing God within the Old Testament's self-understanding.

While acknowledging that there are scattered texts in the Old Testament that might be regarded as stemming from a monotheistic ideology of plundering, Part 2 has confirmed that there are also later arguments that criticize and relativize this view from at least two directions. In Part 3 we shall shift gears and proceed to an examination of the following questions: What happens when we subdivide the original concept of monotheism into monolatry and monotheism? How about when we compare these with polytheism? And in which of these three types is the ideology of plundering primarily rooted?

3 Various Views of God Classified in Terms of Religious Studies

3.1 The Relationship with Polytheism

The general impression gained from a cursory reading of the Old Testament is that it is characterized by lofty monotheism and has rigidly excluded polytheism. In fact, however, the Old Testament has quite a few polytheistic aspects. It is true that the judges and prophets who urge the people to obey the God Yahweh are grandly depicted at the surface level of the Old Testament narrative. Early examples include the judge Gideon, who cut down an Asherah image (Judg 6:25), and Yahweh's prophet Elijah, who emerged victorious in a prayer battle with 450 Baal prophets (1Kgs 18:21). In the period of the writing prophets, Hosea, Jeremiah, Ezekiel, and others leave strong impressions when they severely denounce syncretism with polytheistic Baalism as "fornication" and "adultery" (Hos 2:4 ff.; 4:13 ff.; Jer 2:23 – 24; 3:1 ff.; Ezek 16:15 ff.; 23:3 ff.; etc.).

On reflection, however, we must consider the following point: such rejection of the polytheism of other religions means that polytheism had in fact infiltrated the Yahweh religion to a considerable degree. We may assume that the leaders of this religion felt pressed to reject it precisely because people among the Yahweh religion's laity were converting to or engaging in syncretistic practices with the Baal religion to some extent.

That tendency can be seen not only among the general population, but also among the kings, who filled the role of leader. For example, 1 Kings 11 (vv. 4 ff.) candidly reports how Solomon's heart was "turned away" "after other gods" in his later years. Indeed, this phenomenon occurred to such an extent that one scholar says, "The actual state of Israelite religion during the kingdom period, both at the national level and at the private level, was polytheistic."[13]

This was not only at the secular level, but also at the religious level. We learn from the account in 2 Kings 23:4 ff. and other texts that toward the end of the kingdom period Yahweh's very temple was full of pagan idols and worship utensils (also see Jer 8:1–2; Ezek 8:5 ff.; etc.). Verses 15 onward in the same chapter reveal that this was the situation not only in Jerusalem, the capital of Judah in the south, but also in Samaria, the capital of Israel in the north, as well as in its holy site of Bethel.

Perhaps matters were even worse. In addition to these levels, in fact we cannot strictly say that Yahwistic monotheism was adhered to by even the biblical authors, who shaped and directed Old Testament religion. While the biblical authors denounced polytheistic tendencies at the secular level and enhanced the monotheistic dispositions of the judges and prophets who censured such tendencies, in their theological formulations they themselves drew insatiably from the polytheism around them and assimilated it into their own religion. Based on the results of comparative religious studies, it is possible—, necessary—detect influences from other religions behind the pages of the Old Testament. These are, we must conclude, important historical data that suggest a kind of religious syncretism which, though we might call it monotheism, cannot be regarded as pure monotheism. W. H. Schmidt's *Alttestamentlicher Glaube in seiner Geschichte* is a major work among the body of research that has traced these data widely through comparison with ancient Near Eastern texts.[14] I have written about this elsewhere and do not have space here to treat it in detail. Suffice it to point out that we must pay attention to how much the Yahweh religion was influenced by neighboring polytheistic religions—example, in its notions of God's "royal authority"; the concept of "holiness" (*qadosh*); the understanding of God as "living"; ways of portraying theophanies; the name "El" for God; accounts of battles with the dragon of chaos; the formation of wisdom literature; and so on.[15]

---

13 Akio Tsukimoto, "Kodai Isuraeru Yuiitsu Isshinkyô no Seiritsu to Sono Tokushitsu" (The Formation of Ancient Israelite Monotheism and its Special Characteristics), in *Shûkyô to Kan'yô: Ishûkyô and Ibunka-kan no Taiwa ni Mukete* (Religion and Tolerance: Toward Dialogue among Different Religions and Different Cultures) (eds. Seiichi Takeuchi and Akio Tsukimoto; Tokyo: Taimeido, 1993), 158–9.

14 Werner H. Schmidt, *Alttestamentlicher Glaube in seiner Geschichte*, 1987 6. Aufl.; translated in Japanese as *Rekishi ni okeru Kyûyaku Seisho no Shinkô* (Old Testament Faith in History) (trans. Tetsuo Yamaga; Tokyo: Shinchi Shobo, 1985).

15 Seizô Sekine, *Kyûyaku Seisho no Shisô: 24 no Danshô* (Old Testament Thought: 24 Fragmentary Reflections) (Tokyo: Iwanami Shoten, 1998; Tokyo: Kodansha Gakujutsu Bunko, 2005); see Chapter 9.

3.2 The Law of Monolatry

On those occasions when the biblical authors were influenced by polytheism, did they have any criteria as to what they would accept and what they would ignore or as to which concepts they might recontextualize into Yahwistic monotheism and how? I agree with Schmidt that their fundamental criterion was the spirit of the first commandment in the Decalogue. For example, it is thought that the idea of God's "royal authority" was adopted from Ugarit. In the Old Testament, however, it is the people, not the gods as in Ugarit, who are ruled by God's royal authority. Psalms 5 (v. 2) and other passages attest to this. Although the concept of holy gods is adopted from the Yehimilk inscription and elsewhere, the Old Testament applies this to Yahweh alone, as in Isaiah 5 (v. 16).

In my view, however, Schmidt over-emphasizes the exclusivity of the first commandment. As he himself acknowledges, this is not a monotheistic command, but a monolatrous one. In the parlance of religious studies, "monolatry" refers to the worship of one particular god among "other gods," whose existence is recognized. The first commandment is often rendered in Japanese along the lines of "You shall not deem to be God any[thing] other than me," but because *al-panai* in the original text means "before my face," this commandment, accurately translated, should read as follows:

> I am your God Yahweh, who led you out of the land of Egypt, out of the house of slavery. There shall not be for you other gods before me. (Exod 20:3; Deut 5:7)

Certainly, the first commandment rejects a polytheistic attitude that is calculating and noncommittal on the part of the people and the king. It is a scrupulous standard that strives to be faithful to their past absolute experience of Yahweh in the exodus and rejects anything that runs counter to this.

At the same time, they have not rigidly insisted on their absolute experience with one God to the extent of completely rejecting different kinds of divine experience with other gods on the part of others. The principle of the first commandment was also able to function as a standard that transcended this sort of narrow and exclusive disposition of monotheism and that, through tolerantly accepting heterogeneity, could lead to its own growth. In other words, the principle of the first commandment was able to become a standard whereby, since their past absolute experience also bore the limitation of being interpreted through human wisdom, this experience was perennially relativized and opened to the future and reinterpreted flexibly. At that time their experience was also soundly reinforced through possible experiences concerning "other gods".

The monolatrous spirit of this first commandment continued to underpin the Old Testament. Its legacy can be seen, for instance, in passages such as Micah 4:5, "For all the peoples walk, each in the name of its god, but we will walk in the name of the LORD our God," and it is conceivable that this principle became a healthy criterion and tenet promoting dialogue when the Yahweh religion interacted with other religions. Tenets such as this will always serve as important guideposts in times when religions stand in opposition and their gods contend with one another. To put it another way, we could even say that, based on the first commandment, the Old Testament already advocates the "religious pluralism" found in *shōgi* ("ultimate meaning," or *para-mārtha*)—.e., while choosing faithfulness to the God Yahweh "before me" (i. e., in the context of the relationship with Yahweh), one should also acknowledge that there are "other gods" "other than me" and incorporate understanding about these gods for the sake of understanding the God Yahweh.

Here it has been my aim to confirm that there are in fact polytheistic aspects in Old Testament religion, which generally tends to be viewed as the embodiment of exclusive monotheism. In the process we have seen that the monolatrous law of the first commandment functioned to link polytheism and monotheism and that Judaism and Christianity might be able to free themselves somewhat from the rigid exclusivism of pure monotheism through an awareness of these matters.

It would not do, however, to end the discussion here. After all, Old Testament monotheism progressed from monolatry to monotheism. And surely some will argue that it is impossible to turn back history even if one wished monotheism had stopped at the prior stage, monolatry. Indeed, monotheism is the mature form of the religions of Judaism, Christianity, and Islam, and it is generally believed that the Old Testament prophets were its pioneers. Upon critically reexamining the appropriateness of this widespread belief, I have concluded, however, that in fact the formation of monotheism in the prophets and even the concept itself appear, upon closer inspection, to be quite problematic. It is this point that I wish to discuss next.

3.3 The Formation and Significance of Monotheism

Research on this question has thrived in recent years.[16] In particular, I wish to consider this topic in the light of excellent research close to home. I am referring

---

[16] Limiting ourselves just to notable works in the West during the past two decades, we might mention the following publications. Through detailed analyses of names recorded on inscriptions and elsewhere, Jeffrey H. Tigay (*You Shall Have No Other Gods: Israelite Religion in the Light of Hebrew Inscriptions*, Harvard Semitic Studies 31; Atlanta: Scholars Press, 1987) argues that there was no polytheistic tendency in Israel and Judah during the kingdom period and that, particularly in the southern kingdom, monotheism was recognized as the state religion. In *The Rise of Yahwism: The Roots of Israelite Monotheism* (BETL 91; Leuven: Peeters, 1990; 1997), Johannes Cornelis de Moor boldly challenges the commonly held view that monotheistic Yahwism was shaped late in ancient Israel's religious history, and he points to evidence concerning the powerful El, who already rules over the other gods in place of Baal in early poetic texts. The volume edited by Hershel Shanks and Jack Meinhardt, *Aspects of Monotheism: How God Is One* (Washington, DC: Biblical Archaeology Society, 1997), brought together archaeological discoveries related to monotheism, and it shook the traditional view that regarded Israelite religion as an evolved religion. Building on thirty years of research, Manfred Weippert argues in *Jahwe und die anderen Götter: Studien zur Religionsgeschichte des antiken Israel in ihrem syrisch-palästinischen Kontext* (FAT 18; Tübingen: Mohr Siebeck, 1997) that the religion of Israel and Judah was polytheistic until the Persian Period, if not until the Hasmonean dynasty. Going back to the Bronze and Iron Ages, *Gods, Goddesses, and Images of God in Ancient Israel* (trans. Allan W. Mahnke; Minneapolis, Minn.: Fortress, 1998) by Othmar Keel and Christoph Uelinger chronologically arranges archaeological and iconographic data concerning divine images and argues that Yahwism was established in the ninth and eighth centuries BCE, while admitting the existence of other gods. *Dictionary of Deities and Demons in the Bible* (Leiden: Brill, 1995; second edition, 1998), edited by Karel van der Toorn, Bob Becking, and Pieter Willem van der Horst, is a valuable reference book concerning gods and demons. Patrick D. Miller's *The Religion of Ancient Israel* (Louisville, Ky.: Westminster John Knox, 2000) is a comparative study of Canaanite and Israelite religion. Spanning more than 800 pages, Ziony Zevit's *The Religions of Ancient Israel: A Synthesis of Parallactic Approaches* (London: Continuum, 2001) is a comprehensive overview of various religions in ancient Israel. In Mark S. Smith's *The Early History of God: Yahweh and the Other Deities in Ancient Israel* (San Francisco: Harper & Row, 1990; second revised edition, 2003), the author surveys the biblical and extra-biblical fruits of documentary and archaeological research on faith in Yahweh and other gods in the Old Testament period and undermines the traditional view that Yahwism was free of religious syncretism. Smith presents a bold argument about Israel's polytheism, draws together various views of God, and masterfully explains the circumstances under which Israel's God as known in the Bible was "created." *Der eine Gott und die Götter: Polytheismus und Monotheismus im antiken Israel* (ATANT 82; Zürich: Theologischer Verlag, 2003), edited by Manfred Oeming and Konrad Schmid, is a collection of essays arguing a range of issues, including the relationship between monotheism and polytheism in ancient Israel; the question of whether the Bible was originally monotheistic; the relationship between Yahweh and goddesses in the prophets; Second Isaiah's monotheism; and the prohibition of idols and the existence of other gods. While shining light on Yahweh's relationship to the

to Akio Tsukimoto's contribution to the collection of essays in *Shûkyô to Kan'yô* (Religion and Tolerance).[17]

Tsukimoto argues that "Yahweh, in bringing judgment upon the people of Israel through foreign enemy invasions, outgrows his erstwhile role as ethnic deity or guardian deity of the state. This is because such a God must relate only to the history of his people of Israel or he must be a global deity who rules over all peoples of the earth" (p. 164). As evidence, Tsukimoto points to Amos 9:7, Isaiah 10:5, and Jeremiah 25:9. In my view, all of these passages are in fact riddled with historical problems, so I wish to begin by examining these texts.

First, Amos's statement is as follows:

> Are you not like the Ethiopians to me, O people of Israel? ...
> Did I not bring Israel up from the land of Egypt,
> and the Philistines from Caphtor
> and the Arameans from Kir? (Amos 9:7)

Even if the Philistines migrated as a people from Caphtor—is, from Crete or Cappadocia—the latter half of the second millennium BCE, that event cannot be lumped together with Israel's escape from Egypt's oppressive rule. And even if relocation of the Arameans by the Assyrian king Tiglath-Pileser in 732 BCE actually occurred (Amos 1:5; 2Kgs 16:9), as the book of Kings and others record, the Arameans themselves would not have agreed with the claim that their escape was through the guidance of Israel's God Yahweh. In view of all this, we must frankly acknowledge the strong likelihood that this is a matter of Israel's prophets explaining the situation according to their own needs, rather than it being a matter that transcends historical verification.

The problem only deepens when we consider Isaiah 10 and Jeremiah 25, the other two passages cited by Tsukimoto, because, historically speaking, these two

---

goddess Asherah, William G. Dever's *Did God Have a Wife? Archaeology and Folk Religion in Ancient Israel* (Grand Rapids, Mich.: Eerdmans, 2005) has stimulated debate over views of God in Israel. Other publications are too numerous to mention, especially if research papers were to be included. Although I do not cite works unless I am aware of their direct influence on my thinking, it is only natural that these and other works have indirectly influenced my arguments. Among Japanese contributions other than the essays already cited in note 3, I wish to mention two publications that bring related religions into view: Takashi Katô, *Isshinkyô no Tanjô: Yudaya-kyô kara Kirisuto-kyô e* (The Birth of Monotheism: From Judaism to Christianity) (Tokyo: Kodansha Gendai Shinsho, 2003) and Ryôji Motomura, *Tashinkyô to Isshinkyô: Kodai Chichûkai Sekai no Shûkyô Dorama* (Pluralism and Monotheism: Religious Drama of the Ancient Mediterranean World) (Tokyo: Iwanami Shinsho, 2005).

17 See note 13.

prophecies widely missed the mark. Certainly, as Tsukimoto says,[18] Isaiah 10:5 "called the Assyrian Empire, which waged its campaigns in the west, Yahweh's 'rod of anger' against unfaithful Judah."[19] In my view, however, we must also consider the following text in 10:25. There Isaiah declares, "For in a very little while [Yahweh's] indignation [against Judah] will come to an end, and [Yahweh's] anger will be directed to [the Assyrians'] destruction." In fact, it was 612 BCE when the destruction of Assyria prophesied here actually occurred. Approximately one century had passed since Isaiah's death, and Assyria had suffered gradual attrition through foreign and domestic wars. Even if one were to insist that it was Yahweh who destroyed the Assyrians (a claim that cannot be historically verified), we must note that this prophecy was completely inaccurate regarding the point that it would happen "in a very little while."

The situation is the same in Jeremiah. Tsukimoto says, "As for Jeremiah, he sees in the Babylonian King Nebuchadnezzar, who would eventually bring the nation of Judah to destruction, the 'servant' who would carry out the will of Yahweh."[20] Although some uncertainty remains here because of the problem of Deuteronomistic editing, it is true, at least, that the Jeremiah depicted in the book of Jeremiah sees things this way. Yet the question is the historical validity of this claim. That Jeremiah's self-serving observation did not, in fact, come true, is clear from Nebuchadnezzar's later actions. In 586 BCE, Nebuchadnezzar destroyed the nation of Judah, defiled and sacked Yahweh's temple, and decorated the temple of Marduk, Babylonia's chief deity, with the plundered priestly utensils and treasures. Far from being Yahweh's "servant," he was clearly nothing more than a king serving a pagan god opposed to Yahweh. Jeremiah's monotheistic wishful thinking that Nebuchadnezzar would be Yahweh's "servant" was manifestly betrayed in the ensuing historical events.[21]

---

18 Tsukimoto, "Kodai Isuraeru Yuiitsu Isshinkyô no Seiritsu to Sono Tokushitsu" (The Formation of Ancient Israelite Monotheism and its Special Characteristics), 164–5.

19 This is a point that has generally received attention, up to Baruch A. Levine's paper in the essay collection by Oeming and Schmid. Baruch A. Levine, "'Wehe, Assur, Rute meines Zorns!' (Jesaja 10,5)," in *Der eine Gott und die Götter*, 77 ff.

20 Tsukimoto, "Kodai Isuraeru Yuiitsu Isshinkyô no Seiritsu to Sono Tokushitsu" (The Formation of Ancient Israelite Monotheism and its Special Characteristics), 165.

21 If the "servant" is nothing more than someone used by the world's only God as a marionette, regardless of his subjective faith, then one might still defend the view that Jeremiah's hope was not betrayed. The usage of "servant" ('ebed) in the Old Testament, however, seems to preclude this possibility. As Westermann's research indicates, 'ebed is a special term that is used in three senses ("Kami no Shimobe" [God's Servant], in *Kyûyaku Shin'yaku Seisho Dai Jiten* [Dictionary of the Old and New Testaments] [Tokyo: Kyo Bun Kwan, 1989], 324 ff.): a) in line with the original sense of 'abad (to serve), one who consciously serves Yahweh (the patriarchs in Gen 26:24;

Tsukimoto, however, ignores these historical events and concludes as follows: "In short ... in the prophets' ethical criticisms and judgment prophecies Yahweh is elevated from being Israel's ethnic deity into a global deity invested with transcendence and universality. It is safe to say that, through their 'Yahweh-alone movement' and the prophetic activities based upon this, the people became aware of the God Yahweh's absoluteness and universality. Here we can see the fundamental formation of the concept of ancient Israelite monotheism."[22] However, if we acknowledge the reality we have just noted—when the prophets began speaking about the rule of history by a single God, they were historically wrong on many counts—must conclude that the prophets were rather baffled by these matters all the while they were attempting to elevate the "ethnic deity" Yahweh "into a global deity invested with transcendence and universality." In other words, even if it were the case that they "became aware" of and declared "the God Yahweh's absoluteness and universality," surely they failed to give a persuasive account. I think it is necessary to treat this claim with great skepticism.

Of course, there might a counterargument that the complete formation of monotheism began with the prophet Second Isaiah around the time of liberation from Babylonian exile and that it was not yet fully developed in the prophets from Amos to Jeremiah. Even if we do not appeal to Baltzer and others, the reigning theory is that Second Isaiah was the founder of monotheism, and Tsukimoto agrees with this. Stating that "[the concept of ancient Israelite monotheism] found clearer expression in Second Isaiah's powerful prophetic poetry," Tsukimoto quotes numerous passages from Second Isaiah. For example, Isaiah 45:6 – 7:

Moses in Exod 14:31 and Num 12:7; Job in Job 1:8; the king in 2Sam 3:18; the prophet in 1Kgs 18:36); b) a follower of the God Yahweh (Ps 69:17 [MT 18]; 123:2); and c) those whom Yahweh elects and loves and to whom he speaks with intimacy (Isa 41:8; 44:1, 2, 21; 45:4; etc.). It is highly likely that when Yahweh's "servant" Nebuchadnezzar (Nebuchadrezzar) is mentioned three times in Jeremiah 25:9, 27:6, and 43:10 the term is used as a special appellation for one who stands in a trusting relationship with the God Yahweh. Below I shall discuss Second Isaiah's references to Cyrus as "shepherd" (Isa 44:28) and "anointed" (Isa 45:1). For argument's sake, let us assume that this is not the case and that the prophets of this small state recognize that great-state rulers such as Nechuchadnezzar serve other gods and merely ignore or disdain the small-state God Yahweh. If they are claiming that, even in those cases, they are in fact under the rule of our God, these are nothing more than vain protests. As such, is it not unreasonable to acclaim them for discovering "a global deity invested with transcendence and universality"?

22 Tsukimoto, "Kodai Isuraeru Yuiitsu Isshinkyô no Seiritsu to Sono Tokushitsu" (The Formation of Ancient Israelite Monotheism and its Special Characteristics), 165; also see 159, where Tsukimoto introduces Smith's discussion of "Yahweh-Alone-Movements."

> I am the LORD, and there is no other.
> I form light and create darkness,
> I make weal and create woe.

Or Isaiah 45:21–22:

> There is no other god besides me,
> a righteous God and a Savior;
> there is no one besides me.
> Turn to me and be saved,
> all the ends of the earth!

And so on. Tsukimoto concludes: "Clearly declared here are Yahweh's transcendence as the creator deity of all things; his universality and omnipresence as the ruling deity of all peoples of the world; and his unique absoluteness as the incomparable and unrivaled God."[23]

Yet is this actually so? Is it not true that in Second Isaiah too the historical circumstances are essentially no different from those of the pre-exilic prophets? As in Jeremiah, the strained view of foreign conquerors as Yahweh's "servant" can also be found in two passages in Second Isaiah, though Tsukimoto does not cite them. Second Isaiah calls Cyrus, the first king of the emerging Persian Empire, Yahweh's "shepherd" (Isa 44:28) and even "his anointed" (Isa 45:1). The Cyrus Cylinder testifies that this kind of excessive attachment to a foreign king was a mistake. Following his bloodless entry into Babylon, Cyrus is said to have "worshiped Marduk [Babylon's chief deity] daily." It is clear here that Cyrus did not have the faintest notion of having been commissioned by Yahweh, the God of Israel, a minor nation completely alien to him.

And that is not all. In the first place, how could Second Isaiah so confidently have Yahweh say "there is no other God besides me"? His sole purpose was to ridicule: the pagans, who worship pagan gods that are no more than idols, are ignorant people who bow in worship to wood and stone (Isa 44:9–20).

> No one [among the Babylonians] considers, nor is there knowledge or discernment to say, "Half of [the wood] I burned in the fire; I also baked bread on its coals, I roasted meat and have eaten. Now shall I make the rest of it an abomination [that is, an idol]? Shall I fall down before a block of wood?" (Isa 44:19)

---

23 Ibid., 166.

Recent scholarship on the Near East, however, has demonstrated that this ridicule missed the mark. For example, W. H. Schmidt[24] has carefully analyzed matters pertaining to idol worship in the ancient Near East, starting with Babylonia, and has demonstrated that these people did not bow in worship to "a block of wood," thinking it to be God. Rather, they were worshiping the divinity to which it pointed as a symbol representing God. If this is the case, then Second Isaiah's ridicule of these idol gods was based on fiction-based insults against pagans and was not actually valid. It becomes evident, then, that this fictionally based, enthusiastic confidence in Yahweh as the only true God stood, in fact, on very weak ground. In the light of the above, we must frankly acknowledge that despite what many have said about the formation of monotheism in the prophets, it is a dubious proposition, and the grounds there for viewing Yahweh as the only God were riddled with errors.

Here we have reached a somewhat unexpected conclusion. It is traditionally said that the source of monotheism stems from the prophets of ancient Judaism, and this view has been uncritically accepted up to the present day. We have concluded, however, that in reality the very concept of monotheism is truly ambiguous and its formation was in fact distorted and hypothetical and partly based upon self-serving delusions of grandeur. We are compelled, are we not, to stop and "deconstruct" the very way of thinking about "Old Testament monotheism."

Let me add one more point. At the end of his essay, Tsukimoto asks what becomes of the relationship between this single God of the entire world and the single people of Israel. He makes the following point, with which I agree: "The special characteristic in the concept of Yahwistic monotheism lies not in its absolute transcendence or universality in and of themselves. Rather, it is especially found in the paradox that this transcendent and universal being manifests his will on earth as 'God of the small.'"[25] See, for example, Deuteronomy 7:6 ff., Isaiah 9, and especially Second Isaiah 53.

This point does not, however, necessarily find general acceptance. In an interactive symposium published as an appendix to the volume in which Tsukimoto's essay appears, authors expressed doubt. For instance, Haruyoshi Shibuya offers this criticism: "Saying that a people walking the path of suffering have been chosen is giving a reason that is not a reasonable argument."[26] Seiichi Takeuchi says, "It makes sense to me that internal faith is the answer to the question of

---

24 Werner H. Schmidt, "Bilderverbot und Gottebenbildlichkeit: Exegetische Notizen zur Selbstmanipulation des Menschen," *Wort und Wahrheit* 23 (1968).
25 Tsukimoto, "Kodai Isuraeru Yuiitsu Isshinkyô no Seiritsu to Sono Tokushitsu" (The Formation of Ancient Israelite Monotheism and its Special Characteristics), 169.
26 Takeuchi and Tsukimoto, eds., *Shûkyô to Kan'yô* (Religion and Tolerance), 344.

why Israel. But that is not an adequate explanation for different people [that is, to others of different faiths]."[27] Tsukimoto simply agrees with these views, but I wish to argue the point and ask whether it is not possible to seek an "explanation" for "others" of "different" "faiths." This, however, involves probing the very understanding of God using philosophical and common logic. I wish to conclude Part 3 by advocating the need to deconstruct Old Testament monotheism and the need for philosophical reflection. In Part 4, I shall temporarily set aside the Old Testament and proceed with some philosophical considerations.

4 Philosophical Reflections about the Concept of God

Kitarô Nishida's posthumous "The Logic of Topos and the Religious Worldview" (1946)[28] is a philosophical consideration that employs universal language and that logically and thoroughly probes understandings of God, broadly including within its scope Zen experiences, the Diamond Sutra, and the Old Testament. Because this concerns comprehensive understandings of God, it seems to encompass Old Testament understandings of God. It could also be described as a brilliant explanation of matters about which Old Testament people spoke in intuitively mythological language. Here, in Part 4, I wish to move on to a consideration of the essence of monotheism according to Nishida. This will also lay the ground for our return to the Old Testament in Part 5. However, because I have already discussed Nishida's understanding of God in some detail in Part 7 of Chapter 1, to which the reader can easily refer back, I shall avoid unnecessary repetition here and very simply corroborate the main points.

First, Nishida contests the objective-logical (*taishō ronri-teki*) understanding of God found in traditional Western Christianity, which "sees God externally" "as an object." This understanding reduces God to a relative object that is relative to relative humans, and he ceases to be an absolute existence. On the other hand, in developing his argument concerning the God of creation and history, Nishida says: "Certainly, the absolute transcends the relative, but that which merely tran-

---

27 Ibid., 347.

28 *Bashoteki Ronri to Shûkyô-teki Sekai-kan* (*Nishida Kitarô zenshû*, 11; Tokyo: Iwanami Shoten, 1949 [1946]). Quotations are from Michiko Yusa's translation in "The Logic of Topos and the Religious Worldview (I)," *The Eastern Buddhist* 19:2 (1986), 1–29, and "The Logic of Topos and the Religious Worldview (II)," *The Eastern Buddhist* 20:1 (1987), 81–119. For an alternative translation and extended introduction, see Kitarô Nishida, *Last Writings: Nothingness and the Religious Worldview* (trans. with an introduction by David A. Dilworth; Honolulu: University of Hawaii Press, 1987).

scends the relative is not anything but merely nothing. A God who does not create anything is a powerless God; he is not God."[29] In other words, the true God is
absolute being, but if something relates to being, it is only relative; and if it relates to nothing, it is only nothing. If so, then regarding the true God we must
conclude that "The absolute is truly absolute in facing nothing. By facing absolute nothing it is absolute being."[30] This means we must conclude that if it relates to something—if that something is "nothing"—it is only relative, so the absolute contains nothing within itself. But nothing is the negation of being.
Therefore, "The absolute must contain absolute self-negation within itself. Moreover, this means the self becomes absolutely nothing."[31] Nishida treated this as a
typical example of "the self-identity of absolute contradiction."[32]

After discussing God as having a self-identity of absolute contradiction,
Nishida makes reference to the creator-God such as that of the Old Testament:
"The created world exists because God the Creator exists; God exists because
the created world exists."[33] This is the panentheistic view that the true God,
who is absolutely nothing and also absolute being, negates himself and manifests himself in individual and substantial beings, gives life to each of us, and
lives within the creation.[34]

If there were multiple absolute beings, they would be reduced to relative beings;
therefore, it is correct that there must be only one absolute being. Yet is it not the
case that the Old Testament prophets viewed the absolute being as an individual
and substantial being? If so, it means that one must deny other gods. But if we follow Nishida and reconceive God as a panentheistic absolute nothing, it is no problem at all for there to be multiple gods as symbols pointing to this absolute nothing.
I suggest that the monolatrous law on which we focused in Part 3 comes alive here
with deeper meaning. Nishida goes so far as to say: "This is the only way we can
describe God in a logical language."[35] I think this truly captures the real intent behind what the Old Testament authors could express only in mythical language, and

---

29 Nishida, "The Logic of Topos and the Religious Worldview (I)," 19 (1949:396).
30 Ibid., 19 (1949:397).
31 Ibid.
32 I shall not discuss the validity of this point here. In this essay, Nishida has too much of a
tendency to explain everything in terms of his own philosophical system of "the self-identity of
absolute contradiction." It would be off topic and beyond my ability to discuss the merits of this
tendency here. Regarding the necessary question of why Nishida now, though, see Chapter 1,
section 7.
33 Ibid., 20 (1949:398).
34 Ibid., 20 – 21 (1949:399).
35 Ibid., 20 (1949:398).

to the extent that Nishida's essay stands as a brilliant exposition on our experiences of God, it is not without reason.

Finally, I shall conclude this section by quoting Nishida. This passage relates to the argument I have traced up till this point, and it also refers to the narrative directly connected to the heart of the Old and New Testaments. It is the claim that the transcendent God, who exists in this world in self-negation, is manifested not only in the work of creation, but especially in the salvific work of atonement.

> Christianity, which holds personalistic values, ascribes the foundation of religion to the fall of human beings. It is held that the offspring of Adam who rebelled against God are all tainted by original sin; that we are all sinners by birth; that there is no way out of this predicament for us, except by the atonement of the only Son of God, who was sent to the human world by God's love; and that we are saved by our faith in the revelation through the person of Christ. … [T]his view of human existence which is based on the fall is a very profound religious view of life, poignantly expressing the rudimentary conditions of our existence. Human beings come into being through God's absolute self-negation; and at the foundation of our existence we are destined to the flaming inferno.[36]

5 The Anthropological Significance of Atonement Faith

Here the argument converges with atonement ideology. Nishida argued this primarily from the perspective of theism characterized by a self-identity of absolute contradiction, but what happens when we reconsider this from the perspective of anthropology? And what if we back up and view it from the standpoint of the Old Testament's religious and concrete representations, rather than philosophical and abstract ones? These are the points I wish to raise anew in this final section.

Here, again, previous considerations in this book become relevant. Through my discussion in Chapter 2, I have already attempted to ascertain the vital points of Hebraism and Christianity. I did so by demonstrating that the highest point of atonement ideology in the Old Testament is Second Isaiah's fourth servant song (Isa 52:13 – 53:12) and by then comparing this religious suffering servant with a parallel example from Greece, namely, the philosophy surrounding Socrates' suffering execution.

As we saw in Part 1 of this chapter, though Feuerbach is well-known for his criticism that the essence of Judaism and Christianity is rooted in egoism, when we trace back through the history of Western thought we end up at Aristotle's *Nicomachean Ethics* as the first philosophical text to treat the problem of egoism. There, Aristotle develops his speculations about the relationship between suffer-

---

36 Ibid., 28 (1949:410 – 11).

ing and egoism, most likely with Socrates' death in mind. If so, this attempt at a comparison with Greek thought leads back to a reconsideration of the essence of Hebraic atonement ideology in relation to egoism.

Again, to avoid repetition I shall limit myself to noting the key points while recalling points of argument from Chapter 2.

5.1 Atonement of the Righteous in Judaism and Christianity

In the history of Old Testament atonement ideology, Second Isaiah's fourth servant song is without parallel—human actually "poured out his life to death" (Isa 53:12)—it constitutes the preliminary level that leads to the ultimate level in the New Testament wherein neither animal nor human, but Jesus, the son of God, poured out his life to death. At what point, then, is the redemptive significance of this suffering recognized? Is it during the lifetime of God's servant and during that of Jesus, or is it after their deaths? I concluded in Chapter 2 that it occurred after their deaths, based on my exegesis of Isaiah 53:10b–11 and my interpretation of "Eli, Eli, lema sabachthani," Jesus' final cry on the cross (Matt 27:46 par. Mark 15:34).

5.2 Egoism of Suffering in Greek Philosophy

In ancient Greece, parallel to Israel, Socrates submitted to an unjust execution, charged with "giving a corrupting influence to the youth, and not recognizing the gods that the state recognizes."[37] It was his grandson-disciple, Aristotle, who attempted to elucidate the meaning of this "suffering" in his contemplations on love in Chapter 9 of *Nicomachean Ethics*.

In sum, Socratic sacrificial death constitutes suffering when viewed in the light of the values of everyday people, who place great value on property, honor, and physical pleasure. Yet for the good person who is indifferent to those values and instead strives to obtain goodness and beauty that pertain to *logos* and *nūs*, he is merely choosing to attain what is truly beautiful to him. Therefore, this is nothing more than egoism's accomplishment of *shōgi* ("ultimate meaning," or *paramārtha*), and it is something that can be assigned a positive value.

By contrast, in Hebraic thought deaths of suffering ultimately ended in the absurdity of being cast down into the hopeless place of death, where nothing ex-

---

37 Plato, *Sokuratesu no Benmei* (Apology of Socrates), 24C.

ists. The egoism of humans in general—causes people to hope that they, at least, can avoid suffering and dishonor—crushed through unjust attacks, and in the sufferer's awareness during his lifetime such suffering was assigned only a negative value. Only after the sufferer's death, to the extent that God's redemptive work is recognized in it, is there a faint possibility of transformation into something that can be assigned a positive value. The contrast between Greek and Hebrew thought on suffering is striking.

5.3 Atonement as the Starting Point of Liberation from Egoism

What, then, occurs in deaths of hopeless suffering in Israel? My answer was as follows. For the first time there is a *tariki* religious reversal that transcends common sense, including philosophy. Here for the first time occurs what might be called a reversal of self-pursuit on the part of one striving to "obtain for himself beauty" based on calculation and confidence. In other words, a liberation from the egoism that people continue to display, an egoism that they inherently continue to seek, somehow occurs here.

Egoism frequently becomes the work of self-formation through philosophy and other kinds of reasoning. In religion, it can take the form of the pursuit of self-enlightenment and salvation. I would suggest, however, that a horizon of *tariki* religion that transcends that kind of egoism opens up, at least in the hopelessness of Hebraic suffering.

The German term *Hingabe*, which connotes this kind of self-abandonment, literally means to throw (oneself) away. It refers to the "devotion" of suffering, but not only that. It is deeply interesting that it also refers to "conversion" to the religion opened up by these sufferers.[38] Through devotion to their teacher—who was forced to abandon egoism, and who bore their sins and accomplished an atoning death—and through faith in God's self-denying will for salvation displayed there, a new level of devotion emerges especially because they also deny themselves, become futile and empty, and experience transcendence over egoism. When people devote themselves, do they not eventually discover that they have broken away from the egoism that has become deeply rooted in them?[39]

38 Shojun Bando, "Jesus Christus und Amida. Zu Karl Barths Verständnis des Buddhismus vom Reinen Land," in *Gott in Japan: Anstöße zum Gespräch mit japanischen Philosophen, Theologen, Schriftstellern* (eds. Seiichi Yagi und Ulrich Luz; München: Kaiser, 1973).
39 See ibid., 78.

I have learned from Seiichi Yagi's meticulous argument about the inherent meaning of egoism,[40] and I am aware that Parfit,[41] Wolf,[42] Popper,[43] and other modern ethics scholars have presented detailed discussions of the problems of egoism as me-ism. The breaking away from egoism that I am imagining here, however, is a simpler matter. Let me borrow the example given by Shojun Bando. Someone who simply believes in Amida's self-sacrificial salvation and chants *Namu Amida Butsu* with all his or her heart becomes empty like "a child watching cherry blossoms fall with mouth agape."[44] I imagine this to be of a similar dimension. This is akin to the account where Jesus blesses the children and says that "whoever does not receive the kingdom of God as a little child will never enter it" (Mark 10:15).

Be that as it may, freeing oneself of self-interest is next to impossible for many people. Yet for those who simply devote themselves to suffering, it becomes possible to pull away from self-interest without effort. Without such devotion, however, it is exceedingly difficult to do this, no matter how great an effort they expend on the paths of ascetic practices or philosophy. By contrast, when they do devote themselves, they are already in a state of selflessness without having any intention of returning to such a state of selflessness. No longer, then, can be found the self that has not been liberated from egoism, the self that has been engaged with other things, or the self that, despite having accepted suffering, will not abandon calculations to obtain the beauty of *logos*.

From an anthropological perspective, does not the paradox of atonement boil down to these points? As we saw in 3.3 of Chapter 2, for philosophy, which is the path of rational inquiry, secular suffering was nothing more than a trivial episode from the non-rational world. Yet for religion, no matter how difficult suffering might be, it becomes a God-given opportunity to break free from self-serving egoism, and it can become a path that opens the essential level of salvation to charismatic and ordinary people alike.

This becomes possible because it is a reflection of the way God exists, as we saw in Part 4. God, the "I am who I am" who is absolute being, "contain[s] ab-

---

40 Seiichi Yagi, *Iesu Kirisuto no Tankyû* (The Quest for Jesus Christ) (Tokyo: Sanpo, 1976), especially Chapter 1; Seiichi Yagi, *Ai to Egoizumu* (Love and Egoism) (Hadano, Kanagawa: Tokai University Press, 1979), especially Chapter 1.

41 Derek Parfit, *Riyû to Jinkaku: Hi-jinkaku-sei no Rinri e* (Reason and Persons: Toward an Ethics of Impersonality) (trans. Susumu Morimura; Tokyo: Keiso Shobo, 1998).

42 Susan Wolf, "Happiness and Meaning: Two Aspects of the Good Life," *Social Philosophy & Policy* 14 (1997), 207–25.

43 Karl R. Popper, *The Open Society and Its Enemies* (London: Routledge, 1962).

44 Bando, "Jesus Christus und Amida," 79.

solute self-negation within itself"; that is, God is a being who "becomes absolutely nothing." Because the death of God's servant and the cross are truly the very symbols of this, through being conformed to it humans also come to glimpse the work of God and begin to emulate it.

Conclusion

Finally, I wish to add three concluding statements or personal impressions, while reflecting back on the entire chapter.

My first point relates to the claim in Part 1 that Christian monotheism is an ultra-egoistic ideology of plundering. I have not yet directly responded to this claim. Nevertheless, the answer is already evident if the reader connects my introduction and conclusion in the five-part composition of this chapter. Even if people have repeatedly made ultra-egoistic mistakes throughout the history of Christianity and continue to do so today, Christianity's essence can be found in the antithesis of this—, in the very abandonment of egoism.

I am content for vigilance against the ideology of plundering to function as a helpful barometer that makes us sensitive to our inner egoism. Yet one must rebut the argument that monotheism in its entirety may be rejected from the perspective of egoism characterized by the ideology of plundering, because this criticism misses the point. Certainly, we must cast aside egoistic contaminants that tend to be deeply rooted in monotheism, and we must critically dismantle this ideology of plunder. On the other hand, however, we must again reconstruct the essence of Christian monotheism into a purer form by returning to the point of egoism's abolition by God, whose self-denial finds ultimate expression in atonement, which has lasting revelatory power.

Of course, the path is not easy, and there is no guarantee that those who believe and speak of this "essence" have not fallen away from it. When believers realize this, they become powerless and fall into temptation. This is the temptation to yield to whispers that such faith is nothing but a pious and self-righteous daydream and that "attempting to reform the world politically and economically is far superior to clinging to the meaninglessness of religion (see the temptation story in Matt 4:1–11)."[45] Yet the believer strives to resist this temptation. This does not mean he resists it heroically. Nor does it mean that he takes pride in himself and thinks he can attain Christianity's essence. "The only thing he can do is to endure calmly without losing love and humility. Why? It is not for the sake of the virtue of endurance. Rath-

---

45 Seiichi Yagi, "Buddhistischer Atheismus und christlicher Gott," in *Gott in Japan*, 182.

er, it is because the only thing that can help him is the recognition that his existence is based on that which transcends the oppositions between existence and non-existence, meaning and meaninglessness, and integration and disintegration."[46] He is governed by the prescript on the essence that is egoism's abolition by God, whose self-denial finds ultimate expression in atonement. Is this not why he acts toward that particular end on each occasion?

The second point I wish to add relates closely to the first. Earlier, I discussed deconstructing the concept of monotheism that stemmed from the prophets, especially Second Isaiah. The ethical leap and exclusive self-righteousness by which they treat their own people's God as the ruler of world history must certainly be criticized philosophically, whatever the historical facts. The conflicts among the three major exclusive monotheisms of Judaism, Christianity, and Islam clearly indicate the outcome of this kind of leap and self-righteousness. I wish, however, to draw attention to the fact that Second Isaiah's subtle spirit left the frayed logic untouched when he spoke of this monotheism. Consider when he speaks of the pagan king Cyrus as Yahweh's instrument for dominion over world history. While secretly longing for Cyrus to become a follower of Yahweh (45:3), Second Isaiah confusedly says that Cyrus knew Yahweh (41:25)[47] and then that he did not know him (45:4, 5).[48] Second Isaiah himself stumbles and wavers in his move toward this construction of monotheism. When liberation from exile is actually realized through Cyrus, he perceives that Cyrus was not the political and historical savior of world history or of Israelite history; he stumbles over his own construct of political monotheism, and he shifts to his later hope for a religious savior through the servant (Isa 49 – 55). Ultimately, the culmination of his prophetic activities was that this religious salvation is fulfilled in the servant's substitutionary

---

46 Ibid.

47 If we read the Masoretic Text as it is, Isa 41:25a says, "I stirred up (a person) from the north, and he arose, and from the rising of the sun, he calls my name." There is a proposal to revise a Dead Sea Scroll reading of "he shall call his name" to "I [Yahweh] call his [Cyrus's] name" and thus force it to agree with 45:3 – 5. This should not be adopted, however, because it lacks support in ancient translations. Seizô Sekine, trans., *Izaya-sho* (Book of Isaiah) (Tokyo: Iwanami Shoten, 1997). Also see the note for this passage.

48 Regarding the original version of this chapter, published under the same Japanese title in *Nihon no Shingaku*, Tsukimoto offers the following rebuttal in his recent essay mentioned above (see note 3). "Second Isaiah also called Cyrus Yahweh's 'anointed' because he perceived the will of the God Yahweh, which transcended the subjective intentions of these rulers behind the movements of these great nations. It was not because he thought these kings would become followers of Yahweh" (77, note 43). This paragraph is my response to his rebuttal. I have newly written it together with the preceding paragraph in the course of revising this chapter. I wish to thank Tsukimoto for bringing clarity to this point within the present debate.

atonement (Isa 52:13 – 53:12).[49] Monotheism was established somehow only after passing through such twists and turns and arriving at the discovery of the self-denying God who would kill his very own servant. Is this not the essence signified by original monotheism? We must recognize that we can only speak about the reconstruction of monotheism today by returning to this point.

The third and final point I wish to mention concerns the question of how such a reconstruction of monotheism relates to philosophy. If held forth as one fixed truth, Christianity's atonement faith, at which we arrived in Part 5, might dominate other religions and rekindle egoism in the name of evangelizing pagans. I think it is fitting here, in closing, to give heed to this point one more time. If we understand atonement faith as nothing more than one symbolic manifestation of the absolute who contains within itself absolute self-negation, then we must always be prepared to decode these symbols philosophically. For Christianity to accomplish authentic reforms today and to acquire renewed life force, cooperation with philosophy based on objective analyses of phenomena and universal ethics will be essential.

On the other hand, this symbol is an irreplaceable symbol in the self-understanding of Christians, and it will continue to possess a strong visceral power that transcends the many abstract words of philosophy. Most Christians appreciate the evocative power of personalistic monotheism's image of the servant of atonement more than philosophy's logic of topos. In that sense, too, it is both permissible and possible, I believe, to speak of monotheism's reconstruction. For that reason, cooperation with philosophy must ultimately be carried out based on myths filled with riddles and metaphors and on specific biblical texts filled with visceral power, which are treasure troves of many symbols that need to be decoded.

Today, when Christianity must be open to dialogue with other monotheistic religions, as well as various other religions and ideas, including atheism, all the while maintaining its Christian identity, this complementary and tense relationship between religion and philosophy is essential, as is the dynamism of constant feedback.

My considerations in this chapter—use of the Old Testament text as a starting point, as well as my arguments based on comparisons with the philosophies of Nishida and Aristotle—been an attempt to achieve just such a dialog. Building on Chapters 1 and 2, I have simply traced the general outline of my argument. I now wish to develop this tentative treatise more exhaustively and, through cu-

---

49 Regarding the details of redaction history during this period, see Sekine, *Transcendency and Symbols in the Old Testament*, Chapter 5.

mulative arguments from multiple perspectives, to give at least a modest response to the aspects of monotheism that have faced criticism. Perhaps when that response returns to the respondents themselves it might stimulate them to reflect on where the locus of their own standpoint ultimately lies.

Part II **Old Testament Thought
and the Modern World**

Chapter 4 Modern Aspects of the Old Testament Understanding of God: Qohelet, Schoenberg, Jung

1 Suspicions, Criticisms, and Verbal Attacks against the Old Testament God

Anyone attempting to understand the Old Testament will experience a vague sense of unease. In particular, the God portrayed there is said to have dominion over time, space, history, and nature, but in reality he has difficulty controlling rebellious man. One moment he high-handedly wields justice, and the next he acts like a man spurned by a woman, whimpering for Israel to come home. A God who is a relative being, in that he can be swayed though his relationship with relative humans, is not fitting to be called absolute. Jewish and Christian believers rush to quell as blasphemy such doubts in themselves and others, while non-believers have had a strong tendency to take this for granted rather than argue the point. That is why, I think, the issue has rarely been confronted.

Though few in number, however, there have been some who candidly expressed such doubts—some in the form of criticisms, others escalating into verbal attacks. I, too, have shared these kinds of doubts as a modern Japanese reading the Old Testament. Rather than ignoring or suppressing them, I have put these problems to the text and paid assiduous attention to its response. In my view it is the very process of such dialogue that constitutes the essential elements of a philosophical interpretation of the text. In this chapter I offer a few examples of this kind of dialogue, and through this process I wish to suggest some ways in which Old Testament understandings of God are relevant to us today. I have already written about matters related to research history, text-critical problems, and other hermeneutical issues elsewhere, so I shall set those aside because of space constraints. Here I shall concentrate on bringing the text's main reasoning into relief.

1.1 Qohelet's Suspicions of the God who Requites Good and Evil

Doubts about the God of the Old Testament are in fact already present in the Old Testament itself. For instance, Qohelet, a thinker from the Hellenistic period, which was the final period of the Old Testament, voices his skepticism about the traditional view of God. What I mean by "the traditional view of God" is the retributive concept whereby God requites humans for their ethical good and evil. As stated in Proverbs,

> The LORD does not let the righteous go hungry, but he thwarts the craving of the wicked. (Prov 10:3)

Such was the traditional belief. Yet such a retributive law does not seem to function in reality. To the contrary, evil people who are shrewd and manipulative often prosper, while righteous people make fools of themselves. Qohelet, who cool-headedly acknowledges this reality, has this to say:

> ... there are righteous people who are treated according to the conduct of the wicked [that is, with misfortune],
> and there are wicked people who are treated according to the conduct of the righteous [that is, with fortune].
> I said that this also is vanity. (Eccl 8:14; bracketed insertions here and below are mine)

Because "God will judge the righteous and the wicked" (Eccl 3:17) impartially and, concerning their requital, "they cannot find out what God has done from the beginning to the end" (Eccl 3:11), Qohelet concludes: "vanity of vanities! All is vanity" (Eccl 1:2). It is my view that, in adopting the attitude that everything is ultimately "vanity," Qohelet preached *nihil* and was thus an advocate of nihilism. This can be proven by comparing his thinking with the three stages of nihilism proposed by Nietzsche and Heidegger,[1] although I shall not do so here. Whatever the case, my point here is that Qohelet was someone who frankly doubted and denied the traditional view that God presides over acts of retribution.

1.2 Schoenberg's Criticism of the God who Rejects Idols

The above is a criticism of the Old Testament God from within the Old Testament itself. Outside the Old Testament, such criticisms are harsher. Jewish composer Arnold Schoenberg, born in Vienna in the first half of the twentieth century, regards the Old Testament God as strange for rejecting idols, and he expresses his doubts against this God in the opera *Moses und Aron*. This is a dialogic drama for which Schoenberg wrote both the libretto and the music. He puts these words in the mouth of Moses, who firmly rejects idols. The omnipresent and infinite one cannot be contained in an image (Act I, Scene 2; Act II, Scene 4). It is impossible

---

1 Friedrich Nietzsche, *Sämtliche Werke: Kritische Studienausgabe* (ed. Giorgio Colli and Mazzino Montinari. 15 vols.; Berlin: de Gruyter, 1980), vol. 8:2, 11, etc.

to express in visible form the God who transcends this world and "cannot be seen or represented" (Act I, Scene 4). Therefore idols should be prohibited. The Old Testament itself does not give such explicit reasons for this, but there is no doubt that it fundamentally rejects idols. For instance, the second commandment of Moses' Decalogue strictly commands,

> "You shall not make for yourself an idol" (Exod 20:4; Deut 5:8).

Schoenberg voices criticism of this orthodox view in the Old Testament through the mouth of Aaron, Moses' older brother. "Can [a person] love a God who must not be represented?" (Act I, Scene 2). "There are no peoples who believe in a being that cannot be felt" or that does not dwell in this world (Act II, Scene 4). Based on this perspective, Aaron makes a golden calf for the people during Moses' absence and argues him down upon his return. With this, Act II comes to an end. This opera has music only through Act II; Act III has only the libretto. As a result, oftentimes only the first two acts of the opera are performed. This gives the strong impression that Aaron has won and that idols are enthusiastically endorsed.

1.3 Jung's Statement that "Job's God is a Fool"

Then there is Swiss psychologist Carl G. Jung, who criticized the Old Testament God even more overtly. In his small book *Answer to Job*,[2] Jung expresses his frank doubt that the key question in the book of Job is solved. This is the overriding question of whether the righteousness of God, who irrationally caused the righteous Job to lose his family, possessions, and health all at once, can ultimately be justified. The arguments among Job and his friends concerning this question run through the book. Then, at the end, God appears out of a storm and rebukes Job, Job repents, and the story comes to a close. Yet was the question ultimately solved by this rebuke? Jung's answer is no. This quote is from the climax.

> Yahweh roars his accusatory words against a human [Job] who is like a half-trampled worm: "Who is this that darkens counsel by words without knowledge?" (Job 38:2) Given the words of Yahweh that follow, however, one must ask who darkens what sort of counsel here. The answer to Yahweh's question is this: the fool who darkens his own counsel is Yahweh himself. In his retort, as it were, God blames Job for that which God himself did. ... He takes seventy-one lines to proclaim the sovereign right of the creator to a miserable victim. There is absolutely no call for Job to be astonished by this sovereign right to such a nauseating degree.[3]

---

2 Carl G. Jung, *Antwort auf Hiob* (Zürich: Rascher, 1952).
3 Carl G. Jung, *Yobu e no Kotae* (Answer to Job) (trans. Mikiko Nomura; Tokyo: Jordan), 41–43.

Jung's argument devolves into a verbal attack against God, so perhaps it is only natural that Christians have rejected it as blasphemous or ignored it as unscholarly. In his preface Jung cautions that one must distinguish between God as depicted by the biblical author and God himself. In the body of his book, however, he launches attacks at God himself, as if he has completely forgotten this warning.[4] I do not think that the response by Christians is necessarily unjustified. Yet as far as the point on which Jung expressed frank doubts is concerned—namely, that the question raised in the book of Job remains unsolved and something is amiss in God's speech and behavior—we must acknowledge that Jung's statement continues to bear heavily upon us.

Many other doubts have been expressed about the God of the Old Testament. Back in ancient times, the second-century heretic Marcion distinguished the God of the Old Testament from the God of Christianity and rejected the former. This idea has been repeatedly asserted in many different forms up to Yōji Inoue in recent times.[5] Kant and Buber protested against the cruel God who commanded Abraham to sacrifice his firstborn.[6] Kierkegaard, Derrida, and others have presented yet other arguments. Tetsurō Watsuji cast doubts from a religious studies perspective on the view that worship of a personal God is a mature form of religion.[7] And Levinas has expressed fundamental doubts about a redemptive God, based upon his experience with the Nazis.[8] In recent years I too have called for critical perspectives toward the understandings of God that are expressed in the historical narrative of David's acts of adultery and murder[9] and in the falsification of prophecies through pseudonymous Deuteronomistic redaction.[10] In the limited space available here, however, it is best not to extend the discussion too broadly. The above doubts about the Old Testament God from three different directions are in some sense typical and can be regarded as encapsulating other

---

4 For a balanced consideration of this point based on past research, see Satoko Miyashita's noteworthy doctoral dissertation, "Yungu ni okeru Shūkyō-teki Rinri no Kanōsei" (The Possibility of Religious Ethics in Jung) (Tokyo: University of Tokyo, 2007), Chapter 5.
5 Yōji Inoue, *Namu no Kokoro ni Ikiru* (Living With the Heart of Namu) (Tokyo: Chikuma Shobo, 2003).
6 See Chapter 1.
7 Tetsurō Watsuji, *Fūdo* (Climate) (Tokyo: Iwanami Shoten, 1935), 57 ff.
8 Emmanuel Levinas, *Konnan na Jiyū* (Difficult Freedom) (trans. Tatsuru Uchida; Tokyo: Kokubunsha, 1985), 69 ff.
9 Seizō Sekine, *Kyūyaku ni okeru Chōetsu to Shōchō: Kaishakugaku-teki Keiken no Keifu* (Tokyo: University of Tokyo Press, 1994), Chapter 3. This monograph has been published in English as *Transcendency and Symbols in the Old Testament: A Genealogy of the Hermeneutical Experiences* (trans. Judy Wakabayashi; Berlin: Walter de Gruyter, 1999).
10 See Chapter 7.

questions and doubts as well. Therefore this chapter will focus on these three critiques, and I shall further consider how to respond to them and whether the Old Testament God is so fragile as to collapse under the weight of such doubts.

2 A Response from the Old Testament

2.1 The Nihilism of Qohelet and his Triumph Over It: The Ontological Personal God and the Non-ontological Transcendent One

First, what can be said about the retributive God who falls under suspicion from Qohelet? Qohelet the Nihilist pronounced the death of the "traditional retributive God." While there is room for debate over whether the nihilism of Nietzsche[11] and Heidegger,[12] which spoke of God's death, theorized about a new God to take his place,[13] in my view Qohelet did just that. What kind of being, then, is this new God whom Qohelet encountered after rejecting the traditional God? I think the following words, which are repeated throughout the book of Ecclesiastes in various forms, convey the appearance of this new God, and they also suggest a direction for overcoming the nihilism that announces the death of God:

> I know that there is nothing better for them than to be happy and enjoy themselves as long as they live; moreover, it is God's gift that all should eat and drink and take pleasure in all their toil. ... God has done this. (Eccl 3:12–14) (also see Eccl 3:22; 5:18; 8:15; 9:7)

There is not sufficient space here to trace in various texts how Qohelet arrived at this position. In short, he stopped living the faith in a God who enacts the kind of retributive law whose goals include a society in which the righteous flourish and the evil perish. This was because Qohelet realized that the very mindset that subsumes small everyday relative purposes within that kind of absolute purpose is itself "vanity of vanities" and "meaningless."

Let us consider an example close to home. When people study for entrance exams, being accepted by a particular school is the absolute purpose, and they allow themselves to engage only in those relative purposes that can be sub-

---

11 Friedrich W. Nietzsche, *Die fröhliche Wissenschaft* (Chemnitz: Verlag von Ernst Schmeitzner; New York: E. Steige, 1882), fragment 125.

12 Martin Heidegger, "Nietzsches Wort: Gott ist tot," in *Holzwege* (Frankfurt a. M.: V. Klostermann, 1950).

13 Eugen Fink, *Niiche no Tetsugaku* (Nietzsche's Philosophy), *Niiche Zenshū* (Complete Works of Nietzsche), Supplement (trans. Denzaburō Yoshizawa; Tokyo: Risōsha, 1963).

sumed within their absolute purpose. To the extent that the relative purpose of chatting with friends is refreshing and therefore effectively helps them to fulfill their subsuming purpose, it is permissible to some extent. They cannot, however, afford to talk through the night, even if a friend contemplating suicide comes to them for counsel. Yet relating to people ought to mean accepting others regardless of one's personal convenience and values, so turning away a friend in need would not be truly relating to others. And if the subsuming purpose is one that has been egoistically established ultimately for the sake of one's own convenience and values, it becomes impossible to meet with others who do not align with the means to one's end purpose. Because a person's self does not exist in isolation, but comes into being through relationships with others, one would expect such people to feel as if they were gradually wasting away and that their lives were drying up. Is that not the meaning of "vanity" in the cry of this nihilist? Facing the crisis of such nihilism, Qohelet shifted his thinking and resolutely repudiated a subsuming purpose. This meant accepting only relative purposes, such as "eat[ing] and drink[ing] and tak[ing] pleasure in all [one's] toil." When hungry, one wants to eat. When the desire to eat is met, it disappears. This itself is not the absolute purpose comprising the implementation of retribution in history. It is nothing more than something relative that is born only to disappear and then eventually be born again. Yet when one learns what it is to love this sort of small purpose for its own sake, one discovers in oneself a distinct healing from vanity, even if only slightly so.

Viewed in relation to understandings of God, the subject of this chapter, the point here is as follows. Qohelet started out with doubts about the traditional God, a retributive God who rules over history. He then decided that such a God conflicted with the reality where the righteous suffer and the wicked flourish and that this God should be discarded. Yet rejecting God does not settle the matter. The true God must be sought beyond this rejection. Qohelet does find the true "gift of God" through his search. This God is no longer a retributive personal God who is revealed directly through the history of mercy in the exodus, or through the speaking of the prophets, or through the scourges of storms and wars. This God is nothing more than a being who is faintly perceived in and through the small pleasures of daily life, such as eating, drinking, and working, in that these are "gifts" from him. God cannot be observed as an ontological entity; he is the non-ontological transcendent one whose workings alone can be faintly perceived. This was the new God whom Qohelet found beyond the death of the traditional God.

Questions remain as to whether this discovery by Qohelet truly represents a triumph over nihilism and whether it was connected to encounters with others,[14] but these points are beyond our present scope.

2.2 Schoenberg's Uncertainty: Toward the Idea of Atonement Thought

Next, what can be said concerning the second doubt about the Old Testament God—i.e., Schoenberg's positive view of idols? As noted above, the second act of the opera ends with Moses falling prostrate in despair before Aaron, who made the golden calf, and the people, because of his own inability to represent God. However, there is more to the libretto. In the third and final act of the opera, Moses, having regained his strength, declares that the omnipotent one is one who is "not bound to anything," be that in the form of idols or the duty of retribution. Aaron then dies, and the opera comes to an end. Because the Old Testament takes the position of Moses' rejection of idols, this conclusion is in line with the Old Testament. When performed at concerts, Act III often ends tranquilly, with Moses and Aaron simply speaking their lines. Audiences receive an impression that is directly opposite to that conveyed at two-act performances, which reflect a positive view of idols.

Did Schoenberg himself affirm idols or reject them? I think he probably wavered between the two. After Schoenberg wrote the libretto and composed the music for the first two acts of this opera during the years around 1930, he was driven from his professorship at the Academy of the Arts in Berlin, and he fled to the U.S. He was perfectly capable of composing the music for the third act during the seventeen years before his death in the U.S., but he did not complete it. Perhaps Schoenberg could no longer empathize with the Mosaic concept of God, who allowed six million of his people to be slaughtered, who did not save them though he was immanent in history, and who merely remains transcendent and rejects idols. Whatever the reason, Schoenberg neither rewrote nor scrapped his third act that contradicts Aaron. This gives us reason to believe that Schoenberg wavered on this matter for the rest of his life. In other words, it is safe to say that, while still unsure himself, Schoenberg cast doubt on the Old Testament's categorical rejection of idols.

How can the Old Testament respond to such doubts? There are various reasons that it unabashedly rejects idols, but the following two points are particu-

---

14 Sekine, *Kyūyaku ni okeru Chōetsu to Shōchō* (Transcendency and Symbols in the Old Testament), Chapter 2, esp. 149 ff.

larly important. First is the reason that the prophets often give. Idols falsely represent God, and because they are made of mere wood and stone, worshipping them is nothing more than a risible and pagan act of folly (Hos 8:6; Jer 2:28; Isa 44:9–20; etc.). The other reason is stated in the latter half of the second commandment, which prohibits idols. They are prohibited because "I [Yahweh] … am a jealous God, punishing children for the iniquity of parents, to the third and the fourth generation of those who reject me, but showing steadfast love to the thousandth generation of those who love me and keep my commandments" (Exod 20:5–6; Deut 5:9–10). In other words, Yahweh is a God who extends "steadfast love" and "punishes" people according to their attitude toward ethical "commandments." It is utterly impossible to represent through static idols the God who is made manifest especially in love and righteousness within this dynamism of history, so idols must be rejected.

Ultimately, however, are these reasons compelling? The second reason is difficult to accept for those of us who have suspected, as did Qohelet, that God cannot be counted upon to execute retribution in history. As for the first reason, modern archaeological discoveries and research into idolatry throughout the ancient Near East have found counter-evidence.[15] In pagan idolatry it is not that people were simply worshiping stone and wood. Rather, through them, they were worshiping the divinity that these things symbolized. Hence even if one derides this alleged childish identification between gods and things, this does not constitute a criticism of actual idolatry itself.

Does this mean that the Old Testament ultimately cannot answer doubts such as those of Schoenberg concerning whether idols symbolizing God must necessarily be rejected? I do not think so. There seems to be one more twist in the matter. We should note that Schoenberg inherited the traditional view of an authoritative Moses that had become exaggerated in later Jewish and Christian tradition (Sir. 45:1 ff.; John 1:17; 6:23 ff.; etc.). By contrast, the image of Moses originally depicted in old Pentateuchal sources is that of a weaker and smaller man who was sensitive to his and his people's sins and incapabilities. We must also pay attention to the recognition that love and justice are faintly manifested in history through such small people. If we piece together the old Yahwist or Jehovist source, we can briefly sum up the life of Moses depicted there as follows.

First, the adult Moses appears in the narrative not as an exceptional character revered by everyone, but as an outlaw who commits murder and flees from fear of being discovered (Exod 2:11–15). However, his motive for the murder was a right-

---

15 Werner H. Schmidt, "Bilderverbot und Gottebenbildlichkeit: Exegetische Notizen zur Selbstmanipulation des Menschen," *Wort und Wahrheit* 23 (1968), 209–16.

eous anger against the Egyptian tyrants, coupled with love and compassion for his oppressed people. These same principles of righteousness and love can also be seen when he rescues some women from mistreatment by shepherds in the land of Midian, where he had fled (Exod 2:16–17). Afterward, in this land of refuge, Moses is called by God as the leader of the exodus, but he declines:

> O my Lord, I have never been eloquent … I am slow of speech and slow of tongue. (Exod 4:10)

Here, too, the figure of Moses is not that of a hero who takes the initiative to lead his people. Rather, it is that of a small man ashamed of his inabilities, one who fears he is unworthy of this exceedingly great mission. At the end of his quarrel with God, it turns out that he is appointed as the leader of his people, but afterward he is depicted as slowly maturing while continuing to struggle under the heavy burden of leading his people (Exod 17:1–7).

In particular, Moses appears to have matured into an exceptional leader when he comes down Mount Sinai to where the people have made a golden calf and are reveling around it, and he reprimands them for this. Here, too, we see the aspect of love in his intercession for God's mercy upon the people, who have committed the sin of idolatry (Exod 32:9–13), and the aspect of righteousness is evident in his clear act of punishment and execution of judgment (Exod 23:25–29). What is new here, however, is that Moses desires to die in place of the people, and he offers God this means of overcoming the contradiction, as it were, between love and righteousness (Exod 32:3–32). This indicates the highest point in the Old Testament's genealogy of redemptive death, beginning with animal sacrifice in Leviticus and elsewhere (Lev 5:14–6:7; 7:1–9) and culminating in the suffering and death of God's servant in Second Isaiah (Isa 52:13–53:12). This is a discovery of thought that underpins the Old Testament and aims to sublate the conflict between unrighteousness, which merits death, and love, which desires to forgive and to give life. In other words, the following idea reaches fruition in this intercessory prayer through which Moses, who from the outset has experienced the conflict between love and righteousness, wagers his life. It is the idea that one righteous person, while loving and giving life to many by atoning for their unrighteousness in their stead, might also achieve righteousness for the whole by receiving punishment as the whole.

We should be able to see anew here the significance of the reasoning for prohibiting idols. It is impossible to represent God through idols because God becomes manifest in history through love and righteousness. Therefore the Old Testament was not ignoring a reality whereby the suffering of the righteous seemed to be violating the law of retribution, nor was it falling into high-sounding talk. Rather, it turned this wretched reality on its head and stated that, truly, such a God of atonement is faintly manifested above all in that very site of fracture. It seems that we can recognize here the testimony that the Old Testament God is very much alive in the place of substitutionary atonement above all else. This answers the Schoenbergian criticism, which is a step removed from common sense, that it is better to have idols if they vaguely represent divinity. It also discredits the Qoheletian suspicion that, generally speaking, God is hidden in history.

2.3 What Jung Missed: Demythologizing the Creation Story

Let us briefly consider the third doubt, Jung's criticism of Job. Does the God who appears out of a storm in Job 38 onward merely bully the worm-like Job, as Jung sees it? Is it true that God is only "retorting" threateningly to Job's candid doubts that God is unjust if he imposes hardships on the righteous while failing to carry out ethical retribution?

This is probably not so. Rather, the point here seems to be that, in response to the selfish human desire for God to act in accordance with the law of ethical retribution (Job 9), God reveals the existence of an additional aspect that is rooted in creation and transcends ethical aspects. He says no to human arrogance that would cage God for one's own eudemonic purposes without knowing God as the basis of all created beings beyond the realm of ethical good and evil. It is a rebuke of Job, who forgot that God is not an immanent God measurable by analogy with human ethics, but a transcendent God who completely transcends human ethics. This is the essence of chapters 38 onward. As indicated above, Jung tends to confuse the God portrayed in the book of Job with God himself. Similarly, I think he misses the true significance by failing to distinguish between the reality portrayed in the creation myth and the myth itself, because he lacks the perspective needed to demythologize the latter.

Assuming that faith requires literal belief in every word of the Bible, some believers irrationally seek to believe things that modern scientific knowledge shows to be impossible. There are also unbelievers who simply reject the Bible, regarding it as a collection of absurd stories that are unbelievable for modern people. Both constitute fundamental misunderstandings, however, and both commit the fallacy of literalism. Literalism absolutizes the words of the Bible, which are ultimately nothing more than the words of relative humans communicated within the constraints of particular time periods. In a broad sense, this is idolatry, which deifies the things of this world. As we saw in the discussion about Moses, the Bible itself denounces this. Instead it is more important to clear away such period constraints, relativize the conceptual mechanisms of the period, and thereby hermeneutically untangle the unlimited reality that the author wished to communicate. We must conclude, I think, that because Jung critically lacks this demythologizing perspective, he misses the vital point of God's speech in Chapter 38 onward.

What, then, is this reality? There is not sufficient space here to review the text of Genesis 1, which underpins Job, but here is my conclusion: We can sum up this reality as "the infinite basis of human existence" and as feelings of thanksgiving and awe toward "the being that, with love, transfers humans from the midst of the chaos of formless darkness into the order and fullness of light, and who wishes to have fellowship with them." The texts in Genesis and Job 38 onward "made great efforts to portray symbolically the reality of this unlimited being through representations available to ancient people, even if their schematic representations included embellishments that may be denied by modern science."[16]

3 How Does the Old Testament Understanding of God Challenge the Modern World?

After reviewing radical challenges to the Old Testament God from three different directions, I have explored here the possibility of responding to these challenges by probing deeper into Old Testament thought. In sum, my argument is as follows. God manifests his true form in the following ways. Contrary to Qohelet's suspicions, God must in fact be perceived within non-ontological works. Contrary to Schoenberg's criticism, God manifests himself instead as the being who integrates love and righteousness through atonement. And contrary to Jung's verbal attack, God manifests himself as the transcendent basis of surpassing the ethical realm. In what ways, then, does the existence of the Old Testament God, which can also respond to various modern doubts—Schoenberg and Jung were of course modern thinkers, but Qohelet also exhibits modern aspects as a Nihilist—challenge us today? I would like to conclude by reflecting on this and suggesting some new ways of looking at it, boiling matters down to the topic of "challenges from monotheistic civilization."[17]

---

[16] Concerning the details regarding interpretation of this text, see Seizō Sekine, *Kyūyaku Seisho no Shisō* (Old Testament Thought), Chapter 4, especially page 52.
[17] This chapter originated as part of a series of lectures at Komaba, but various people have considered this topic.

3.0 What Kind of Age is this Modern Period?

So from the perspective of understandings of God, just what kind of age is this modern period? Let us briefly consider this point. Firstly, we can say that it is an age of autonomous humanism and an age that has pronounced the death of an ontological God who exists outside of the self. There are valid reasons that have led up to this pronouncement. At its root lie the experiences of modern people who have witnessed tragedies such as massive slaughters of innocent peoples and who have achieved material well-being through the results of scientific developments that exclude God. These alone are defining factors of modernism. It would not be an overstatement, however, to define this modern age, secondly, as one that has experienced violations against the law of retribution within history, and thirdly, as an age that lauds dominion over nature through science. In fact, my description here of the three doubts about the Old Testament God as "modern" is not merely because their proponents are modern, but also because they accord with these three definitions of modernity. Let us review them in order.

3.1 Doubts about the Concept of God

First, I think that the understanding of God as the transcendent one discovered beyond Qohelet's doubts and perceived in non-ontological works challenges the modern age, which has pronounced the death of the ontological God, in the following way. Contrary to the perfunctory understanding of God as one who can be discarded because it is no longer possible to believe in an old, bearded man riding on the clouds, God is actually the very entity with which that person relates unlimitedly. To the person who relates unlimitedly with money, money is god, and to the person who seeks to relate unlimitedly with romantic love, romantic love can become god, although there are authentic and counterfeit gods. We discover that unlimited being through and beyond our deciphering of the symbols of this world, whether that be the biblical text, prayer or meditation, or individual experiences of everyday life.[18] Furthermore, just as individual nails align when placed in a magnetic field, so too are individual, self-absorbed egoists able to form a community only when placed in the magnetic field of love. In figurative terms, God is like a magnetic field, itself invisible, in which love is at work, and the personal representation of this is nothing more than an ontological personal

---

18 Paul Tillich, *Shinkō no Honshitsu to Dōtai* (Essence and Movements of Faith) (trans. Michio Taniguchi; Tokyo: Shinkyo Publishing, 2000).

God.[19] This is an example, I think, of how the understanding of the non-ontological transcendent one challenges our modern superficial understandings of God.

3.2 Sensitivity to Suffering

Secondly, the understanding of the redemptive God found beyond Schoenberg's criticism richly challenges the modern world, which has witnessed violations against the law of retribution. Nevertheless, because atonement thought has itself been subject to criticism in modern times, it is first necessary to address this criticism.

Here I shall use Nietzsche's criticism as a typical example. According to Nietzsche, atonement thought is a hypothetical construct fabricated to justify the ressentiment of the weak. He argued that this ideology regards sinners and the sick as blissful, turns all values upside down, and is eerily seductive (F. Nietzsche, *On the Genealogy of Morals*). I think that the following rebuttal from the side of atonement thought is possible. It is not that there is value in the sins of sinners or in the sicknesses of the sick, as Nietzsche charges. Rather, these people are assigned value as those whose sins have been forgiven and whose diseases have been healed. By contrast, from the outset Nietzsche's master morality takes into account only sinless nobles and the disease-free healthy, abandoning sinners and the sick. Atonement thought, however, supports them, and its true value lies in its declaration to them of forgiveness and healing. Other criticisms against atonement thought have received considerable attention, such as those by I. Kant (*Philosophy of Religion*), the young G. W. F. Hegel (*Bern Fragments 44 – 46*), and E. Levinas (*Difficult Freedom*). Regarding the possibility of responses to each of these, I would simply point the reader to my *Rinri no Tansaku* (The Quest for Ethics)[20] and move on.

For instance, the following section of Tadao Yanaihara's *Dai-ni Izaya-sho Kōgi* (Lectures on Second Isaiah),[21] which he delivered during World War II, epit-

---

19 Seiichi Yagi, "Makusa no Rikiryō: Dōgen Zenji to Seisho" (The Power of Prohibitions: Zen Master Dogen and the Bible), in *Dōgen Zenji Kenkyū Ronshū* (Studies of Zen Master Dogen: Collected Essays) (Eihei, Fukui: Eihei-ji, 2002).

20 Seizō Sekine, *Rinri no Tansaku: Seisho kara no Apurōchi* (The Quest for Ethics: An Approach from the Bible) (Tokyo: Chuko Shinsho, 2002), Chapter 1, section 4.

21 Aware that this was a lecture given at Komaba, I have intentionally quoted from Tadao Yanaihara, the dean at that campus of the University of Tokyo a half century ago. These wartime remarks resulted in Yanaihara's dismissal from the university because of his criticism of the war.

omizes a challenge rooted in atonement thought and directed at the modern world, which had experienced violations against the law of retribution:

> Settle your hearts, now, and listen quietly to the world. Many sounds reach our ears from places far and near—groans seeking liberation, voices filled with distress. It is the violence of those who commit injustices. The cry of a child who has lost his parents, the lament of the young wife who has lost her husband, the person with no rice to eat, the person with no wood coal for keeping warm, the cries and screams of the battlefield, voices from the leprosy ward, voices from the mental ward—the world heaves its breath. The world is filled with the cry to "loosen the chains of confusion." Amidst those bitter noises and hysterical voices, you can hear a calm, clear voice. It is the voice of the servant of Jehovah. He neither shouts nor raises his voice. He teaches, he prays. He is struck, he is trodden upon. Without resisting, he quietly dusts himself off and rises and speaks Jehovah's words once again.[22]

This very "servant of Jehovah" is the redemptive servant of God who stands at the pinnacle in the above-mentioned line of Moses' intercessory prayer; he is the one who atoned for people's sins, endured suffering, and went calmly to his death. This individual can be seen in suffering people around the world, and he finely hones their sensibility to suffering. Yanaihara's words advocate for the need to listen quietly to those voices. In bringing my commentary to a close here, I challenge us, too, to listen quietly.

3.3 The Givenness of Existence

Lastly, the understanding of God as the transcendent basis of existence beyond the ethical realm, which we saw beyond Jung's criticism, issues an important challenge to this age that lauds dominion over nature through science. I wish to conclude by directing our attention to this point.

The Jewish philosopher A. J. Heschel, who was a near-contemporary of Jung and who, like Schoenberg, went to America to escape the Nazis, commented as follows based on his experience of war:

> Perhaps this is the essence of human misery: to forget that life is a gift as well as a trust.[23]

---

22 Tadao Yanaihara, *Iwanami-ban Zenshū Dai-jūni-kan* (The Complete Works, Iwanami Edition, Vol. 12) (Tokyo: Iwanami Shoten, 1978), 591.
23 Abraham Joshua Heschel, *God in Search of Man: A Philosophy of Judaism* (New York: Farrar, Straus & Cudahy, 1955), 352.

Moderns may be quick to rebut such words along the following lines. The notion that life is a trust given by something that transcends humans was thought up by ancient people and is nothing more than a childish myth that religious people wish to believe. After all, we are reaching a day and age when it is possible to create human clones by human hands. In response to such an argument, however, one must ask whether, to the contrary, this modern tendency to deny the concept of God as the transcendent basis of existence is itself nothing more than a myth that fails to recognize the fundamental limits of science. Certainly, modern science has discovered a way to reproduce DNA by linking it to certain viruses using enzymes. Fundamentally speaking, however, that is as far as modern science can understand. Science cannot know why DNA reproduces through this kind of procedure or why DNA already exists here in the first place. In other words, science can only accept nature and the natural laws at work within it as they already exist. Herein lies the limits of science, as well as the limits of humans. The very fact that nature, the natural laws at work within it, and especially life itself are bestowed on us as gifts is utterly mysterious and amazing. Is not contemplating this fundamental fact, which we all too easily forget, one way—but also the most essential way—to escape "human misery"? I think that this third understanding of God as the transcendent basis of existence will continue to challenge the modern world.

I might attempt to summarize the argument of this chapter in these final words. Behind its ancient and mythical surface-level manner of speech, the Old Testament understanding of God has at least three modern implications for three essential problems that continue to challenge us today. That is the conclusion of this chapter—a temporary anchorage point after having left the moorings of Abraham's understanding of God, and a foothold for achieving further understanding.

Chapter 5 Toward Regenerating Ethics: Seeking an Ordered Path of Joyful Coexistence

Introduction

As an ethicist aware of the ethical and moral collapse that has been a focus of attention for some time now, I have struggled to find a way to somehow contribute to moral education in school settings. I am deeply grateful for this opportunity to discuss moral education with teachers who have leadership roles in local school settings. Although I have very little knowledge and experience in school education, I think about ethics and morals on a daily basis. My aim is to provide at least a springboard for debate so as to facilitate a candid exchange of opinions by both researchers and teachers.

Here I mainly use the term "ethics," but in a sense nearly synonymous with "morals." The original terms *ēthos* in Greek and *mōrēs* in Latin both mean "folkways, customs," and there is little difference in their meaning. As Tetsurō Watsuji has explained in detail,[1] however, the Japanese word *rinri* ("ethics") refers to the *ri* (reason, order, coherence) of *rin* (a company of people and the terms of their relationship). This is very close in meaning to the "ordered path of coexistence" in my title. Watsuji defined ethics as the "order" or "reason" (*dōri*) of "betweenness among people" (*aidagara*). Nevertheless, today many use the term "environmental ethics" to include not only human relationships but also our relationship to the natural environment, so I will use the term "coexistence" to refer to living together with other humans as well as the natural environment. By itself, the expression "ordered path" (*riro*) refers to the order or coherence of things. Here, however, I use this not only in that sense, but also to connote a sense that distinguishes between "order" or "coherence" (*ri*) and the "path" (*ro*) by which this is realized. It is with reference to an "ordered path of coexistence" in this sense, then, that I wish to use the term "ethics" below. Since it is too abstract and difficult to understand through definitions alone, let us consider some specific situations.

A recent TV segment titled "Are Japanese Morals Collapsing?" by NHK, Japan's national broadcaster, introduced various examples suggesting that Japanese morals are dangerously on the verge of collapse.[2] Examples included people driving through highway toll gates without paying the toll, writing in library

---

1 Tetsurō Watsuji, *Ningen no Gaku toshite no Rinrigaku* (Ethics as the Study of Man) (Tokyo: Iwanami Shoten, 1934). See Chapter 1, section 1, "'Rinri' to iu Kotoba no Imi" (The Meaning of the Term "Ethics").

2 On the television program "Kurōzu-appu Gendai" (Today's Close-up), August 1, 2006.

books and tearing out the pages, and disposing of household trash in trash bins at train stations and convenience stores. According to an NHK poll taken around the same time in 2006, the number of Japanese who think that recent Japanese morals are low or somewhat low had risen to 77 percent.

Yet there is also a counterargument against this. Some people commented online that they were fed up with NHK's bias, as reflected in this program, that "the Japan of yesterday was better." They argued that the public morals of Japanese were worse in the past. Rush hour, for instance, was a combative sport. Coffee shop employees were completely untrained, and shopping at street markets was like a fight. And they pointed out that there were more juvenile crimes in the past, many of them heinous.[3]

Moreover, the collapse of morals could be viewed as a worldwide tendency not limited to Japan. For instance, Mr. Sarkozy's critical remarks before France's presidential election on May 1, 2007 are still fresh in my memory: "Particularly the 1968 Paris May Revolution [which was the precursor of student movements worldwide] led to the collapse of France's morals, and since then one no longer hears the word 'morals' in France. Victimizers have run rampant over victims, and there has ceased to be a hierarchy of values. Schools, too, have become corrupt." This drew protests from baby-boomer intellectuals, who had been behind the student movements. And since being elected president, Sarkozy himself has drawn criticism for his divorces and fondness for vacations, with many questioning his morality.

In this way, it is easy to fall into arguments for and against what one considers to be ethical and unethical. Here, therefore, I wish to focus on a careful argument about an unethicality that we can all agree clearly runs counter to "ethics" as an "ordered path of coexistence." The vast majority of people acknowledge that murder is unethical. Murder is truly a rebellion against coexistent living with others, and if we cannot regard this as unethical, there are no longer any unethical acts. In fact, debates about the collapse of ethics in recent years stem from murder cases that many might wish to describe as satanic, such as Aum Shinrikyo's sarin gas attack, the Kobe child murders by a 14-year-old boy, the HIV-tainted blood scandal, and the 9/11 simultaneous terrorist attacks. What shall we do, then, to overcome the unethicality of such murders, to discover an ordered path of coexistence, and to regenerate ethics? Here I wish to limit myself to considering this point.

Before proceeding to this question, however, we must first explore the background behind why our society has neglected ethics in this sense in the first

3 For example, see http://homepage.mac.com/naoyuki_hashimoto/iblog/C1310380191/E20060 801202336/index.html.

place, and we need to recognize at least part of the reason for that. Hence this chapter consists of the following three parts. Part 1 notes the postmodern ethical conditions underpinning modern society. Based on this, in Part 2 I consider the reason (*ri*) that murder is wrong to begin with. Part 3 explores a specific path (*ro*) we might take to arrive at an understanding of this reason.

1 Two Attitudes Toward Ethics

1.1 Emotional Draconianism and Ethical Education

From the Aum Shinrikyo attacks to the HIV-tainted blood scandal, these various incidents are antisocial occurrences that deviate from ethics as an ordered path of coexistence. When we witness the tragic deaths caused by these crimes, we feel anger toward the perpetrators, along with sympathy and sadness for the victims.

Anger against the perpetrators is natural, especially when one considers the pain and suffering they have caused their innocent victims and the bereaved family members. Beyond this, we might also feel anger against the current judicial system, which neglects the human rights of the victims and mainly emphasizes those of the perpetrators. It might be an anger that we do not know where to direct, or an anger arising from internalized fear that those close to us, our loved ones, might become victims of such misfortune. Or it might stem from growing apprehension that we would break down should something like this occur. When these types of anger become entangled within us it is natural, I think, to have thoughts of anger against the perpetrators and not only to feel sad for the victims.

1.2 Theoretical Ethical Relativism and Skepticism

Nevertheless, we must stop and consider that today there is, on the other hand, a deeply rooted tendency not to approve of unbridled displays of such anger. Perhaps this could be explained as a "postmodern tendency," but here I must forego that analysis because of space constraints. For a detailed discussion of this point, I recommend Ryōhei Matsushita's excellent and substantial *Dōtoku no Dentatsu: Modan to Posuto Modan o Koete* (Transmission of Morals: Beyond the Modern and the Postmodern).[4] In any case, postmodern intellectuals attempt to curb their emotional anger against perpetrators.

In response to unethical acts, on the one hand there is an emotional tendency for some simply to clamor for discipline, education of the heart and mind, and severe punishment. On the other hand, there is an extremely calm-headed postmodern trend aimed at restraining this tendency. Postmodernists criticize emotionalists for letting their emotions get ahead of them and falling into a kind of aphasia, whereby they are unable to explain logically the deep roots of modern ethical issues.

More specifically, postmodernists maintain that people who make emotional assertions are unaware of the resulting paradox whereby the ethical values they preach deviate from their original intention and operate in reverse.[5] For instance, emotionalists assert that it is important to teach values such as "respect for life," "respect for human rights," "caring," and "democracy" systematically through education. The more they assert this, however, the more they deviate from their original intention and perpetuate the existing social system. They wind up alienating those who are critical of their approach or people who do not fit into the system; paradoxically, they fail to "respect" the "human rights" of others or to "care" for them. In other words, those who enjoy benefits within problem-filled social systems—such as modern capitalistic institutions, the information society, consumer society, the modern education system, or the modern nation-state—are vocal in support of the values that sustain society in order to preserve their own vested interests. They succumb to structures of power that suppress dissenters and elements critical of these structures. Whether the emotionalists recognize this paradox or not, it does not present any problem for them. This is the sort of incisive criticism that postmodernists level against them.

1.3 Aphasia and Working to Overcome It

In sum, there is a confrontation between support for emotional Draconianism and ethical education on the one hand, and postmodern criticism based on theoretically grounded ethical relativism and skepticism on the other. This confrontation constitutes the difficult circumstances surrounding modern ethics.

---

4 Ryōhei Matsushita, *Dōtoku no Dentatsu: Modan to Posuto Modan o Koete* (Transmission of Morals: Beyond the Modern and the Postmodern) (Tokyo: Nihon Tosho Center, 2004).
5 Ibid., 22.

The difficulty is exacerbated because both sides have fallen into a state of aphasia, as it were. The emotionalists are not theoretically equipped, so they simply spout off about "severe punishment" and "disciplinary education," but they are unable to address how to cope with the paradox this entails. Postmodernists criticize them for aphasia, but what about the postmodernists themselves? They are so apprehensive about getting caught up in structures of power when discussing ethics that they become highly relativistic and skeptical on the question of ethics and cannot easily discuss it. They back away from ethical matters and fall into a state of enforced silence.[6] In that sense, postmodernists also lapse into a state of aphasia.

These are the difficult circumstances confronting modern ethics. I wish first to investigate the loci of this contemporary issue.

What will it take to overcome these circumstances? Aphasia concerning ethics is the loss of a means to talk effectively about ethics. We do not know how to speak about ethics properly, so we have neglected it for now. This neglect has come back to bite us, however, and it has led to deviant behavior. Antisocial and brutal murders are rampant, and the result is a society filled with the groans and laments of the victims of senseless violence. If the emotionalists and theorists would listen to this, surely they would both realize the severity of the suffering and sad conditions resulting from this neglect of ethics. Are we not facing a desperate situation in which, given the realities, we can no longer remain paralyzed in a state of aphasia? An awareness of this fact is the starting point for overcoming this problem.

Having experienced postmodernity, however, we must give heed to the following point. We must take special care that speaking about ethics does not devolve into a form of suppression of the weak in order to perpetuate a society in which society's winners can enjoy their personal benefits. As long as we keep this in mind, there is no reason to be fearful or reluctant about overcoming aphasia in practical ways or about attempting a "regeneration of ethics" in some form or another. Rather, moving toward such ethical practice is now the most urgent task facing us.

Here, therefore, I am using the term "ethics" to mean "an ordered path of coexistence wherein people do not commit murder." What, then, can we do to recover this sort of ethics? In one sense, it should be a simple matter, because it would be sufficient for everyone to agree on why murder is wrong. After the Kobe child murders, in particular, this issue was debated from various perspec-

---

6 Ibid., 28.

tives. I have written about how one might address this argument in my *Rinri no Tansaku* (The Quest for Ethics),[7] so I shall not repeat myself here.

Instead, I wish to focus on how, by looking back at the Old Testament's "Mosaic Decalogue," which is the oldest text that issues the command "you shall not murder," we might gain some hints of an essential insight that our postmodern age tends to forget. Perhaps I should reflect on whether I am turning this to my own advantage as an Old Testament scholar, but I think that a study of the history of ethical thought will demonstrate that this is not the case and that the insights of ancient people contain important understandings that we moderns tend to forget. That is my conclusion at present.

Since I have pointed out the Old Testament way of thinking in my book,[8] I wish to begin with a summary of this thinking

2 Two Grounds for Rejecting Murder: Awareness of Order (*Ri*)

There are four main answers in the Old Testament to the question of "Why must we not murder?" For the sake of brevity, however, I wish to focus on two of them thought to be especially important. One is a ktisiological answer, and the other is a soteriological answer.

2.1 A Ktisiological Reason[9] (*Ri*)

Let us begin with ktisiology, or the theology of creation. This answer goes as follows: "You shall not murder because life was created by God." In fact, however, this alone will persuade few modern people, who would regard it as a *deus ex machina* (god from the machine), an answer that evades the issue by bringing God into the matter when logical evidence cannot be provided. On top of that, many tend to view belief in the creation of all things by a personal God as having been rejected by modern science, especially the theory of evolution. So we need to delve a little further into the significance of this.

The conflict between the scientific theory of evolution and religious fundamentalism has persisted down to the present day. The theory of evolution says the Bible is mistaken because the Old Testament's opening account, whereby

---

7 Seizō Sekine, *Rinri no Tansaku: Seisho kara no Apurōchi* (The Quest for Ethics: An Approach from the Bible) (Tokyo: Chuko Shinsho, 2002), Chapter 3.
8 Ibid., 120 ff.
9 From "ktisis," the Greek word for creation.

God created all things in the span of seven days, conflicts so radically with modern science. By contrast, fundamentalism asserts that because this is what the Bible says, it is the theory of evolution that is mistaken, and we must believe in a seven-day creation as taught in the Bible.

I would argue, however, that both sides are operating on the basis of the same mistaken assumption, that of textual literalism. Literalism is the attempt to understand the text literally, according to the letter. Reading the Bible literally, evolutionary theorists assert that its account must be rejected because it conflicts with modern science, while fundamentalists assert that science must be rejected in order to believe the Bible literally word for word. Their common assumption is precisely that of textual literalism.

Basically, however, a text is something that communicates some kind of meaning through linguistic symbols. The important thing, therefore, is not to interpret its language literally word for word, but to explain the significance of that to which it points. Furthermore, because linguistic symbols are created within the constraints of a particular period, it is only natural for them to become outdated as time progresses.

So even if the biblical authors were filled with divine inspiration, what is wrong with acknowledging that they merely wrote in the words of their time, using symbols that modern science has now deemed to be outdated and limited? Instead, the important thing for interpreting the text is to ask what the ancient authors wished to express through their conceptual mechanisms, even if these appear outdated from a contemporary perspective.

The Old Testament account of creation expresses the belief that all beings—from individual lives to all of creation—were not created by humans but were already given by something. That is, this account shows "the givenness of existence," and it also expresses feelings of wonder, thanksgiving, and awe toward that fact. This is the substance that we must interpret when deciphering symbols that today are outdated conceptual mechanisms; this ought to be a message that we can read from the text. Decoding the reality to which it points—not the surface-level meaning—is what interpreting the text today means, and that is the task facing philosophical interpretation, which harnesses its true significance for modern times.

Discussing the specifics of this approach is beyond my scope here. Nevertheless, by adopting this approach to interpreting the text, instead of interpreting it literally, we can detect therein the ancient people's feelings of wonder and awe toward the givenness of being, the fact that existence has already been given, and the fact that it is not of our own making. This, I think, is the heart of the issue here.

There might still, however, be some objections on this point. In 2007 the establishment of iPS (induced pluripotent stem) cells by a team led by Kyoto University's Professor Shinya Yamanaka caused a sensation. Some people might be particularly quick to think, "Now we can make human clones. Life is not something given, it is now something that science can create." But let us consider this coolheadedly. The news is reporting that if one injects four particular genes (Oct3/4, Sox2, c-Myc, Klf4) into existing human skin cells, the skin cells are transformed and cells with the ability to divide as ES cells are established. This is nothing more than the discovery and development of natural laws and the technology to implement them. Of course, it is wonderful that this valuable research means there is hope for discovering new ways to treat diabetes, diseases caused by degeneration of the cerebral nervous system, myocardial infarctions, and other severe conditions through cell transplants. In fact, however, neither science nor humans can produce particular genes or natural laws themselves. In that sense, fundamentally speaking, we cannot take a single step beyond pregivenness. No matter how much science progresses, this remains an unshakeable, brute fact.

When we get back to this, we become aware of the limits of science and human beings and feel a humble fear of overstepping those limits and a renewed and deep sense of amazement that, indeed, this life has been given to us by something. Whether we view that "something" as a personal creator-God, such as in the Old Testament, or as a cosmological principle, or as the Gaia of the Gaia Hypothesis, or as absolute nothing or something else, in truth, humans do not know (John 1:18). It is better, then, to describe this state of affairs carefully in terms of our lives having been given to us—a passive non-religious statement—rather than as God having given us our lives, which constitutes an active religious statement.

Whatever the case, our entire existence, including life itself, has been given us in advance by something that absolutely transcends us. Whether or not one believes in a specific religion, it is appropriate to acknowledge that this givenness of existence is the fundamental fact that determines human life. When we return to this fact, which we are apt to forget in our daily lives, and when our wonder and gratitude are renewed, we realize the preciousness and dearness of each life, which is mysteriously and irreplaceably gifted from somewhere. It then becomes unthinkable that we would resort to violent acts such as killing such a life. That is why one must not murder. When the question of why we must not murder is brought back to this foundation, the answer becomes readily apparent. This approach should also be applicable to environmental ethical issues, among others, but because I am focusing here on the ethical issue of murder, I shall not develop the discussion any further.[10]

---

10 Because I am limiting my discussion in this chapter to a recognition of fundamental ethical bases or orders (in this case the rejection of murder), I shall merely point out the givenness of

The above represents an outline of a ktisiological answer to the question of "Why must we not murder?"

2.2 A Soteriological Reason (*Ri*)

There is another answer in the Old Testament to the question of "Why must we not murder?" This is a soteriological answer, to which I shall now proceed. The answer becomes apparent when we examine both the meaning of the original Hebrew wording in the Mosaic Decalogue, which is usually translated as "you shall not murder," and the historical context in which the Decalogue was given.

The words translated as "you shall not murder" are "*Lo tirtsach*" in the original Hebrew. This is a construction in which the negative particle *lo* precedes the imperfect form of the verb *ratsa*. In conceptual terms, this originally connotes an assertion of the impossibility of murder, as in "it is impossible for you to murder." Yet although impossible, murders do occur in reality. In view of this, because one must not do the impossible, this phrase is usually translated as a prohibition, "you [absolutely] shall not murder." I wish to note first, then, that the Hebrew *Lo tirtsach* is an expression that has this dual meaning. This applies also to *Lo tin'aph* ("you shall not commit adultery"), *Lo tignob* ("you shall not steal"), and other commandments, but because I wish to confine the present discussion of "ethics" to "the ordered path of coexistence without people committing murder," I shall limit my considerations to *Lo tirtsach*.

The next question we must ask is where does the ideal "it is impossible for you to murder" come from. The answer lies in the historical setting of the Mosaic Decalogue. It is the salvation-historical context within which the people of Israel received the God Yahweh's love and were saved from a state of slavery in Egypt. Having been awakened by this love of God, the people themselves overflowed with love, and it should have been unthinkable to kill their own people, who were likewise objects of God's love. That is why murder was impossible. This is an outline of a soteriological answer.

---

nature. I must note, however, that each specific ethical issue can be further developed. For instance, see Tomonobu Imamichi, *Shizen Tetsugaku Josetsu* (Introduction to Natural Philosophy) (Tokyo: Kodansha Gakujutsu Bunko, 1993) concerning important possibilities beyond what I have discussed here. In particular, see Imamichi's powerful thoughts concerning the fact that not only is nature given, but humans also have an obligation to form it together. This is in Chapter 9, "Kankyō no Keisei" (Formation of the Environment), and Chapter 10, "Shizen to Ai" (Nature and Love).

Nevertheless, I think that doubts remain for us moderns. It is natural to question the connection between the particular ethnic God Yahweh bringing salvation 3,000 years ago to a single Middle Eastern nation, the people of Israel, and us living in modern Japan. The two are like night and day. Instead, I would like to think of this in the following manner.

The Old Testament is not monolithic. Beginning with the Mosaic period there is a gradual maturation, and especially in the prophet Second Isaiah during the Babylonian exile the Old Testament begins to speak of salvation for all humanity, not just the single nation of Israel. After passing through the New Testament, stripping everything away, and continuing on up to the present day, modern Christian philosophy has progressed to the point of re-expressing this soteriology as follows. It is none other than the idea of "an insubstantial[11] magnetic field of love." This is a brilliant metaphor used by the New Testament scholar and religious philosopher Seiichi Yagi. If soft-iron nails are lying around on a desk, they will remain apart without a magnetic force. If there is an active magnetic field, however, the individual nails will attract one another and form a connection.

In the same way, from the time we are born we are egoists and individually self-absorbed. Yet when we realize that the invisible magnetic force of love is at work there and we consciously yield to this force, we are drawn to one another and establish connections. Ancient people represented this invisible, insubstantial magnetic field of love in personalized terms as "God" during historical events such as the exodus. Ultimately, however, "God" is nothing other than "the work of love" that works universally among people, or an invisible, "insubstantial magnetic field."[12]

Today even Old Testament soteriology can be demythologized and interpreted in this way. When our thinking progresses to that point, we become aware of the insubstantial magnetic field, and it becomes impossible for us to commit murder, an act that fundamentally denies the existence of the other, who is an irreplaceable object of love. That is why ethics can be spoken of as an assertion of impossibility, as in "it is impossible for you to murder," and not merely as the prohibition "you shall not murder."

Also important here is the fact that this idea includes an answer to issues raised by postmodernism. The following is the source of skepticism among postmodernists. Rulers impose self-serving ethics upon the ruled, so in that sense ethics is a mechanism that entrenches power structures. Therefore, they say, we must be on

---

11 "Insubstantial" in the sense of "having the characteristics of nothingness."

12 Seiichi Yagi and Katsumi Takizawa, *Kami wa Doko de Miidasareru ka* (Where Can God be Found?) (Tokyo: San'ichi Shobo, 1977), 82.

guard. In response, however, I would argue that the idea of such an insubstantial magnetic field, a magnetic field of love among individuals, is an acknowledgment of the equality of individuals who are drawn to each other. And because it is an idea whereby individuals together and voluntarily build this sort of relationship, they escape from the power structures that force rulers to fix social relationships in place or individuals to sacrifice themselves and submit to the whole.

2.3 Summary

The two ideas of "the pregivenness of existence" and "an insubstantial magnetic field of love" find their sources in Old Testament ktisiology and soteriology. We arrived at these ideas not through a literalistic reading, but a broadly philosophical hermeneutical approach whereby we interpreted their true significance in a contemporary manner. When we correctly understand these two ideas, we can arrive at a lucid understanding that "it is impossible for [us] to murder."

If we fail to reach this understanding, then "you shall not murder" lapses into enforcing a dead-letter norm or regulation. As such, it merely suppresses our desires or is something we begrudgingly follow simply because we are afraid of punishment. Or we impose it upon ourselves and others for the sake of preserving old-fashioned societal order so that we can protect our own vested interests.

Yet once we arrive at this understanding, we can return to the way of being that tends to be forgotten in the darkness of daily life, and we can feel the vibrant breath of life that attempts to protect this order (*ri*) of coexistence. That is because ethics points to this natural way of human life, and it can become a call to practice it collectively.

These two understandings of ktisiology and soteriology—recognition of the givenness of existence and of the insubstantial magnetic field of love—are the most important for considering this basic ethical problem of "why must we not murder?" It is only when we arrive at an understanding of this "order" (*ri*) that we can establish a foothold for taking a step toward regenerating "ethics" as an "ordered path of joyful coexistence."

3 Seven Paths (*Ro*) for Arriving at the Two Understandings of Order (*Ri*)

How, then, can we arrive at an understanding of these two "orders"? In this final part I wish to consider seven specific "paths," keeping local school settings in mind.

3.1 Religion

First is the path of religion. "Ktisiology" and "soteriology" in Part 2 are expressions from Christian theology. Here, however, rather than focusing on specifically Christian thought, I shall redirect my attention toward explaining the universal significance or general meaning contained therein. In fact, I think that excellent paths for constructing this ethic have also been proposed in various forms within religions other than Christianity.

For instance, A. J. Heschel, a leading twentieth-century Jewish philosopher, comments as follows about the Mosaic Decalogue given after the exodus:

> Indeed, there is no perception that may not be suspected of being a delusion. But there are perceptions which are so staggering as to render meaningless the raising of such a suspicion. A cosmic fear enveloped all those who stood at Sinai [this refers to the Israelites who were given the Mosaic Decalogue after the exodus], a moment more staggering than the heart could feel. ... At that moment the people of Israel not only were able to entertain a feeling but also to share in an awe that overtook the world. Only in moments when we are able to share in the spirit of awe that fills the world are we able to understand what happened to Israel at Sinai.[13]

Thus writes Heschel in his *God in Search of Man*. I think this is a brilliant testimony that religious experience is experienced together with an absolute authenticity and glorious thoughts. Heschel says that this experience of awe-inspiring thoughts given by that which transcends us is what happened to the whole nation of Israel at Sinai, and he emphasizes that modern religious rites exist precisely for the purpose of renewing this experience daily.

My aim here is to point out that religion, in that sense, can be viewed as one powerful path that inspires awe at the fact that our existence is indeed something which is given and that we are loved and given life by something transcending us.

Here I have presented an example from Judaism, but of course we could also consider examples from Christianity or, when we speak about an insubstantial magnetic field of love, from Buddhism. This is noticeable in the case of the Jōdo Shinshū sect of Buddhism, which Karl Barth called Japanese Protestantism.[14] Shojun Bando, who passed away in 2004, explains very clearly in his

---

13 Abraham Joshua Heschel, *Ningen o Sagashimotomeru Kami* (God in Search of Man) (trans. Kōji Moriizumi; Tokyo: Kyo Bun Kwan, 1998), 247. English quotation from Heschel, *God in Search of Man*, 196; note in brackets is mine.
14 Karl Barth, *Die Kirchliche Dogmatik: Die Lehre vom Wort Gottes Prolegomena zur Kirchlichen Dogmatik*, Vol. I/2 (Zürich: Evangelischer Verlag, 1960), 374.

comparative study of Barthian Protestantism that Amida's long-cherished desire is an insubstantial magnetic field of love and that chanting "Namu Amida Buddha" involves participating in this insubstantial magnetic field.[15] The religious philosophy of the Kyoto School, going back to Shin'ichi Hisamatsu and Kitarō Nishida, very strongly attests to the fact that this branch of Buddhism and also "the true nature of enlightenment" in Zen Buddhism relate to these matters.

In any case, my primary aim has been to point out that these various religious directions are excellent paths for experiencing the givenness of existence and the insubstantial magnetic field of love, the two understandings described above.

3.2 Philosophy

I now wish to consider philosophy, which can also be regarded as providing important paths for arriving at these two understandings.

3.2.1 The Philosophical Hermeneutics of Gadamer and Ricœur

The philosophical hermeneutics of H. G. Gadamer and P. Ricœur are important for their rejection of literalism, which we discussed above. If one of philosophy's tasks is to interpret religion's concrete representations more theoretically or, in the terms of the religious philosophy of P. Tillich, to explain unlimited being, then philosophy also suggests an important method for arriving at these understandings through its supplementing of religion.

3.2.2 Plato's Criticism of Democracy

We can also count among philosophy's contributions its criticism of democracy. This relates to the fact that postmodernism's skepticism toward ethics has been partly triggered in Japan, in particular, by certain mistaken educational approaches of postwar democracy. There is an aspect whereby postmodern ethical skepticism has been readily accepted because people have asserted their individual freedoms and rights to the neglect of their responsibilities and duties to society. Philosophy presents a richly critical perspective on this mistaken form of democracy.

---

15 Shojun Bando, "Jesus Christus und Amida. Zu Karl Barths Verständnis des Buddhismus vom Reinen Land," in *Gott in Japan: Anstöße zum Gespräch mit japanischen Philosophen, Theologen, Schriftstellern* (eds. Seiichi Yagi und Ulrich Luz; München: Kaiser, 1973), 75 f.

Next, I wish to consider a passage that actually comes from the crux of Book VIII in the *Republic* by the Greek philosopher Plato more than two thousand years ago.[16] It reads as if he were criticizing today's postmodern condition. Plato expresses this along the following lines.

Democratic politics glorifies the freedom of the people and promotes dissipative desires, calling "modesty" silliness and "temperance" a lack of bravery and twisting things so that "moderation and thriftiness" are regarded as vulgarity and meanness and are cast out. Conversely, democratic politics mistakes "insolence" for good breeding and misconstrues "anarchy" as liberty, applauding "waste" as magnanimity and "impudence" as bravery. Young people brought up in this way spend their lives indulging their passing whims. At times they become intoxicated, while at other times they drink nothing but water and exercise in an attempt to lose weight. Or they remain idle, or pretend to immerse themselves in philosophy. One moment they are dabbling in politics and sounding off about their views, the next they are envying warriors and businessmen and trying their hand at those ventures. Hence their whole lives lack order and certainty. Such a climate gives rise to a state of anarchy, and fathers fear their children, while children have no respect for their fathers. Teachers pander to their students out of fear, while students despise their teachers. Older people ingratiate themselves with the young and try to please everyone. This too is an attempt to avoid being regarded as uninteresting or authoritarian. People become overly sensitive, and when subjected to even the slightest repression they cannot take it and lose their temper. They no longer care even about the laws, determined as they are to have no master. Once things reach this state, excessive freedom leads to a yearning for barbaric enslavement, and the situation can easily degenerate into a dictatorship.[17]

This somewhat lengthy, concatenated passage is Plato's criticism of democracy. Because he grew up witnessing the turmoil of democratic politics in Athens after Pericles, Plato critiques with an extremely sharp pen the corruption of democracy, the turmoil of societal order in the broad sense, and the disregard for ethics. Such observations by philosophers point to the current state of our modern democracy and to one of the sources of the moribund state of ethics, and hence they are highly suggestive.

---

16 Plato, *Kokka* (Republic), *Puraton Zenshū*, Dai Jū-ichi-kan (Complete Works of Plato, Vol. 11) (trans. Norio Fujisawa; Tokyo: Iwanami Shoten, 1976), 591 ff.

17 With permission, this paragraph is slightly adapted from the translation in Seizō Sekine. *A Comparative Study of the Origins of Ethical Thought* (trans. Judy Wakabayashi; Lanham, Md.: Rowman & Littlefield, 2005), 75–76.

Yet is Plato's criticism of democracy connected to the two understandings discussed above—i.e., the givenness of existence and the insubstantial magnetic field of love? I think that it is.

3.2.3 Wonder (*thaumazein*) is the Beginning of Philosophy (*philosophiā*)

Plato is the first philosopher, at least within the extant texts, to say that wonder (*thaumazein*) is grounded in philosophy (*philosophiā*). This expression appears in the dialogue of *Theaetetus*, where he speaks of "wonder" in the sense of intellectual curiosity.[18] Instead it is in *Phaedrus* where he discusses wonder in relation to Ideas, which fundamentally transcend us, which are the archetypes of being in this world, and which bring things into being. Plato also attests to the importance of recovering that wonder. In that context he does not use the well-known term *thaumazein*, but *ekplēttō* (amazement).[19]

As is well known, philosophy means the love of knowledge. Ultimately, criticism of democracy is also based on a philosophy of love directed toward such knowledge of Ideas. The fallen state of democracy forgets love, loses sight of Ideas, which are the basis of this world's existence, and idly doubts and sneers at the basis of ethics, thereby turning into something destructive. Plato was voicing a warning and criticism against these things based on a philosophy of the love of knowledge. Both the suggestion to return to love of knowledge and the importance of awakening to love are implied here.

In Aristotle's *Metaphysics*, the expression "it is wonder that is the beginning of philosophy [love of knowledge]" is repeated numerous times.[20] The task of metaphysics is to recognize that which transcends us and gives us being. I think this is an example, therefore, of philosophy providing us with insights that point to the fact that we have been given our existence by something that transcends us, or to the importance of recognizing the invisible magnetic field of love.

This is the second path, that of philosophy. Other examples from philosophy are too numerous to mention, and they are often obscure and perhaps of little benefit for elementary and junior high school moral education, so I shall move on to the next section.

---

18 Plato, *Teaitetosu* (Theaetetus), 155D.
19 Plato, *Paidorosu* (Phaedrus), 250 A.
20 For instance, see Aristotle, *Metaphysics* I, 2, 982b12 (Loeb Classical Library [1933]).

3.3 Science

Limiting its focus to surface-level issues in the natural world, modern science has produced spectacular results. Nevertheless, there is a postmodern situational awareness that something is lacking. Nor must we forget that on another front postmodern science has contributed hypotheses such as the "Anthropic Cosmological Principle."

Playwright and former Czech president V. Havel made the following statement in his lecture, "The Need for Transcendence in the Postmodern World,"[21] regarding the creation myth to which I referred in 2.2:

> After all, the very principle of inalienable human rights, conferred on man by the Creator, grew out of the typically modern notion that man—as a being capable of knowing nature and the world—was the pinnacle of creation and lord of the world. This modern anthropocentrism inevitably meant that He who allegedly endowed man with his inalienable rights began to disappear from the world: He was so far beyond the grasp of modern science that he was gradually pushed into a sphere of privacy of sorts, if not directly into a sphere of private fancy ... .[22]

Havel continues, however, in developing his argument.

> Paradoxically, inspiration for the renewal of this lost integrity can once again be found in science, in a science that is new—let us say post-modern—a science producing ideas that in a certain sense allow it to transcend its own limits. ... The first is the Anthropic Cosmological Principle. ... [According to this theory,] we are not at all just an accidental anomaly, the microscopic caprice of a tiny particle whirling in the endless depths of the universe. Instead, we are mysteriously connected to the entire universe, we are mirrored in it, just as the entire evolution of the universe is mirrored in us. ... [T]he moment it begins to appear that we are deeply connected to the entire universe, science reaches the outer limits of its powers. ... With the formulation of the Anthropic Cosmological Principle, science has found itself on the border between formula and story, between science and myth. In that, however, science has paradoxically returned, in roundabout way, to man, and offers him—in new clothing—his lost integrity. It does so by anchoring him once more in the cosmos.

The American biologist R. Carson, who became a pioneer of environmental ethics through her book *Silent Spring*, which warned of environmental pollution through pesticides, says the following in her posthumous book *Sense of Wonder*.

21 Václav Havel, "The Need for Transcendence in the Postmodern World." This was a speech given at Independence Hall in Philadelphia on July 4, 1994. It can be read in its entirety at http://www.worldtrans.org/whole/havelspeech.html.
22 http://worldtrans.org/whole/havelspeech.html

> A child's world is fresh and new and beautiful, full of wonder and excitement. It is our misfortune that for most of us that clear-eyed vision, that true instinct for what is beautiful and awe-inspiring, is dimmed and even lost before we reach adulthood.[23]

And, in

> preserving and strengthening this sense of awe and wonder, this recognition of something beyond the boundaries of human existence ... I am sure there is something much deeper, something lasting and significant. Those who dwell, as scientists or laymen, among the beauties and mysteries of the earth are never alone or weary of life.[24]

Havel's "Anthropic Cosmological Principle" and Carson's "something beyond the boundaries of human existence" relate to the pregivenness of nature discussed above. Science must recover a sense of wonder concerning these things, and through science, everyone must learn about the "antidote" to "boredom and disenchantments."[25] This is what modern intellectuals have pointed out. In that sense, science, too, can suggest paths for arriving at an understanding of the order that we consider to be important. We should focus our attention on producing this type of science today.[26]

3.4 Summary

These three paths of religion, philosophy, and science are at the front and center of ethical education. And though these paths open the way for frontal attacks on the castle of ethics, today it is also important to attack from the rear. That is the aim of the fourth, fifth, and sixth paths.

How can we approach people who have already committed murder or are likely to commit murder? Even if we express high-sounding sentiments about

---

23 Rachel Carson, *The Sense of Wonder* (New York: Harper & Row, 1965; 1998), 54. The Japanese version comes from Rachel Carson, *Sensu obu Wandā* (The Sense of Wonder) (trans. Keiko Kamitō; Tokyo: Shinchosha, 1996), 23.
24 Carson, *The Sense of Wonder*, 100; Carson, *Sensu obu Wandā* (The Sense of Wonder), 50.
25 Carson, *The Sense of Wonder*, 54; Carson, *Sensu obu Wandā* (The Sense of Wonder), 23.
26 For further possibilities of connecting 3.3. "Science" with 3.2. "Philosophy," I wish to point out the excellent considerations in Haruyoshi Shibuya, "'Uchūron-teki Nihirizumu' to Jinsei no Sho-ruikei" ("Cosmological Nihilism" and the Various Typologies of Life), in *Gyakusetsu no Nihirizumu*, Shinpan (Paradoxical Nihilism, New Edition) (Tokyo: Kadensha, 2007), 11 ff.; and especially 67, 119. Drawing on modern scientific findings, Shibuya asserts that humanity's place in the cosmos is baseless and meaningless, and for that very reason he recognizes there "the outflow point of complete human freedom."

an insubstantial magnetic field of love, how can this reach people who have never had a formative experience of love and who have lived in environments where they were unable to recognize its importance? And no matter how much we might stress a sense of wonder over the givenness of existence, what about people whose sensibilities have been deadened or who cannot feel anything in the first place (perhaps we are among them)? If we fail to consider how to approach these people, the issue will take on even less concrete shape. I wish, therefore, to suggest the following three paths for rear attacks.

3.5 Law

The first one is "law." The seventeenth-century English thinker J. Locke has given us a brilliant insight into this issue. Here is a passage in *Two Treatises of Government* about the natural state of humans.

> [E]very man, in the state of nature, has a power to kill a murderer, both to deter others from doing the like injury, which no reparation can compensate, by the example of the punishment that attends it from every body, and also to secure men from the attempts of a criminal, who having renounced reason, the common rule and measure God hath given to mankind, hath, by the unjust violence and slaughter he hath committed upon one, declared war against all mankind, and therefore may be destroyed as a lion or a tyger, one of those wild savage beasts, with whom men can have no society nor security.[27]

In short, two reasons are given here why a murderer should be executed.

The first is that it is necessary for the prevention of murder by arousing fear in potential criminals and showing them that murder will mean execution and thus is not worth it. The second reason is that a "murderer" has renounced the reason given to humans and has declared war against all humanity. Thus "the death penalty" will secure humanity from further crimes by that criminal.

I think this parts ways with the Draconianism of emotionalists; although similar, the thought here is different. Whereas emotionalists are entirely driven by retributive anger when they say that a murderer must be severely punished, Locke's purpose is not merely crime prevention—that is, the protection of people—but also concern for criminals or potential criminals. This purpose is the result of logical and calm analysis, and I think that it is here that his propos-

---

27 John Locke, *Shimin Seifu Ron* (Theory of Civil Government) (trans. Nobushige Ukai; Tokyo: Iwanami Bunko, 1968), 17; English quotation from John Locke, *Two Treatises of Government* <http://www.gutenberg.org/files/7370/old/trgov10 h.htm> (Sec. 11).

al parts ways with emotionalism. This line of argument tends to be suppressed by postmodern trends, but we need to return to classics such as Locke's and calmly reconsider our options.

Human rights advocates have staunchly argued to the contrary, maintaining that severe punishments do not lower crime rates. In particular, they have cited statistics from certain states in the U.S. for support. We must carefully consider, however, whether this is relevant to those youths in Japan who have complacently said they wanted to experience killing while still protected under the Juvenile Act. There are many issues involved here. We must rigorously consider people's temperaments, educational backgrounds, and the like and recognize the differences between a society with many people who fly off the handle and murder without any concern or knowledge of the law and a society with a sizable number of people who cunningly calculate their actions based on legal loopholes.

The following related statistics appeared recently. In Japan 2,263 youths were charged with violent crimes in 1997, and the number stayed at around 2,000 in the following years. After the Juvenile Act was revised, however, 2004 witnessed a 28.3% drop to 1,584 incidents. In the first half of 2005, the number fell even further, with 747 people charged, amounting to a 7.2% decrease. One can only interpret this as evidence that in Japan, at least, tougher punishments had the effect of deterring crime.

In other words, we might conclude that because until now we did not uphold strict laws such as this, our society has needlessly produced many victims and victimizers. The time has come to reflect on how this came about. Although there are many difficult issues surrounding this problem, it is important to rethink Locke and other important classics that are brimming with suggestive ideas.

In short, ethical education must also launch a rear attack, and we must concern ourselves with preventing potential criminals from committing crimes by firmly upholding severely punitive laws. My point here is that the time has come to discuss this at a level removed from emotional endorsement of vengeance; furthermore, this concern is in fact one aspect of the work of an insubstantial magnetic field of love and it is yet possible somehow to make the person who cannot see this insubstantial field aware of it. We must remain hopeful that if one obeys the laws that regulate coexistence there will come a time when he or she will be able to see the ordered path of coexistence at work there.

3.6 Politics

Together with law, politics can also become a path to understanding the ordered path of coexistence. Indeed, it can be an excellent way to attack from the rear. I know of no better work paradoxically suggesting this than *Around the Cragged Hill: A Personal and Political Philosophy*,[28] by G. Kennan, a twentieth-century American diplomat and political thinker.

In Chapter 3, "On Government and Governments," Kennan declares that "the institution of government bears, in essence, no moral quality. It could be said to be morally neutral."[29]

> ... I should make it clear that I am wholly and emphatically rejecting any and all messianic concepts of America's role in the world: rejecting, that is, the image of ourselves as teachers and redeemers to the rest of humanity, rejecting the illusions of unique and superior virtue on our part, the prattle about Manifest Destiny or the "American Century"—all those visions that have so richly commended themselves to Americans of all generations since, and even before, the foundation of our country. We are, for the love of God, only human beings, the descendants of human beings, the bearers, like our ancestors, of all the usual human frailties.[30]

Kennan also says:

> We have great military power—yes; but there is, as Reinhold Niebuhr so brilliantly and persuasively argued, no power, individual or collective, without some associated guilt. And if there were any qualities that lie within our ability to cultivate that might set us off from the rest of the world, these would be the virtues of modesty and humility; and of these we have never exhibited any exceptional abundance.[31]

Kennan is arguing that, after all, politics is a power game with "associated guilt" and it is ridiculous for a citizenry who are merely "the bearers ... of all the usual human frailties" to engage in "moralistic preaching" at the level of diplomatic politics. Yet if that citizenry has "the virtues of modesty and humility," surely Kennan would not deny that moral qualities would emerge concomitantly in a government that "bears, in essence, no moral quality."

Kennan says that Americans "have never exhibited any exceptional abundance" of "the virtues of modesty and humility." Yet there is a citizenry that has exhibited these virtues at a near-comical level, one that grovels with inces-

---

28 George F. Kennan, *Nijusseiki o Ikite: Aru Kojin to Seiji no Tetsugaku* (Living Through the Twentieth Century: A Personal and Political Philosophy) (trans. Hajime Seki; Tokyo: Dobu Shoin International, 1994); translation of George F. Kennan, *Around the Cragged Hill: A Personal and Political Philosophy* (New York: W. W. Norton & Company, 1994).
29 Kennan, *Around the Cragged Hill*, 53; Kennan, *Nijusseiki o Ikite* (Living Through the Twentieth Century), 85.
30 Kennan, *Around the Cragged Hill*, 182–83; Kennan, *Nijusseiki o Ikite* (Living Through the Twentieth Century), 294.
31 Kennan, *Around the Cragged Hill*, 183; Kennan, *Nijusseiki o Ikite* (Living Through the Twentieth Century), 295.

sant apologies. It is we, the Japanese. For better or for worse, practically every-one acknowledges this.

Allow me to digress for a moment. At an international conference in Sloven-ia last summer, an elderly, renowned German scholar waited at the entrance to the meeting hall, holding the door for me as I approached. Feeling obliged, I has-tened to the door and expressed my gratitude. He told me, "I have had several Japanese students. There is no other nation as humble and as courteous as yours. I thought I might try to follow your example a bit, so I waited for you." A quarter-century ago, when I was studying in Germany, there was a tendency for Japanese to be viewed somewhat humorously as overly humble and insuffi-ciently self-reliant, but I do not think this renowned scholar was necessarily making fun of Japanese.

Upon returning to Japan, I came across a report about an interesting interna-tional poll (*Yomiuri Shimbun*, Nov. 23, 2007, Morning Edition, special feature "Japan"). A joint poll of 27 nations around the world from March of that year con-cluded that "the countries with the most positive influence around the world are Japan and Canada." Again, in a poll of 15,000 people in Europe in May as to "Who are the best tourists in the world?" Japan was reported as ranking first. In an era when nations lock horns with each other in S. Huntington's "clash of civili-zations," construing this as due recognition of Japanese humility is not necessarily mere self-serving talk. As Tenshin Okakura once pointed out, Japan, which has ac-cepted and protected other civilizations with respect and has taken on aspects of an Asian cultural museum, has the power to mediate peacefully without injecting our-selves much into the clash of civilizations. I think this reflects a recognition of the desirability of the disposition of a non-self-asserting civilization, not that of a self-asserting civilization, as Shunpei Ueyama claims. Or it is affirmation that Japan con-veys a sense of what twenty-first-century peace might be like. As for why we have this sort of humility, I think it is because Japanese are not at all large in size, nation-al character, or culture, and we have an awareness of our many weaknesses. This is why we do not become entrenched and absorbed in self-reliance but instead have feelings of respect for other civilizations and why we are open to the insubstantial magnetic field of love. The insight of Kennan, who went through many hellish sit-uations, is correct after all: it is such people who are first qualified to speak of mo-rals in the political arena.

However, Kennan does not credit Japan with this, and if we lift Japan too highly we will fall into the comical self-contradiction of taking pride in humility. So let us leave matters here.

3.7 The Arts

Next, I shall discuss "the arts" as the sixth path. Again there are numerous examples, but I wish to focus on G. Puccini's opera *Turandot*. In recent years the story of Princess Turandot has become well-known to everyone through figure skating music and commercials, so I shall give only a very brief overview of the plot.

Its setting is Beijing's Forbidden City in ancient China. Turandot is a cold-hearted princess who lives in the Forbidden City and does not know love. And she is an extremely beautiful woman. An endless number of men fall desperately in love with her beauty and come seeking her hand in marriage. Each time, however, she gives three riddles, and many men are executed because they cannot solve them. Such is Turandot, a cold-hearted murderer.

Prince Calàf of Tartary arrives there on his journey of exile following the destruction of his country. He falls in love with Turandot at first sight and accepts the challenge of the riddles. Amazingly, he solves all three. Turandot, however, is a maiden unable to open her heart to love, so she rejects Calàf's courtship. Making various excuses, she resists becoming the wife of this young man.

Seeing this, Calàf feels sympathy for her and says, "Then I shall also give you a riddle. What is my name? If you are unable to answer by tomorrow, then you must become my wife. But if you are able to answer, then I shall willingly accept execution."

At this point, Liu, a slave girl from Tartary, passes by. She secretly had feelings for Calàf at the palace, but ever since their country was destroyed she has been roaming the land while kindly leading Timur, the blind king and Calàf's father. Turandot's officials suspect that Liu is from the same country as this young man, so they torture her in order to learn his name. While enduring torture, Liu confesses her love and passionately sings the aria "Tu che di gel sei cinta" (thou who in ice art girt). Although she is in love with Calàf, they are of different social ranks, and she knows that Calàf loves Turandot. There is no hope for me, she says. But, she continues, she wishes for the love of the one she loves to be fulfilled, and she longs for Princess Turandot's icy heart to be melted by Calàf's love and for her to know love.

Thinking, "I must not cry out Calàf's name should I be unable to endure any more torture," she suddenly grabs the dagger of an official by her side and takes her own life. Many audiences cry at this scene. Puccini, too, seems to have considered it to be the climax of this opera. Having written up to this point, he succumbed to cancer at age 66, but this was the scene he most wanted to write. The opera ends in a love duet between Turandot, whose heart has been melted by Calàf's love, and Calàf. This part was written by Alfano, Puccini's student, in accordance with Puccini's deathbed instructions. Because of its poorer musical quality, however, in recent years Berio rewrote a quieter finale that mourns Liu's death, and the opera is often performed in this newer version.

In any case, such a story is a good example of the essence of tragedy, which, as Aristotle (*Poetics*, Part 6) pointed out, evokes catharsis. In other words, when love enters from the front or main gate, this becomes a story where love directly participates in the insubstantial magnetic field of love. In most cases, however, things are not so straightforward. Perhaps the reason so many people (including myself) cry during the suicide scene after the aria is that they are somehow twisted and require not a frontal approach but one from the rear. Many people who commit murder have not experienced sufficient love from their parents, or they have not known love at all. The cathartic tears evoked by tragedies such as *Turandot* could be one means of teaching love to such people. Liu and Calàf each possess a precious love. They have their lives, and they live with hope. The murderer Turandot suddenly cuts this off. What sorrow is caused by this! Also, when murderers open their hearts to love, they understand for the first time that their act of murder was wrong. Upon witnessing Liu's sacrifice, Turandot, as well as audience members like Turandot, awaken to love. The point is that tragedies can serve a certain instructive role toward this end.[32]

That is why I wished to introduce an example from the arts. Of course, this also relates to religion. To express it in terms of John's understanding, humanity does not genuinely know love. Rather, it first came to know love through the love of Jesus' cross, or sacrifice, which atoned for humanity's sins (1John 3:16). Yet this, too, is a tragedy possessing artistic aspects. Indeed, it became the source of a great number of artistic works, including St. John's Passion. Hence it has been my aim to point out that catharsis-evoking tragedies and other arts are an important rear path for arriving at an understanding of the order of coexistence that would render murder impossible.

3.8 The Art of Discovering Good Things

Among these six paths for arriving at the two orders of coexistence, paths one to three have been straight roads from the main gate, while paths four to six have been back roads. The seventh and final path, however, represents something of a

---

32 I am unable to treat opera music analysis or performance theory in this chapter. For a fresh examination of questions of ethics and the arts from the performance perspective, see Haruyoshi Shibuya, "Nomosu to Pyūshisu no Benshōhō: *Opera Aurisu no Ifigeneia* no Enshutsu o Megutte" (The Dialectic Between Nomos and Physis: On the Performance in the Opera *Iphigénie en Aulide*), in Shibuya, *Gyakusetsu no Nihirizumu* (Paradoxical Nihilism); see 209.

shortcut. As such, perhaps it will produce the quickest results in educational contexts. I hope it will act as a path or method that enables people simply to experience first-hand how ethics is the order or reason of "joyful" coexistence.

Although I have given this the grandiose title of "The Art of Discovering Good Things," the basic idea is this: at school and at home, reflect back upon the day and report the good things to one another. Or even alone before bedtime, simply remember what made you happy that day.

For some reason, we are prone to fall into negative thinking, and we often wander futilely in a vicious cycle whereby we criticize and speak ill of others, or even bully them, become hurt ourselves, and hold grudges against people. Is this the result of wisdom and customs from primitive times enabling us to survive by detecting negative danger, or is it the nature of competitive society wherein people must discover and correct their faults in order to stay in the race? Do we wish to forget our own inferiority for a while by being judgmental of others, or do we make excuses to avoid shouldering risk and taking positive action? Is it laziness that leads us to cling to the status quo and hammer the nail that sticks out and therefore goes against the virtue of humility? The reasons are not clear, but negative thinking takes a firm hold on us. This occurs not only at the individual level; it also appears to be a flaw that is deeply ingrained in society. For instance, it strikes me as odd that the Japanese media made light of the above-mentioned positive report that Japan ranked number one, or even ignored it for half a year. I recall the novelist Shūsaku Endō's lament that the sensational human-interest sections of newspapers are full of dark reports and that he longed for a section packed with cheerful news. If we are to break this vicious cycle that has become deeply entrenched at the individual and societal levels, we need to seek and find things that are simply good. And it is important to actually speak out about them. Even if one abstractly attempts to change one's mindset in an effort to become a positive thinker, patterns of negative thinking that have become second nature over many years do not change that easily.

For instance, basking in the morning sun after you wake up and open the shutters is simply a good thing. The star that is our sun, at a distance of 150 million kilometers from the earth, has continued to emit energy through a nuclear fusion reaction for 5 billion years, and it will continue to shine and provide heat for another 5 billion years. I cannot help but feel glad that today I can again take pleasure in this environment that was given without me doing anything. After a deep sleep I feel energetic, recovered from my tiredness of yesterday. That is happiness. My family's smiles greet me when I go downstairs for breakfast. In the darkness of night, any of us could have died of a heart attack. I am overjoyed that I can see them again. My breakfast toast and tea are delicious. Today's tea was a gift of Fortnum & Mason's Assam Golden Broken Orange Pekoe, meaning it was picked in the Assam region of the Himalayan foothills, blended in the UK, and shipped to Japan from the store in Piccadilly, London. From beginning to end, how many people must have worked to bring its fragrance to my breakfast table this morning? The freshness expiration date has not been altered, and (probably) no pesticides were used. One might take all this for granted because it was a business transaction. Yet I cannot help but be thankful when I consider the honest work at each step along the way. When I think about the friend who gave me this gift of tea, the book that taught me how to make delicious tea, and the delicious water piped in and purified, I am full of gratitude for all those who made this possible. The same for my bread. And my butter. Today I take out the trash because my wife seems to be coming down with a cold, and I run into a neighbor I haven't seen for some time. I enjoy chatting and catching up. Once we begin taking stock, we find that our lives are overflowing with good and positive things.

Ultimately, these are the joys of becoming aware of the two orders (*ri*) of pregivenness and an insubstantial magnetic field discussed in Part 2.

Rather than closing the shutters and withdrawing into one's room or staying uninvolved with others, it is more joyful to be given the morning sun, to be given life, to coexist with this given environment, and to coexist with others while being drawn to and helping one another. Of course, there are rainy days and days when we struggle with others or withdraw into solitary contemplation. Yet that too should be able to become part of our vicissitudinous coexistence. In the final analysis, ethics is nothing more and nothing less than wisdom for joyful coexistence, which we become practically aware of in our simple everyday life.

Because of intimidating sermons and because we take ethics too seriously, we come to suspect that it restricts the freedoms of self and others and is a tool for dominating other people, so we get completely turned off. Also, we make ethics unnecessarily complicated, and our reflections are overly timid, so it has long become removed from the exuberance of life-settings. Yet ethics is similar to how riding a bicycle is terribly difficult to explain but simple when we actually move our arms and legs. When we experience the exuberant operation of ethics in actual daily life, we find that it is surprisingly simple, and also a joyful thing. And just as it is easy to get the hang of riding a bicycle once we give that first push-off and pick up momentum, ethics functions simply after giving a small push and picking up momentum. The simple step of counting good things in our everyday life can act as that first, small push. Is it too optimistic to say that this can ultimately become a driving force and ethics as the order of joyful coexistence will then run well on its own?

Perhaps this entire discussion, in which I have considered ethical issues while reflecting on the history of ideas, has seemed futile or sounded like run-of-the-mill practical advice. But the reason we can confidently step out in this sort of practice is of course because we have recognized that pregivenness and an insubstantial magnetic field are the pillars of ethics as the two reasons (or orders) of joyful coexistence. It would be building a castle in the sky, though, to end a discussion of ethics, which concerns practical matters, with theory alone. That is why I have attempted, in closing, to complete the picture with this finishing touch.

The six paths in Part 3 take us in a practical direction, but they might be somewhat difficult to implement in practice. By contrast, the seventh and final path is the wisdom that is easiest to implement. Perhaps many teachers are already putting this into practice at their schools. When I tried this myself, however, it was unbelievable how the prevailing vicious cycle of negative thinking disappeared, and I experienced tremendous happiness. Therefore, I would like to add one more remark.

During their early years of elementary school, apparently my own children and their schoolmates would report to the class about good things. It is fine just to say that the bread in the school lunch tasted really good or that one was happy because it snowed. If possible, though, I hope the reports will go deeper to include the fact that the bread was produced as the result of the work of many people, or that snow is like a gift from heaven, thereby helping us to become more deeply aware of how we are connected to other people and to nature.

Conclusion

I would like to conclude by briefly summarizing my argument.

In Part 1, I noted and analyzed the perilous state of ethics in connection with postmodernism. How can we regenerate ethics in such circumstances? Exploring ways to do this has been the focus here. After carefully defining ethics, I limited myself to the ordered path of coexistence wherein people do not commit murder.

In order to regenerate such ethics, it was important to understand why murder is wrong in the first place. If we can arrive at this understanding, people will be persuaded to stop committing murders. I found a hint for approaching this problem in the Old Testament. I explored this hint, though, by "demythologizing" it and interpreting it in modern philosophical terms, not by reading the text literally.

Firstly, I argued that there exists an order (*ri*) of pregivenness. Once we become aware that life and being have been given by something that transcends us, we should no longer be able to destroy this irreplaceable gift. Secondly, I pointed out the existence of an order (*ri*) consisting of an insubstantial magnetic field. When self-absorbed individuals recognize that they are placed in a magnetic field wherein they are drawn to one another, they can no longer act counter to this work of love and kill others.

My conclusion in Part 2 was that these are the two grounds, or orders, for why murder is wrong. How, then, can we arrive at an understanding of these orders? In Part 3, I specifically suggested seven paths. These were religion, philosophy, science, law, politics, the arts, and lastly, the art of discovering good things. No doubt there are other paths, but I think it is possible to arrive at an understanding of the above two orders through these paths at least.

My point there was that this is the ordered path of "joyful" coexistence in keeping with how humans were originally intended to exist. Because ethics is prone to impose formalistic norms and fall into stifling power structures, people tend to go to great lengths to avoid it. Given this situation, I focused on the question of the primary sources of ethics and what we can do to restore the joy of ethics.

Our task is not complete once we have arrived at the two essential understandings in the form of the givenness of existence and the magnetic field of love. Because our understanding becomes clouded and our cause weathered, adults as well as children must repeatedly learn from these seven paths and constantly refresh our understanding. In that sense, perhaps I have been speaking to and challenging myself here.

The time has come when we must act "toward regenerating ethics." I think that many will acknowledge the need for this. What, then, shall we do? My hope here was to present at least a starting point for thinking about these matters, and so I have discussed them while groping in the dark for a large roadmap. Ethics need not be something that lapses into stifling enforcement or manipulation of power. Rather, it can be an ordered path of joyful coexistence that revitalizes our lives by returning them to their natural state. I would be delighted if this preliminary discussion triggers further development of this point into a much broader theory and practice. I would appreciate readers' honest criticisms and suggestions.

Part III **The Prophets and Soteriology**

Chapter 6 A Genealogy of Prophetic Salvation: Isaiah, Second Isaiah, and Jeremiah

Introduction

The Iwanami Translation of the Old Testament was completed in March 2004. After its completion, the translators, who were each responsible for a specific section, gathered to check and take note of where their translations differed from previous Bible versions.[1] I was responsible for the books of Isaiah and Jeremiah. Looking back at the footnotes, I counted about five hundred passages where I had noted major and minor differences based on variant readings and interpretive issues. I certainly cannot go into all of these in the space available here, nor would it be interesting just to enumerate them without any coherent basis.

Therefore, I shall set aside variant readings that have little impact on the overall interpretation of the books of Isaiah and Jeremiah, including well-known variants in the history of interpretation, and base the following argument on a selection of only the relatively major points that affect the overall interpretation. I wish to focus my final attention in this chapter, then, on the coherent picture that emerges concerning the genealogy of salvation declared in these two books.

1 From the Book of Isaiah

1.1 The Call of Isaiah

First I wish to consider the ending to the prophetic call of First Isaiah. My translation reads as follows:[2]

> Though one-tenth will remain within it,
> This, too, in the end, will be devoured like the terebinth and the oak.
> *But the terebinth* will be cut down
> —the stump is a holy descendant in *them*—
> It will leave behind *its* stump. (Isa 6:13)

---

1 Old Testament Editorial Committee, *Seisho o Yomu: Kyūyaku-hen* (Reading the Bible: The Old Testament) (Tokyo: Iwanami Shoten, 2005).

2 Seizō Sekine, trans., *Izaya-sho* (Book of Isaiah) (Tokyo: Iwanami Shoten, 1997). Except where noted otherwise, all quotations from the book of Isaiah are from this translation.

(The words in italics are the particular focus of my discussion here and in subsequent sections.)

In previous translations, this has been rendered as "'... even if one-tenth of the people remain within it, this will also be burned and destroyed. As the stump remains when the terebinth or oak is cut down.' The holy seed [nation] is that stump." (Colloquial Version; Japanese), or as "Though one-tenth will remain there, it will also be burned up. Like the felled terebinth or oak. But even then, the stump will remain. That stump is the holy seed." (Japanese New Interconfessional Translation; Japanese). The translation tradition of the former (including KJV, NKJ, NRS, LUT, NEG, LSG, Masao Sekine, and Wildberger) compares that which does not remain with that which remains, and so it falls into a logical contradiction. And the latter tradition (New Japanese Bible, Kōki Nakazawa, Kaiser) presents the difficulty of not strictly translating the pronominal suffix at the end. Translated literally, the final phrase should be, "Her stump is the holy seed in them."

By contrast, my translation focuses on the third-person, feminine, singular suffix *ah*, attached to the line-ending *matsebet* (stump), which has almost completely been ignored in previous versions. I understand its antecedent strictly to be the nearby feminine noun *'ela* (terebinth). If this is correct, it is natural to understand the immediately preceding relative pronoun *'asher* as also referring back to *'ela*, alone. It is thus appropriate to read it adversatively, so I concur with Wildberger and others. I do not follow Budde, Kaiser, and others in treating the phrase omitted in the Septuagint, which is between the dashes, as having been omitted simply due to a straying of the eyes (*aberratio oculi*). Because of the Hebrew syntactical problems, I think it is appropriate to regard it as a later insertion, in line with the prevailing view. In terms of meaning, however, this is a correct explanatory gloss. It is necessary, therefore, to translate accurately the pronominal suffix *am* attached to the preposition *b* as "them" and to understand this as referring back to both "the terebinth" and "the oak." In Isaiah 10:19 and elsewhere the remnant is likened to the trees of the forest, and the "them" here refers specifically to the ones remaining and "the terebinth" becomes one of Isaiah's metaphors for this. By accurately showing the referent of the pronominal suffix, my translation allows the connotation that, among the perishing remnant, only Isaiah will leave "its [the terebinth's] stump," namely, his disciples, for posterity.

It is only when we accurately translate the Masoretic Text of the ending of this call narrative, which inaugurates Isaiah's prophetic activities, that we can correctly understand where it will lead and also prospects concerning the genealogy of prophecies reaching down to Second Isaiah, who follows. I wish to consider that point below.

1.2 Early Messianic Prophecies

> 8:23 But where there was agony, there will be darkness no more.
> Though formerly *a person made light of the land of Zebulun and the land of Naphtali*, he later esteemed *the coastal road, the place beyond Jordan, and Galilee of foreign people.*
>
> 9:1 The people who were walking in the dark saw a great light.
> The people living in the land of the shadow of death, light shined over them.
>
> 2 You increased *the nation for him*, you enlarged the joy.
> As they rejoice at harvest-time,
> As they cheer when they divide plunder,
> They rejoiced before you. ...
>
> 5 Truly, *a child was born for us*,
> *A boy was given to us.* ...
>
> 6 The dominion will increase, the peace will be endless,
> On *David's throne*, he will rule his kingdom,
> He will establish it, and expand it, with justice and righteousness,
> From now until forever.
> *The zeal of Yahweh* of hosts *will accomplish this.* (Isa 8:23–9:6)

Despite the hopeless prophecy at the time of his call that even the ones remaining would be destroyed, it appears that the early Isaiah placed his hope in the messiah's salvation.

In 8:23, at the opening of this unit, I translated the third-person, masculine, singular verbs *qalal* and *kabad*, both in the causative Hiphil form, as "made light" and "esteemed." Their subjects are not specified, so it is possible to understand the subject to be "God" instead of "a person." The land of Naphtali lay to the west of the Sea of Galilee, and the land of Zebulun lay adjacent to Naphtali further west, possibly reaching as far as the Mediterranean Sea coast (Gen 49:13). These regions in northern Israel were captured by Assyria during the Syro-Ephraimite War. Afterwards, however, in 732 BCE, Tiglath-Pileser III valued the Mediterranean coastal region, the region of Gilead to the east, and the region of Galilee as administrative districts. As do many other commentators, it is correct to view this verse, which is based on those historical events, as a later addition whose aim was to connect the previous unit with the following messianic prophecy while giving it historical specificity.

If we read *haggoi lo'* in 9:2 as it appears in the Masoretic Text, the translation "who are not a nation" is not impossible, but it is quite unlikely in terms of both syntax and meaning. Nor does reading it as the single term *haggila* and translating it as "exult" find any support in the ancient manuscripts and versions. Therefore, following multiple manuscripts, the Dead Sea Scrolls, and the Talmud, I have read *lo'* as *lo*. "Him" refers to "the people" in verse 1. If we were to connect the people here with 8:23, it would refer to northern Israel. But because Isaiah does not sunder northern Israel from southern Israel (7:17), we can understand it as referring to both kingdoms from the time of David (9:6). Furthermore, the reference to the birth of the child in 9:5 can be interpreted as referring to the king's enthronement (Ps 2:6–7).

Reading it in this way, I understand this entire unit as a messianic prophecy. Certainly, the king is "the anointed" (messiah; *mashiach* in Hebrew; *meshicha* in Aramaic; *messias* in Greek), but in fact nowhere in the Old Testament is the term *messiah* used with reference to an eschatological savior. That is a usage that emerges in later Judaism (Psalms of Solomon 17:32; 18:5, 7; Ethiopian Book of Enoch 48:10; 52:4), so in order to avoid confusion some scholars do not call it the birth of the messiah. There are a number of theories, including one that relates this entire unit to Hezekiah's enthronement and one that, while understanding it as a messianic prophecy, attributes it to the post-exilic period and not to Isaiah. In terms of its meaning, however, I understand it as a prophecy of the ideal king's birth in the end times, a turning point in history. I think it is appropriate, then, to call it a messianic prophecy, and I see no definitive reason for not attributing its composition to Isaiah. As verse 6 indicates, this king is an eschatological king who shall legitimately ascend the Davidic throne in order to accomplish eternal peace through Yahweh. And it can be understood as agreeing with the messianic prophecy in Isaiah 11, which refers to Jesse, the father of David.

1.3 David's Scion

> 1 A shoot shall grow out of *the stump* of *Jesse*,
> A branch shall bear fruit from his roots.
>
> 2 *Yahweh's spirit shall rest* on him.
> This is the spirit of wisdom and understanding,
> The spirit of judiciousness and valor,
> *The spirit of knowing and fearing Yahweh.* ...
>
> 8 *The nursing child shall frolic over the hole of a poisonous snake,*
> *The weaned child shall reach out his hand over the lair of a viper.*
>
> 9 They will not harm or lay waste any place in my holy mountain.
> For *knowledge about Yahweh* will fill the land as the waters cover the sea. (Isa 11:1–2, 8–9)

Following 9:1–6, 11:1–9 is a prophecy that announces peace from the ideal king, though it does not use the term "messiah." Based on the readings below, I understand this unit, which emphasizes the spirit and also refers to peace in the animal world, as a further development of the prophecy in chapter 9. There are differing theories concerning this passage as well—ones suggesting that it was composed after the prophet experienced disappointment in Hezekiah around the mid-point of his ministry; or that it is a composition from the post-exilic period and not Isaiah's; or that at least verses 6–9 were a later addition dependent upon Third Isaiah 65:25 or Habakkuk 2:14. I think it is possible, however, to understand this as a messianic prophecy from around the end of Isaiah's early ministry.

The fact that the text names "Jesse," David's father (1Sam 16), instead of David himself, is often understood as an implicit criticism of the actual Davidic Dynasty. This criticism is off target, however, because Isaiah 9:7 and 16:5 mention David by name. It is better to understand this as a way of referring to someone by using his father's name, such as in Isaiah 7:6 and 1 Samuel 16:18. If so, it means that Yahweh's spirit shall rest on the scion of David as it rested on David himself (1Sam 16:13; 2Sam 23:2–3).

"The stump" (*geza'*) is noteworthy in that it corresponds with "the stump" (*matsebet*) in 6:13. I shall discuss "a shoot" (*choter*) and "a branch" (*netser*) further below in connection with the messianic prophecy in Jeremiah 23:5. It is said that "fearing Yahweh is the beginning of knowledge [wisdom]" (Prov 1:7; 9:10; 15:33), and throughout the Old Testament God is often depicted as one to be feared (Isa 6:5; Eccl 12:13; Gen 32:42, 53; Deut 7:21; Neh 1:5; 4:14; etc.). Here, too, "the spirit of knowing and fearing Yahweh" does not rest on the messiah alone. "For knowledge about Yahweh" will overflow on all people and animals, and it will "fill the land." The flood of this "knowledge" (*de'a*) is a beautiful representation of the end times that also relates to Jeremiah's "new covenant" (Jer 31:34), discussed further below.

Apparently peace still existed between humans and beasts at the time of creation (Gen 1:28–30), but it was broken after Noah's flood (Gen 9:2–3). The restoration of this peace during the end-time salvation is another promise envisioned in prophetic eschatology (see Hos 2:20), and we can also note it here in Isaiah's messianic prophecy.

1.4 Those Who Received Instruction

> Bind up the testimony, seal the teaching among *those who received* my *instruction*. (Isa 8:16)

In his early ministry, Isaiah offered counsel to King Ahaz at the time of the Syro-Ephraimite War, but the king did not heed it. Isaiah also prophesied Assyrian attacks, but this was not immediately fulfilled. It is thought that these are the reasons that Isaiah temporarily halted his public activities and went into seclusion, where he turned to the work of confining his "teaching" (*tora*) to a few disciples. In this verse, "those who received instruction" (*limmud*)—who were faithful to Yahweh—is understood as specifically referring to Isaiah's group of disciples.

I do not think it is satisfactory, however, to translate the occurrences of *limmud* in the book of Isaiah as the unrelated terms "disciple" and "received instruction," as various versions have done until now (the Colloquial Version, New Japanese Bible, New Interconfessional Translation, and Masao Sekine version all do so; also, the NKJ and others have "disciple" and "the learned"). *Limmud* occurs only six times in the Old Testament. Excluding two occurrences in the book of Jeremiah, where it carries the sense of "accustomed to" (Jer 2:24; 13:23), the remaining four occurrences are concentrated in the book of Isaiah, all with the sense of "received instruction" (besides Isa 8:16, *limmud* occurs three times in Second Isaiah: twice in Isa 50:4, and once in 54:13). Furthermore, two of these occurrences refer to the servant in a song of Yahweh's servant. If we pay attention to this fact, we can, together with Buber[3] and others, recognize the following roadmap of salvation envisioned by the editors of the entire book of Isaiah. Isaiah suffers a setback and is "cut down," as seen in his prophetic call, but he "leave[s] behind [the] stump" of his disciples. And this stump, especially Second Isaiah's servant of Yahweh, "receives [special] instruction" as "a holy descendant" and follows the deceased Isaiah's wishes.

Incidentally, the end of the book of Second Isaiah concludes with a passage in which the "cypress" and "myrtle" trees "shall be for Yahweh's memorial, for an everlasting sign that shall not be cut down [*yikkaret*]" (Isa 55:13). We can understand this as a corresponding expression announcing where the specific fulfillment of Isaiah's salvation prophecy—that, while the terebinth would be "cut down" (*shallekhet*), it would "leave" a "holy" "stump"—has been seen. In the footnotes to various passages and in the general commentary, my translation draws attention to these points and emphasizes the special weight of this verse within the book of Isaiah.

1.5 Second Isaiah's Suffering Servant

How, then, did Second Isaiah's servant of Yahweh fulfill Isaiah's salvation prophecy? The answer to this is in Second Isaiah's fourth servant song (Isa 52:13 – 53:12). I have translated its beginning as follows:

---

3 Martin Buber, *The Prophetic Faith* (New York: Macmillan, 1949), 202–5.

Behold, my servant *shall be satisfied*,
Raised and lifted,
Greatly exalted. (Isa 52:13)

The original term *yaskil*, which I have rendered as "shall be satisfied," occurs here in the causative Hiphil form and has traditionally been translated in Japanese as "prosper" (Colloquial Version, New Japanese Bible, New Interconfessional Translation; also following this tradition are the NAB and NRS in English and the LSG and NEG in French) or as "complete the work" (Masao Sekine version; the LUT and EIN in German tend to go in this direction). The simple Qal form of this verb occurs only in 1 Samuel 18:30, where it carries the sense of "to succeed, to have military success." Except for an Aramaic Hithpaal form, the remaining sixty occurrences are all found in the Hiphil form. Not all of these occurrences, however, necessarily relate to the Qal sense of "to succeed" or "to prosper" (such as in 1Sam 18:5, 14, 15; 2Kgs 18:7; Jer 20:11; 1Kgs 2:3). Instead, most of the occurrences relate to an intellectual understanding, such as "to have insight" (Job 34:35; Prov 1:3; 10:5, 19; 14:35; 17:2; 19:14), "to make wise" (Gen 3:6; Ps 36:4), and "to give understanding" (Ps 32:8; Prov 16:23; Isa 41:20; 44:18; Jer 9:24). Furthermore, for the Isaiah passage in question, the Septuagint has *sunēsei* and the Vulgate has *intelliget*, both of which strongly connote the sense of "to understand" (many German versions, including ELB, ELO, and SCH, which have "einsichtig [weisheitlich] handeln," also emphasize this connotation). My translation considers Second Isaiah's own parallel instances in 41:20 and 44:18, as well as "to justify many" and "enlightened sages" in Daniel 12:3, and uses "to be satisfied" (*tokushin suru*) in the sense of being satisfied after having been enlightened on his own.

This rendition has two merits. First, within verse 13 itself, if "prosper" were added to the three verbs "raised," "lifted," and "exalted," it would be unnecessarily saying the same thing four times. Inasmuch as "shall be satisfied" refers to the inner disposition of "my servant," while the other three verbs refer to outward things, this rendition strikes a good balance between the inward and outward exaltation of the servant.

Of course, if this is not the poet's perspective, it would be a simple case of reading too much into the text. However, the poet also shows concern for the balance between inward and outward exaltation in Isa 53:11–12. There, the passage "Through knowing, he [my servant] shall be satisfied" (53:11) speaks about his self-satisfaction, and the passage "Therefore, I [Yahweh] shall divide and share many with him, and he shall divide and take the strong as plunder" (53:12) describes his outward prosperity in relation to others. And in the first place, this fourth servant song consists of a three-part structure wherein 52:13–15 and 53:10aβ–12 correspond to each other and frame 53:1–10aα. The balance would be destroyed if one half of the symmetrical frame had no internal perspective. In other words, here lies the second merit of translating 52:13 as "shall be satisfied": it adds the finishing touch to the frame's symmetry.

In this way, the translation of the opening of the first half of the frame relates to that of the ending of the second half of the frame. I have attempted to reflect accurately in translation the contrast between the perfect and imperfect forms, which appears strange at first glance.

> It is he who *bore* the sin of many.
> And *he shall intercede* for the unrighteous ones. (53:12b)

Traditionally, this verse has been translated in either the imperfect or perfect tense, such as "He shall bear the sin of many, and he shall intercede for the transgressors" (New Japanese Bible and BBE) and "He bore the sin of many, and he made intercession for the transgressors" (Masao Sekine version, New Interconfessional Translation, NRS, RWB, LUT, ELB). In the original text, however, the perfect *nasa'* and the imperfect *yaphgia'* do not occur in a chiastic structure or in waw-consecutive form, but in a strange construction where the two simply appear in contrasting forms. My translation above treats them as they occur in the text. It is only when we intentionally go against traditional translations and render the text as it is that the significance and logic of the contrast between the imperfects in 10b to 12aα and the perfects in 12aβ become clear.

First, consider v. 10aβ: "If you⁴ make his [Yahweh's servant's] life an atonement offering, he shall see the days of his descendants last long." This indicates that, with Israel's conscious acceptance of the servant's redemptive act, one condition for the servant's prosperity will be fulfilled. Continuing, then, it is v. 10b's "And Yahweh's will shall be accomplished in his hand" which declares that this shall be an accomplishment of Yahweh's intentions for redemption. In this way, it becomes evident to the servant himself, together with Israel and Yahweh, that the servant's suffering did not end futilely in death but carried the definite significance of atonement: "After the tribulations of his life, he [Yahweh's servant] shall see. Through knowing, he shall be satisfied" (v. 11a). And in this way, the "satisfied" "righteous servant shall make many righteous, he himself shall bear their sins" (v. 11b). In other words, atonement is not yet entirely completed. It is only when the servant understands the redemptive significance of his suffering and when he consciously bears and accomplishes it once more that the servant "shall bear" the "sins" of "many." This is the reason for the imperfect form. If

---

4 Although the Vulgate has 'he,' this is a poor strategy in that it removes thoughts of 'you'—i. e., Israel—from the poet's perspective.

he "bears" and accomplishes it, "I [Yahweh] shall divide and share many with him, and he shall divide and take the strong as plunder" (v. 12aα). That is, the servant shall be "raised and lifted" (52:13). Isaiah 53:12aβ, bα uses the perfect form and expresses matters as an established fact: "Because he poured out his life to death, and he was counted among the unrighteous ones" (53:12aβ)—that is, because "he [already] bore the sin of many" (v. 12bα)—his exaltation is sure. However, the servant, who died without understanding the meaning, shall only be "satisfied" when he becomes enlightened about his death's redemptive significance, and once again, consciously, "he shall intercede for the unrighteous ones" (v. 12bβ). At that time, "Yahweh's will" for substitutionary atonement will be completely fulfilled for the first time. That is the conclusion of this fourth song.

Some have suspected that Israel's sinners who tormented and killed the innocent servant triumphantly invented a passive story, according to which they had received atonement for their sins from the servant as a fiction to relieve their own sense of guilt—a Freudian "work of mourning," as it were. This suspicion disappears, however, when we translate the original text of the song accurately in this way. This is because we can now recognize that the text is speaking about preparation for an active and bitter future where the work is accomplished only when the three conditions are fulfilled—namely, the servant's taking Israel's sins upon himself once again; the accomplishment of Yahweh's will; and the servant's "satisfaction" after death, that is, his conscious "intercession." When we go against the traditions of existing translations and accurately translate this contrast between perfect and imperfect forms in the ending of the fourth song, which appears odd at first, not only can we reconstruct the original significance of *yaskil* in the opening, but the deep implications of this song also become apparent for the first time.

As far as I know, this point has been overlooked until now in the existing Japanese, English, German, and French translations. I wish to conclude my references to the book of Isaiah by noting two additional points that have been debated in the history of translation, along with some extraneous comments.

> 53:8 By cruel justice, he was taken away.
> And who considered his *clan?* ...
>
> 9 He lined up his own grave with the wicked,
> And he joined *the rich* in his death.

As I indicated in the footnotes to my translation, many scholars take *dor* as meaning "fate" in v. 8. We must, however, pay attention to the fact that *dor* typically means "generation" (Gen 6:9; 7:1) and, by extension, "descendants" (Exod 16:32, 33; Josh 22:28), as well as "tribe" (Ps 14:5; 24:6). In view of the connection with "descendants" (*zera'*) in v. 10 and the fact that a look at the sorrow of the clan of one who dies in this way would deepen the sense of the servant's suffering, my translation renders this text straightforwardly.

Also, though some have proposed replacing "the rich" with "those who do evil" in v. 9, I have not adopted this reading because it lacks support in the ancient manuscripts and versions. Counter to the traditional view that riches are God's blessings (e. g., Deut 28:1–14), unrighteous wealth and luxury are often impeached in the prophets (Amos 6:4–6; 8:4–6; Isa 3:16–23; 5:11–12; etc.). Therefore, I read this as it is in the Masoretic Text, and it is possible, of course, to take it in the negative sense. The point is that, even in a translation faithful to the Masoretic Text, we can also recognize here an allusion to the fact that this servant's honor is not restored after death. Therefore, we can already detect here the need to refer to "satisfaction" in the opening and to the imperfect "intercession" in the ending of the fourth servant song.

2 From the Book of Jeremiah

2.1 Jeremiah and the Deuteronomistic Historian

Next, I wish to consider the book of Jeremiah. I shall begin with the following passage, where Jeremiah's prophecy and an editorial revision by the Deuteronomist are juxtaposed. The italicized words are problematic for translation because of various issues related to the ancient versions, Hebrew grammar, and the Deuteronomistic Historian.

> Truly, from long ago *you* broke your yoke.
> You cut off your bonds.
> And you said,
> "I *will not become a slave.*"
> Truly, *on every high hill, and beneath every green tree*,
> You crouched like a prostitute. (Jer 2:20)[5]

In the first line, "you" can be taken in the first-person form, such as in the NKJ, so the first two lines can be translated as "For of old I have broken your yoke and burst your bonds." In that case, "yoke" and "bonds" can be understood as foreign oppression that binds Israel in a state of slavery. It is also possible, however,

---

5 Seizō Sekine, trans., *Eremiya-sho* (Book of Jeremiah) (Tokyo: Iwanami Shoten, 2002). Except where noted otherwise, all quotations from the book of Jeremiah are from this translation.

to connect it with 2:2 and interpret it as pointing to the faithful marriage relationship with Yahweh. Alternatively, since the Yahweh religion had ethical purity based upon holy laws as its foundation, in contrast to the Baal cult's principal interest in sexual orgies and religious ecstasy, which lies in the background of 2:20, it is not impossible to understand this as also implying ethical laws. Additionally, it is possible to understand the two verbs that end with -*ti* as the archaic form of the second-person, feminine, singular verb, which ends with *t*. The *ketib* in nearby 2:33 occurs in this form, and the Septuagint also reflects this in its second-person translation. My translation follows this form. The first two lines mean, therefore, that Israel has loosened its relational ties to Yahweh.

In line with this, in my translation I understand Israel as arrogantly saying "I will not become a slave." This is based on the *ketib*, which is read *'e'ebod*. The *qere*, the Cairo Genizah, and the Targum, which have *'e'ebor*, mean something like "I will not pass over [and go]." The NKJ's "I will not transgress" follows this reading, and it seems to imply "I will not betray Yahweh." If so, however, this would generally emphasize Yahweh's salvation and Israel's obedience. This creates the difficulty of not fitting the context of this unit, from "When on every high hill and under every green tree You lay down, playing the harlot" (NKJ) down to v. 25, where the prophet impeaches Israel's adultery against Yahweh. This is why my translation follows the *ketib*.

Following the *ketib* makes for a smooth connection to the following v. 20b. The pagan cults of Baal and of other gods in Canaan were practiced on the hills and mountains or on "the high places" in the plains (1Kgs 18:19 ff.), and they entailed sexual orgies with temple prostitutes (Hos 4:14). Here, therefore, the text likens Israel, who has run after these things, to a prostitute seeking foreign men. The expression "on every high hill, and beneath every green tree" is found in 1Kgs 14:23 and 2Kgs 17:10. As pointed out in Thiel's groundbreaking research,[6] it should be attributed to the Deuteronomistic Historian. In other words, my translation of 2:20 treats the entire verse as an editorial addition by the Deuteronomistic Historian to Jeremiah's prophetic impeachment of Israel's desires and impurities.

There are many other instances in the book of Jeremiah where we find amalgamations of texts composed by Jeremiah and the Deuteronomistic Historian.[7]

---

6 Winfried Thiel, *Die deuteronomistische Redaktion von Jeremia 1–25* (WMANT 41; Neukirchen-Vluyn: Neukirchener Verlag, 1973); and Winfried Thiel, *Die deuteronomistische Redaktion von Jeremia 26–45* (WMANT 52; Neukirchen-Vluyn: Neukirchener Verlag, 1981).
7 These are the passages in the book of Jeremiah that Thiel attributes to the Deuteronomistic Historian: 1:1–3, 7bβ, 9–10, 16–19; 2:5b, 20b, 26b; 3:6–13 (excluding 12aβ, 13bα), 14–18; 4:3–4; 5:18–19; 6:18–19?; 7:1–8:3 (excluding 7:4, 9a, 10a, 12?, 14, 18abα, 21b, 28b, 29); 8:19b; 9:11–15;

2.2 False Prophets

How did the early Jeremiah view salvation? And what of his relationship to false prophets? In my view, the following verse offers an important clue for answering these questions.

> Then *I said*,
> "Ah, Lord, Yahweh.
> Indeed, you have completely deceived
> This people and Jerusalem,
> Saying, 'Peace will visit you.'
> Instead, a sword is touching the throat. (Jer 4:10)

Based on the Alexandrian manuscript of the Septuagint and the Arabic version, BHS emends "I said" to the third-person "they said." The EIN, for instance, also follows this reading. The likely reason for the change is that voicing the complaint "you have completely deceived," "saying, 'Peace will visit you'" must have seemed unbefitting the prophet. Among the Septuagint texts, however, the Vatican and Sinaitic manuscripts, which are about a century older than the Alexandrian manuscript, have the first-person form, as in the Masoretic Text. Moreover, the Arabic version is not authoritative for text-critical purposes because it includes a mixture of interpretive traditions from the tenth century onward. By contrast, if we read the Masoretic Text as it is, it means that the early Jeremiah believed the prophecies of peace. His ignorance was corrected by God at around the point of 14:14, and this eventually resulted in the public confrontation with the false prophet in chapter 28. When we read the text in this way, the prophet's trials and errors and the dynamics of his thought formation become clearer.

"Peace will visit you" is Jeremiah's quotation of popular prophets who spoke as if speaking God's words. Because of them, Jeremiah earnestly spoke in good faith based on the dogma concerning the inviolability of the holy city of Zion and

---

10:1–16; 11:1–14; 11:15–12:6 (excluding 11:21–23?; 12:1–5); 12:14–17; 13:10a, 11, 12–14; 14:1–15:4 (excluding 14:2–10); 16:3b, 4b, 10–13, 16–18, 19–21; 17:19–27; 18:1, 7–11, 12, 18; 19:2b–9, 11b–15; 20:1, 6; 21:1–10; 22:1–5, 8–9, 11–12, 17b, 25–27, 28, 29?, 30b?; 23:1–4, 7–8, 17, 32, 34–40; 24:1–10; 25:1–38 (compare with 26:3, 4b, 5, 6, 13); 27:5–10, 12–15, 16–22; 28:1aα, 16bβ; 29:2, 4b, 8–24, 25, 31aβb, 32aβb; 30:1–3; 31:27–34 (35–40); (32:1–6a) 32:16–44; (ch. 33); 34:1, 2ab, 8a, 9aβb, 12b, 13b–17, 18aβ, 19–22; 35:1, 7bβ, 13–18; 36:2b, 3, 7, 31; 37:1–2, 19; 38:2, 22–23; 39:1–2, 4–10, 13, 15b, 16aβ, 17, 18b; 40:1, 2b–3; 42:10–16, 17aβbβ, 18–22; 43:1, 4, 7 (13); 44:1–14, 15, 17aβ, 18b, 20–23, 24aαb, 25a, 26a, 27, 28b; 45:1b, 2, 5bα. Thiel also considers the possibility that the following passages in Jeremiah's so-called "confessions" come from the Deuteronomistic Historian, but he is not conclusive concerning them: 11:18–12:6; 15:10–21; 17:12–18; 19:19–23; 20:7–18.

the temple and based on God's eternal covenant with the Davidic dynasty. If the early Jeremiah trusted in the reliability of their words, then the problem runs even deeper than one might be inclined to think. This problem with false prophets is developed in 14:10–16, 23:9–40, and chapters 27–29, and the intention behind my translation of 4:10 is to foreshadow that development.

2.3 Messiah

Next, I wish to consider the somewhat lengthy passage in 23:2–6. My translation is as follows.

> 2 Therefore, thus says Yahweh, the God of Israel, concerning the shepherds who shepherd *my* people. "You *scatter* my flock, you only drive it away, you did not reward them [with good things]. Behold, I will reward your evil deeds. This is the oracle of Yahweh.
>
> 3 But I will gather the remnant of my flock from all the lands where *I have dispersed* them, and I will return them to their pasture. ...
>
> 5 Behold, such days are coming.
> This is the oracle of Yahweh. —
> And I will raise up
> *For David's sake one righteous branch.*
> He shall reign as king, and he shall prosper,
> He shall perform justice and righteousness in the land.
>
> 6 It is Judah who will be saved in his *time.*
> Israel will dwell securely.
> This is the name by which he will be called,
> '*Yahweh is our righteousness.*' ... (Jer 23:2–6)

The italicized parts pose important interpretative problems. Some translations, such as the New Japanese Bible and the TEV, have "his" instead of "my" in v. 2, but this finds no support in the manuscripts and ancient versions. Although it is not impossible to take this as meaning "Jeremiah's," "my pasture" occurs with the first-person suffix for Yahweh in v. 1, and it is not uncommon for first-person and third-person forms to become mixed up in God's speech. It is appropriate, therefore, to translate it in the first person as meaning "Yahweh's."

In vv. 1–2, "to scatter" (causative form of *puts*) is used to mean that Judah's upper class did not lead the people as they should have done, but in vv. 3 and 8, the text uses "to disperse" (causative form of *nadach*) to mean the dispersion of the people through exile. Along with Thiel, we can treat vv. 3 and 8, together with the related v. 7, as an insertion by the Deuteronomistic Historian or a later editor.

"For David's sake" and "branch" (*tsemach*) in v. 5 can be understood as referring to the messiah as a savior who will appear in the future (in Zech 3:8 and 6:12 *tsemach* is used with reference to the messiah). This expression also corresponds to the "shoot" (*choṭer*) and "branch" (*netser*) that shall come from the "stump" of "Jesse," the father of David, found in Isaiah's messianic prophecy in 11:1. Furthermore, we can understand it as having been implicitly and explicitly influenced by Isaiah's identification of the "stump" as the "holy descendant" at the end of his call narrative in Isaiah 6. However, elements that are usually included in messianic prophecies, such as the messiah's miraculous birth, glory, the transfiguration of nature, and eschatological depictions (for instance, see Isaiah 9 and 11, discussed above), have been removed in the Jeremiah passage, where conciseness is a distinctive feature.

Translated literally, "time" in v. 6 would be the same as "days" in v. 5. The original phrase that I have translated as "Yahweh is our righteousness" is *yahawe tsidqenu*. One theory connects this to King Zedekiah (*tsidqiyahu* in Hebrew), but I have not done so here because words from the same root—*tsaddiq* (righteous) and *tsedaqa* (righteousness)—are used in the preceding verse, and the tradition of connecting the coming messiah with righteousness existed from the time of Isaiah's messianic prophecies (9:6; 11:4–5).

Whatever the case, prophetic prospects of salvation through the "remnant," which were proclaimed from the time of Isaiah's call, lay in two directions. In the direction of Second Isaiah, fulfillment would come through the atonement of Yahweh's servant, while in the direction of Jeremiah, it would come through the renewal of a new covenant. Adopting a translation that attends to these related points, one should be able to recognize that chapter 23 is preparing for the latter.

Scholarly views are divided, however, as to whether chapter 31's prophecy of the new covenant goes back to Jeremiah or the Deuteronomistic Historian. Before considering that point, though, I wish to look at a typical passage that presents a case study for distinguishing between Jeremiah's authentic prophecies and the pen of the Deuteronomistic Historian. The passage is 7:21–26.

2.4 Sacrifices

> 21 Thus says Yahweh of hosts, the God of Israel: "Add sacrifices to your *burnt offerings*, and *eat the flesh*. 22 Truly, when I brought your fathers out of the land of Egypt, I did not speak to them, and I did not command them, concerning burnt offerings and sacrifices. 23 Only, I commanded this thing to them, saying, "*Listen to and follow my voice. Then* I will be your God, and you shall be my people. Walk in every way that I command you. In order that you may obtain happiness.

24 But they did not listen, they did not incline their ear; they walked according to their various plots, according to *the stubbornness of* their evil *heart*; turning backward, they did not head forward. 25 From the day when your fathers came out of the land of Egypt until today, I sent to you all of my servants. *I repeatedly sent the prophets from early in the morning every day.* 26 But they did not listen to me, they did not incline their ear; *they stiffened their neck*; they did more evil than their fathers. (Jer 7:21–26)

Among the sacrifices offered to God, the "peace offering" (*zebach shelamim*) could be eaten by the priests and worshipers after offering a portion to God (Lev 3:6 ff.), but the "burnt offering" (*'ola*) was an animal sacrifice that was completely consumed by fire and given to God. Its meat must not be eaten, and it was the most important sacrifice (Lev 1:5 ff.; Num 28–29). It is Thiel's view that the call to "eat" it in 21b is Jeremiah's, but that the rest is from the Deuteronomistic Historian. Amos 5:21–27 states that the cult did not exist in the time of Moses. Jeremiah does not question whether or not the cult existed, but at least he says it was not something commanded by God. Despite some differences, criticism of the cult is part of the prophetic tradition. Therefore, Thiel attributes 21b, the core of this passage, to Jeremiah. Deuteronomistic phraseology is markedly noticeable in the rest, however, and he attributes this to the Deuteronomistic Historian.

God commanded morally righteous acts, not the cult. The expression "Listen to and follow my voice. Then I will be your God, and you shall be my people" is from the Deuteronomistic Historian and, in the book of Jeremiah alone, also appears in 1:4, 13:11, and 26:19. The expression "I repeatedly sent [to you]" in v. 25 is also repeated in the book of Jeremiah in 25:4, 26:5, 29:19, 35:15, and 44:4, and many scholars attribute these and the surrounding prose accounts to the Deuteronomistic Historian. The idea of God sending to the people a line of prophets with Moses heading the list is clearly the Deuteronomistic Historian's thought (Deut 18:15–19; 34:10). It is also true, however, that one might wish to question Thiel's theory, which attributes all but 21b to the Deuteronomistic Historian, and to ask "what kind of person is this 'historian' who would add such a long and independent historical explanation to Jeremiah's few words."[8] Instead, it is probable that, besides 21b, 28b, and 29, which Thiel attributes to Jeremiah, there were more of Jeremiah's words in 21–29. Nevertheless, because the Deuteronomistic Historian embellished them with his historical phraseology, it is appropriate to conclude that we are no longer able to distinguish between them today. (There is some dispute about whether the statement in vv. 24–26, that Israel was persistently rebellious against God from the time of the Exodus, conflicts with Jer-

---

8 Masao Sekine, *Eremiya-sho Chūkai (Jō)* (Commentary on the Book of Jeremiah: Part 1) (Tokyo: Taishindo, 1962), 158.

emiah's words in 2:2, which says that Israel was faithful to God during the wilderness period [for details, see the note at 7:26 in my translation[9]]. However, from the time of Isaiah's call prophecy, the recalcitrance of their "stubborn hearts" and "stiff necks" is the fundamental sin of the people seen by the prophets, and it would not be surprising if, at some point, Jeremiah viewed this as already existing in tandem with their purity in the wilderness.) These matters relate deeply to the interpretive problem in 31:31–34, which is the best-known and most important passage in the book of Jeremiah. Therefore I wish to conclude this chapter, whose goal was to use the wording of the translation as a basis for developing a discussion of the overall thought here, with an overview of the prophecy of this "new covenant".

2.5 The New Covenant

> 31 Behold, the days are coming when I will make a *new covenant* with the house of Israel and the house of Judah. This is the oracle of Yahweh. 32 That *covenant* is not like the *covenant* that I made on the day when I grasped their fathers' hand and brought them out of the nation of Egypt. They broke that *covenant* of mine, Even though I was their lord. This is the oracle of Yahweh. 33 This is the *covenant* that I will make with the house of Israel after the days with them. This is the oracle of Yahweh. *I will place my law within them, I will write it in their heart. I will be their God, and they shall be my people.* 34 People shall no longer teach their neighbor and their brother, saying, "Know Yahweh." Because truly, from the least to the greatest, *they shall all know me.* This is the oracle of Yahweh. Truly, *I will forgive their iniquity, I will not remember their sin again.* (Jer 31:31–34)

This brief unit is one of the most important passages in the book of Jeremiah, and as is well-known, it has become a bridge connecting the Old and New Testaments. Primitive Christianity believed that the promise of the "new covenant," or the "new testament," was fulfilled in the life and death of Jesus Christ (Heb 8:8–12; 2Cor 3:5–18; also see Matt 14:23–25). Scholars have debated how to treat, overall, this unit in which Deuteronomistic expressions can be found here and there: (1) attribute it to the Deuteronomistic Historian; (2) treat it as Jeremiah's original composition; or (3) while recognizing it as a Deuteronomistic revision, maintain that its core is essentially authentic to Jeremiah. If we consider the points discussed above, however, I think that the question of authorship can be settled to some degree.

Certainly, there are numerous Deuteronomistic expressions here. For instance, the covenant formula in 33b is also used in Deuteronomy and by the Deu-

---

9 Sekine, *Eremiya-sho* (The Book of Jeremiah), 59.

teronomistic Historian (Deut 26:17, 18; 29:12; 2Sam 7:24), and it appears in passages usually attributed to the Deuteronomistic Historian in the book of Jeremiah (7:23; 11:4; 24:7; 31:1, 33; 32:38). Among these passages, scholars who follow (1) above think that 24:7 corresponds not only to this covenant formula, but, importantly, also to the reference to "Know Yahweh" in 31:34. Conversely, scholars who follow (2) regard chapter 24 as an editorial revision with chapter 31 at its base, and they explain similarities to Deuteronomistic texts on the grounds that Jeremiah himself was in a Deuteronomistic environment. The image of "they shall all know [*yada'*] me [Yahweh]" to the extent that no one says "Know [*yada'*] Yahweh," as also seen in Isaiah's messianic prophecy that "knowledge [*dea'*] about Yahweh will fill the land" (11:9), is one of the constants in general eschatological imagery.

As scholars who follow (1) point out, it is also true that the Deuteronomistic Historian heavily uses "covenant" (*berit*) and "forgive" (*salach*) (for the former, see Jer 11:2, 3, 6, 8, 10; 22:9; for the latter, see Num 14:19, 20; 1Kgs 8:30, 34, 36, 39, 50; Jer 36:3). However, scholars who follow (2) rebut this argument, stating that although few in number, these terms also occur in Jeremiah's original passages—"covenant" in 34:8, 10, 18, and "forgive" in 5:7—and so it is not impossible for Jeremiah to have used these terms in chapter 31.

Nevertheless, because these terms and formulae frequently occur in passages by the Deuteronomistic Historian, the odds favor the compromise embodied in approach (3), and I conclude that we should view them as essentially authentic (for a detailed discussion, see Chapter 7). Of course, based solely on the probability of terms, (1) might also appear likely. From an ideological perspective, however, it is difficult to accept that the Deuteronomistic Historian was the author of 31:31 ff. There are primarily three aspects to this conclusion.

According to the thought of the Deuteronomistic Historian, salvation is attained, in the first place, when people meet the condition of performing righteous deeds on their own accord (7:1–3, 5:8, 9b, 10b, 13, 15; 11:1–14; 17:19–27; 18:8–10; 26:3, 4b–6; or 21:8–10; 29:12–14; 38:2; 42:21–22; also 6:19; 9:12–15; 16:10–13; 26:4–6; 7:5–7; 19:4; 22:3; 11:1–13). Secondly, in line with this, it is inconceivable that human sins could be so severe that they cannot be wiped away without clinging to the deeds of another (though there are mentions of sin in 7:26 and 16:12, these are merely Israel's sins, not his own). Thirdly, God was understood intellectually and rationally within the framework of moral retribution, and he was not a being one would encounter in the faith struggles of an irrational and emotional person, such as those in Jeremiah (therefore, as we see in 11:14, he refuses intercessions by the prophet that contradict rational, retributive law).

Ideologically speaking, therefore, it is difficult to view the "new covenant" prophecy in chapter 31 as the work of the Deuteronomistic Historian. This prophecy is so far separated from the basic thought of the Deuteronomistic Historian that it cannot be his (their) work. Instead we must conclude that Jeremiah arrived at this conclusion at the end of his lifelong struggles with God and through his deep understanding of sin and forgiveness.

Precisely because these were Jeremiah's own thoughts, he was aware that not only must Israel's sin be impeached but that sin had also established its hold within himself (10:23–24). His awareness of sin, into which all people fall, culminated in a hopeless recognition that the manipulations of intricately entangled sin ultimately stem from the fact that the human heart is naturally recalcitrant. This awareness is revealed in passages such as "Can Cushites change their skin, or leopards their spots?" in 13:23 and "Unrighteous above all else is the heart, it is sick" in 17:9. People refuse obedience to God because it is in their nature to do so—they cannot help it. The spring of rebellion lies especially in their uncircumcised hearts (6:10; 9:24–25). Jeremiah arrived at a hopeless insight into original evil or sin, which rules all of human existence. Yet the ray of hope he left in the end was the transformation of the human heart (31:33) and the forgiveness of sin (31:34) based on the "new covenant" from God.

If we read it in this way, then the author of the core section of 31:31 ff. must have been Jeremiah. A Jeremiah prophecy lacking the new covenant passage would ultimately be lost in the quagmire of disgust and judgment of the people's sin. By contrast, the prophecy comes full circle for the first time with the ignition of this hope. It resolves the hopeless awareness of human original sin, which is otherwise an object of disgust and judgment, and leads one to discover the necessary path of salvation, where hope rests only in the "new covenant" from God. Based on a distinction between Jeremiah's original prophecies and the pen of the Deuteronomistic Historian, which I have presented in my translation and commentary, we reach the conclusion that the essence of thought in Jeremiah's prophecies requires the prophecy of the "new covenant" as a necessary hope.

And that conclusion also suggests the following. Prophetic prospects of salvation through the "remnant," which were proclaimed from the time of Isaiah's call, took concrete shape in the direction of Second Isaiah through the atonement of Yahweh's servant and in the direction of Jeremiah through the renewal of a new covenant. In other words, it again clearly declares the formation of two unique, prophetic types of soteriology based on the work of another, and these exist in a dimension that differs from Deuteronomistic self-salvation based on one's own strength.

Chapter 7 The Prophets and Deuteronomism: The Book of Jeremiah

1 Questions about Authenticity

It was the height of spring 2002 when I completed my translation and notes on the Book of Jeremiah for Iwanami's Old Testament series. In the final stages, it was a race to see whether I could finish before the closing of an exhibition at the Tokyo National Museum in Ueno of the works of Sesshū, a leading 15th-century sumi-e painter. Somehow I managed to complete my work, and I remember setting off for the woods in Ueno Park with a spring in my step. I realize that some might find it distasteful for me to commence an academic essay with a personal anecdote, but I am taking this liberty in order to explain the roots of my perspective in this chapter. Therefore, I beg the reader's indulgence.

The exhibition was a large-scale and quite exhaustive collection of Sesshū's works. It included not only genuine pieces, but also ones whose authenticity could not be verified, as well as obvious forgeries by Sesshū's disciples. This prompted me to reconsider matters concerning authenticity in paintings. While at the exhibition, I recalled a short but thought-provoking essay entitled "Shin-gan" (Authenticity) by the 20th-century literary critic Hideo Kobayashi. "According to experts, there are only about a dozen or so original works by Sesshū. But as long as a countless number of people wish to hang Sesshū on their walls, art and antique circles will be jeopardized unless we accept that fakes have their uses,"[1] reasons Kobayashi in a humorous story of his own misadventures in having mistakenly acquired many fakes. He wrote as if he enjoyed this game of wits. Referring to this article by Kobayashi, the leading contemporary music critic Hidekazu Yoshida penned a piece entitled "Mō Hitotsu no 'Shingan'" (Another 'Authenticity') on the occasion of an incident involving the sale of fake antique musical instruments at a university on the edge of the Ueno woods. After fully acknowledging the great difficulties involved in determining the authenticity of antique musical instruments, just as with other antiques, Yoshida also discusses questions of money and ethics, issues that Kobayashi did not address directly. Yoshida arrives at the forceful conclusion that dealing in forgeries and re-

---

1 Hideo Kobayashi, *Jōshiki ni Tsuite* (On Conventional Wisdom) (Tokyo: Kadokawa Bunko, 1986), 52.

ceiving money for erroneous or false appraisals "should be emphatically censured, criticized, and denounced."[2]

We must keep in mind the obvious fact that counterfeiters lack creative originality and are con artists who swindle people out of money by preying on their weakness of desiring antiques, including antique musical instruments. Although I had arrived at the Sesshū exhibition with a light heart after completing my Jeremiah translation and commentary, I departed with heavy steps. This incident recalled to mind these articles and the question of prophetic authenticity, making me aware of the difficult assignment ahead of me, which I had left unresolved in my translation and commentary.

Like the field of art, religion also involves economic issues. And because its concern with ultimate meaning surpasses even that of the arts or music, the influence of fakes in religion can present even more serious issues. In my view, the question of forgery in the book of Jeremiah is two-fold. A false prophet falsifies the word of God, and subsequent redactors falsify the words of the prophet. Past discussions of questions about authenticity have focused only on the former aspect, but here I wish to concentrate on the latter. That is, I will focus from the viewpoint of redaction history on how the original text underwent transformation and emerged into its present form during the redactional stage of the various transmissions, based on certain redactional intentions. Conventional redaction-history research has typically been content with extracting redactional passages and expounding on the redactor's intents, but what happens when we return to the essence of the matter—i.e., the fact that the redactional passages are actually forgeries purporting to be the work of a true prophet—and examine this critically in terms of its thought content? In other words, what fresh insights can be gained by taking a step from historical examinations toward philosophical interpretation? This perspective constitutes this chapter's immediate point of departure.[3]

---

2 Hidekazu Yoshida, *Mono ni wa Kimatta Yosa wa Naku* ... (Things Have no Predetermined Quality ...) (Tokyo: Yomiuri Shimbunsha, 1999), 102.
3 The book of Jeremiah is also an important text for discussing questions about the composition of Old Testament books. Jeremiah 36 records the writing with "ink" on a "scroll" made of papyrus or leather. Although I had intended to discuss the establishment of the text as a physical artifact, space does not permit me to do so here. Instead, I would direct readers to a fine work that addresses text-critical matters as they relate to the composition of texts. See Ernst Würthwein, *Der Text des Alten Testaments* (Stuttgart: Deutsche Bibelgesellschaft, 1988), especially Chapter 1.

2 True and False Prophets

Of these two questions about authenticity, in this section I wish to discuss briefly the first one concerning true and false prophets. The problem of false prophets in the book of Jeremiah is scattered throughout Jeremiah 27–29 and several other passages. Particularly notable among recent studies that have approached this from the perspective of redaction history are the works by Thiel in the 1970s and 1980s[4] and by McKane in the 1980s and 1990s.[5] I shall begin by outlining the main points of their studies, which represent classic yet contrasting approaches to redaction history.

Thiel systematically identified the redactions by the Deuteronomistic Historian throughout the whole book of Jeremiah and presented a monumental work that became the standard for subsequent studies. On the question of false prophets, he hypothesizes that the Deuteronomistic Historian made major additions to the transmitted texts about the salvation prophets and that he collated them into three large blocks: (1) Jeremiah 14:13–16 (a text by the Deuteronomistic Historian, who borrowed Jeremiah's words on a similar theme), within the rite during the drought in 14:1–15:4; (2) Jeremiah 23:9–32, the received anthology of the anti-prophets (the additions by the Deuteronomistic Historian are restricted to verses 17 and 32); and (3) Jeremiah 27–29, the complex related to the unified theme of "false prophecies." Of these, (3) is linked to the specific examples reported in Jeremiah 28 and is thought to have been composed by the Deuteronomistic Historian (the texts by the Deuteronomistic Historian himself are Jer 27:9ff; 28:16bβ; 29:8–9, 15; and in chapter 29, verses 21–23 and also parts of verses 24–32). The criterion used by the Deuteronomistic Historian for identifying false prophets is taken from the definitions of a prophet in Deuteronomy (Deut 13:2ff; 18:9ff). Judah's destruction in 587 BCE and the Babylonian exile demonstrated decisively that the prophecies of misfortune were accurate and that prophecies of salvation were mistaken. This settled the question of which prophecies derived from Yahweh. Thiel concluded that the Deuteronomistic Historian carried out these redactions based on this unwavering perspective.[6]

---

4 Winfried Thiel, *Die deuteronomistische Redaktion von Jeremia 1–25* (WMANT 41; Neukirchen-Vluyn: Neukirchener Verlag, 1973); Winfried Thiel, *Die deuteronomistische Redaktion von Jeremia 26–45* (WMANT 52; Neukirchen-Vluyn: Neukirchener Verlag, 1981).
5 William McKane, *Jeremiah*, Vol. I (International Critical Commentary; Edinburgh: T. & T. Clark, 1986); William McKane, *Jeremiah*, Vol. II (International Critical Commentary; Edinburgh: T. & T. Clark, 1996).
6 Thiel, *Die deuteronomistische Redaktion von Jeremia 26–45*, 110. A historical note is in order. Jeremiah was mainly active before Israel's destruction and the Babylonian exile in 587 BCE,

While criticizing Thiel's research, McKane's study was seminal in that it represented the first comprehensive comparison of the Masoretic Text and the Septuagint, which is about one-eighth shorter in length. For instance, in relation to the false prophet passages (chapter 28 in the Masoretic Text, chapter 35 in the Septuagint), where there are striking anomalies between the two texts, McKane constructs his argument along the following lines. First, translating the opening of the Masoretic Text results in "In that same year, at the beginning of the reign of King Zedekiah of Judah, in the fifth month of the fourth year, the prophet Hananiah ...," but the Septuagint has "In the fifth month of the fourth year of King Zedekiah of Judah ... the false prophet ... Ananiah ...." This is inconsistent with, and secondary to, the opening of Jeremiah 27—"In the beginning of the reign of Jehoiakim"—which deals with Zedekiah's times, and it suggests that 28:1 in the Septuagint and in the shorter Hebrew text on which this was based originally applied to both chapters. Perhaps in the longer Masoretic Text, Jeremiah 27:1 was also originally "In the fourth year of Zedekiah" and 28:1 read "In that same year." As far as the term "prophet" is concerned, the Septuagint describes "Ananiah" as "the false prophet" (*o pseudoprophētēs*), but in verses 5, 6, 10, 11, 12, 15 and 17 both Ananiah and Jeremiah are mentioned by name only, with no descriptive label. In this respect the Septuagint differs from the Masoretic Text, which refers to both as "the prophet" (*hannabi'*) throughout verses 1–17. McKane argues that wording not present in the original short version was added to the long version at the redactional stage.[7]

By amassing such arguments, McKane concludes that the Septuagint suggests the existence of a Hebrew text that is shorter than the Masoretic Text and that this shorter text was expanded into the longer Hebrew version. Rather than consisting of redactions based on a literary configuration and a theologically consistent system, as Thiel postulates, McKane argues that there is a strong possibility that this expansion was much more the outcome of happenstance and whim, with exegetical changes, expansions, and deletions in relation to just a single verse, or the outcome of a few verses merely piling up without any overall perspective or framework.[8]

---

whereas the Deuteronomistic Historian was active during the exilic period. Based on the book of Deuteronomy, the Deuteronomistic Historian is thought to have edited the historical books comprising the Deuteronomistic History (the books of Joshua, Judges, Samuel, and Kings) by evaluating Israel's history leading up to its destruction and to have redacted prophetic texts according to the same terminology, style, and thought.

7 McKane, *Jeremiah*, Vol. II, 709 ff.

8 McKane, *Jeremiah*, Vol. I, xvff.; esp. 1 ff.

2 True and False Prophets —— **185**

These studies by Thiel and McKane are classic formulations of two directions in redaction-history research. One postulates a systematic redactional intention on the part of a specific redactor, while the other assumes no such intention. Nevertheless, research must set out on the basis of some kind of hypothesis, and the fact remains that both theories are founded on unverifiable assumptions. Yet if pressed as to which hypothesis is more significant, I would have to conclude that it is the one proposed by Thiel. Although textual interpretation is driven by a certain methodology, we should not be so overly constrained by this methodology that the text is weakened to no purpose. By restricting himself to comparing the Septuagint and the Masoretic Text and to identifying the individual detailed phrases added in the transition from the shorter version to the longer version of the Hebrew text, McKane lost sight of the redactor's overall ideological context. For his part, by no means does Thiel neglect a detailed comparison of the wording. In particular, he makes a thorough comparison with the wording in Deuteronomy and the Deuteronomistic History. Yet he also discovers new meanings in the text by postulating a broad ideological framework. We might even say that, unlike McKane, Thiel has actually strengthened the text. Yet if we suppose that we should also allow such eisegetical readings as long as the interpretation does not conflict with exegetical readings—i.e., if we suppose that it is enrichment of the text's meaning that should especially be increased—then, while incorporating individual points from McKane's empirical study, I would evaluate more highly the significance of redaction-history research that postulates a systematic redaction along the lines of Thiel's approach.

What new meanings become apparent in the false prophet texts when we follow Thiel's lead? Because of space limitations, I can cite only a few typical examples. For instance, in Jeremiah 28, where there is a contest with Hananiah ("the false prophet" in the Septuagint, and "the prophet" in the Masoretic Text), according to Thiel, the only redactional passages by the Deuteronomistic Historian are v. 16bβ and probably also v. 1aα. After his prophecies, Hananiah is roundly and prophetically condemned here in wording similar to Deuteronomy 13:6—he has "spoken rebellion against Yahweh" (the only other example in the Old Testament is Jer 29:32). To the Deuteronomistic Historian, who lived in the period of exile after Judah's destruction, it was obvious that such salvation prophecies had been wrong.

By contrast, the condemnation of Hananiah is not so straightforward in the narrative passages that are thought to convey Jeremiah's authentic words. Our attention is drawn to this difference: Jeremiah lived in a time of turmoil, causing him to speak a little more hesitantly and to waver, thinking or hoping that perhaps the salvation prophecies were correct. For instance, Hananiah breaks the yoke that Jeremiah wears around his neck as a symbol of the yoke of Babylonian exile (27:2, 8), and he announces the advent of peace (28:10). Jeremiah's response is as follows: "Amen! May Yahweh do so; … But … the prophets from long ago came and prophesied war, misfortune, and plague against many lands and large kingdoms. As for the prophet who prophesies peace, when that prophet's word is fulfilled, then it will be known that it was a prophet truly sent by Yahweh" (28:6 – 9). Some commentators interpret this as sarcasm on the part of the judgment-prophet Jeremiah, but it should be construed as an expression of his hope that Hananiah's salvation prophecies might be true. This is because in other passages, too, Jeremiah adopts a stance that relativizes himself as he compassionately desires peace for the people (15:11; 18:20; see also 4:19 – 20; 8:18 – 19a, 20 – 23; 9:9 – 10, 16 – 21; 13:17; etc.) while announcing judgment (3:25; 9:22 – 23; 13:18), and we can also see here a reflection of Jeremiah's genuine feelings.[9] The attitude of Jeremiah, whose yoke was broken by Hananiah and who departed wordlessly (28:11), also accords with this and can be regarded as a reaction stemming from his characteristic weakness.

Although Thiel does not draw attention to these points, I think that when we develop his redaction-history considerations of false prophets in this direction we can detect the striking contrast between the Deuteronomistic Historian's redactional intentions and the meaning and characteristics of Jeremiah's original words.

3 An Examination of Thiel's Theory about the Deuteronomistic Historian's Redactional Intentions

Of the two questions about authenticity in the book of Jeremiah, in the previous section I began my argument with a discussion of the first question concerning false prophets. This has naturally led us to the second question about the comparison between Jeremiah's authentic texts and the Deuteronomistic Historian's forged texts in the book of Jeremiah. Thiel's research has subsequently met with arguments by many scholars both for and against it (Smend, Kaiser, and others agree with him, while scholars such as Weippert, Holladay, M. Sekine and McKane have criticized or partially modified Thiel's argument). Discussion has focused mainly on the parts containing Deuteronomistic redactions, and to the best of my knowledge it did not move on to an examination of the authentic parts by Jer-

---

9 For interpretations along these lines, see, for instance, Masao Sekine, *Eremiya-sho Chūkai (Ge) Chosakushū Dai-jūgo Kan* (Commentary on the Book of Jeremiah, Vol. 2; Collected Works, Vol. 15) (Tokyo: Shinchi Shobō, 1982), 72; and McKane, *Jeremiah*, Vol. II, 717– 20. As a representative of those who regard this as sarcasm, see E. W. Nicholson, *The Book of the Prophet Jeremiah, Chapters 26 – 52* (London: Cambridge University Press, 1975), 37.

emiah, with which these redactions are contrasted, or to a meaningful comparison of the two. Nevertheless, if we assume that in certain areas there is still room to round out research along Thiel's lines, then surely this lies in demonstrating the extent to which the systematic redactional intentions and thought of the Deuteronomistic Historian as identified by Thiel can be separated out as an independent entity from the parts that are authentically by Jeremiah. If this can be demonstrated, then the next step is to compare the fundamental ideas of the two. Because it would take too much space to discuss every passage, here I simply note the results of my examination with just chapter and verse citations.

3.1 The Theology of Thiel's Deuteronomistic Historian

After identifying each of the redactional passages in the book of Jeremiah, Thiel summarizes the main theological ideas of the Deuteronomistic Historian extracted from these passages.[10] These ideas can be summed up in the following twelve points. After each number I have summarized the Deuteronomistic Historian's thought (Thiel generally gives citations, but here I omit those), and if a similar idea exists in the parts that are authentically Jeremiah's, I cite the passage(s) in parentheses. Therefore, items not followed by parenthetical citations are exclusive to the Deuteronomistic Historian, with no similar idea found in Jeremiah's original work.

1. The Deuteronomistic Historian regards the exile in 587 BCE as a judgment on the people's sin (Jer 27:1–4, 11[11]).
2. Specifically, the Deuteronomistic Historian portrays sin in terms of the worship of pagan gods, syncretism with pagan cults, and a disregard for Yahweh's will. These practices have been going on ever since the exodus from Egypt, and Yahweh has reached the limits of his patience (Jer 2:8, 11, 13, 23–25, 27–37; 3:1–5, 20–21; 4:14, 22; 5:5–8;[12] etc.).

---

10 Thiel, *Die deuteronomistische Redaktion von Jeremia 26–45*, 107 ff.

11 The authentic passages in Jeremiah 1:13–15 and 2:17–19 mention enemies from the North, and 13:18–19 mentions the exile in 597. These should be regarded as similar ideas in the sense that Israel's defeat was a judgment on the sins of the people.

12 Here "unrighteousness" and "adultery" entail syncretism with pagan gods, and the "yoke" and "bonds" appear also in Jer 2:20. If linked with Jer 2:2, this is construed as referring to a faithful marital relationship with Yahweh. This "honeymoon period" refers to the exodus from Egypt and the wandering in the wilderness. In that case, the statement from that period that "from long ago you broke your yoke, you cut off your bonds" is an argument by Jeremiah in 2:20, and Thiel's purported second point in the thought of the Deuteronomistic Historian is shared by Jeremiah.

3. Judgment was not something initially desired by Yahweh. If Judah would only repent and behave obediently, Yahweh is ready to change his mind about destroying it.[13]

4. Although this judgment also has overtones of collective retribution for the sins of the fathers, it fundamentally consists of individual retribution whereby one is punished for one's own sins. Either way, one cannot clearly distinguish between the two in this age when the individual is more sinful than the fathers had been (Jer 3:25).[14]

5. Deuteronomy was given to Israel by God at the time of the exodus from Egypt, and it expresses God's will as a reliable interpretation of the Decalogue.

6. The prophets who were sent repeatedly by God throughout Israel's history are preachers of repentance calling for a return and obedience to God's will as revealed in the Deuteronomic laws.

7. Judah's destruction demonstrated that those who speak of salvation during this period are false prophets.

8. The salvation prophets are enemies of Yahweh's final prophet, Jeremiah, and it was their success among the priests and people that was particularly responsible for provoking judgment (Jer 4:9 – 10; 5:31; 6:13 – 14; 7:4, 10a; 8:8, 11; 23:16, 25 – 31; 28:1b–16bα, 17; 29:16 – 30).

9. The Deuteronomistic Historian takes a negative attitude toward, or has no interest in, the cult and the holy place(s) (Jer 6:20).

10. "On the day of the exodus from Egypt" Yahweh did not require sacrificial worship but instead demanded obedience to ethical laws (Jer 6:20).[15]

---

13 The citations given by Thiel include Jer 26:3, 13, and, in principle, 18:8 and 42:10 ff. Yahweh's declaration through Jeremiah that he "will not regret, neither will [he] reconsider [his judgment]" (4:28) constitutes a clear contrast with these. Nevertheless, Jeremiah adds the proviso that "yet I will not utterly destroy" (4:27).

14 The Deuteronomistic Historian speaks of individual retribution in Jer 31:29 – 30, but he also suggests collective retribution in 32:18 – 19. Thiel points out that both individual and collective retribution are in harmony because the Deuteronomistic Historian views individuals in this age as more sinful than their fathers (7:26; 16:12).

15 Thiel adds, however, that there are exceptions, with the Deuteronomistic Historian adopting a positive attitude toward the cult (in particular the Sabbath regulations) in Jer 17:21– 27. Likewise, in relation to item 9, Thiel recognized that the situation with regard to the cult "is not unambiguously clear," but this statement means that the parts attributed to the Deuteronomistic Historian are mutually contradictory, thereby possibly refuting Thiel's own argument.

11. As stated in the threat of judgment that ends in the form of setting out a choice, there is a possibility of judgment against those who stay behind, unlike for those in exile.[16]
12. It is under the rule of Babylon that both the exiled and those who remain can hope for developments that will be peaceful and bear much fruit[17] (Jer 29:5 – 7; 30:10 – 31:26; 38:17 – 18).

Above I have listed the twelve points regarded by Thiel as constituting the Deuteronomistic Historian's main thought, and after each item I have given in parentheses just the results of my analysis of whether the idea is unique to the Deuteronomistic Historian. From this it is evident that items 3, 5, 6, 7 and 11 are ideas particular to the historian, while the other items are similar to the ideas in Jeremiah's authentic passages. If we accept this analysis, it means that Thiel chalks up five wins and seven losses. The question is how to evaluate this. Simply because Thiel's losses outnumber his wins does not necessarily invalidate his argument. We could also evaluate this result in a positive light, taking the view that the differences between the Deuteronomistic Historian and Jeremiah are obvious even on the basis of these five points. In any case, the analysis needs to be extended in the following directions: supplementing Thiel by asking whether, in addition to these twelve points, there are any other ideas exclusive to the Deuteronomistic Historian and, conversely, asking what happens if we more actively seek out characteristic ideas in Jeremiah's authentic passages. This might further accentuate the differences between the thought of the Deuteronomistic Historian and Jeremiah.

---

16 For this point alone Thiel suddenly fails to give any citations, but we could cite the following. With regard to the choice whereby failure to obey the law will lead to judgment while obedience results in salvation: Jer 7:1– 3, 5 – 8, 9b, 10b, 13, 15; 11:1– 14; 17:19 – 27; 18:8 – 10; 26:3, 4b–6; with regard to the choice whereby if one remains in Israel one will die, while if one descends into captivity one will live: Jer 21:8 – 10; 29:12 – 14; 38:2; 42:21 – 22; etc. These are all passages that Thiel attributes to the Deuteronomistic Historian. He does not attribute to the historian 38:17 – 18, which offers such a choice to Zedekiah—although Gunther Wanke, *Untersuchungen zur sogenannten Baruchschrift* (Berlin: de Gruyter, 1971), and others do make such an attribution. Nor does Thiel regard this as having been written by Jeremiah. Hence this choice format can be regarded as a characteristic of the Deuteronomistic Historian that is not present in Jeremiah.
17 Thiel goes on to say that the fact that the Deuteronomistic Historian also takes into consideration the demise of Babylonian rule differs from Jeremiah and that the change of heart in Jer 31:31ff occurs at the time of its demise. However, this relates to the point of debate in part 5 below and is a tenuous matter, so I shall not go into it here.

3.2 Ideas and Expressions Unique to the Deuteronomistic Historian (Other than those Cited by Thiel)

Here I can do no more than sum up my conclusions, but I would like to add to Thiel by noting the following four points as ideas and expressions unique to the Deuteronomistic Historian (citations are in the footnotes):

(a) The Deuteronomistic Historian states that judgment will be handed down if the "law" is not carried out to the letter.[18]

(b) He literally states that "if you act justly, if you do not oppress the resident alien, the orphan, and the widow, if you do not shed blood of the innocent, and if you do not follow other gods, then I will dwell forever in this land that I gave to your fathers."[19]

(c) He thinks that people who do not keep the words of the "covenant" merit a "curse."[20]

(d) He forbids intercession on behalf of the people.[21]

3.3 Ideas Unique to Jeremiah

Thiel's study, which focused on Deuteronomistic redactions, tends to overlook ideas unique to Jeremiah, but in my view the following twenty items can be identified even if we restrict ourselves just to the main points:

(i) Jeremiah intercedes on behalf of the people.[22]

(ii) He feels compassion for the people and grieves for them (the subject is Yahweh or Jeremiah, with the two frequently being conflated).[23]

(iii) Jeremiah asks for punishment and compassion for himself.[24]

(iv) He asks why the wicked prosper.[25]

(v) He asks why Yahweh does not save us.[26]

(vi) He recognizes original sin in people.[27]

---

18 Jer 6:19; 9:12–15; 16:10–13; 26:4–6.
19 Jer 7:5–7; 19:4; 22:3 (see also 12:16–17).
20 Jer 11:1–13.
21 Jer 7:16; 11:14; 14:11–12; 15:1.
22 Jer 15:11; 18:20.
23 Jer 4:19–20; 8:18–19a, 20–23; 9:9–10, 16–21; 10:17–22, 13, 27; 13:17.
24 Jer 10:23–24.
25 Jer 12:1–4.
26 Jer 14:8–9; 15:18.
27 Jer 13:23; 17:1, 9.

(vii)   He mentions sacrificial atonement.[28]

(viii)   He speaks of salvation and consolation.[29]

(ix)   He chastens Israel, but declares that it will not be annihilated.[30]

(x)   He is of the view that it is Yahweh himself who will heal Israel's backsliding.[31]

(xi)   He points out his awareness of his own sins and the people's lack of awareness of their sins.[32]

(xii)   He complains that the God who spoke of peace has deceived us.[33]

(xiii)   Jeremiah is of the view that if he can find even one righteous man, God will forgive the whole of Jerusalem.[34]

(xiv)   To those who have become rich by exploiting the weak and to those who have deceived their fellows, Jeremiah announces the vengeance of the God of retribution.[35]

(xv)   He is of the view that because of the folly of its leaders Israel will be judged.[36]

(xvi)   He is of the view that Israel should wear sackcloth and lament.[37]

(xvii)   He predicts that Israel will experience the suffering of a woman in childbirth.[38]

(xviii)   He is of the view that "we" will be judged.[39]

(xix)   He is of the view that the people should humble themselves.[40]

(xx)   He asks that God act for his name's sake.[41]

Here, in no particular order, we have ascertained that there are at least these twenty ideas[42] unique to Jeremiah, with no counterpart in the passages redacted

---

28 Jer 30:21; 31:11; 50:34.

29 Jer 30:7–31, 26; 32:15.

30 Jer 30:11; 4:27.

31 Jer 3:22.

32 Jer 3:25; 8:6.

33 Jer 4:10.

34 Jer 5:1–5.

35 Jer 5:26–31; 6:13–15 par. 8:10–12; 9:7–8.

36 Jer 10:21–22.

37 Jer 4:8; 6:26.

38 Jer 4:31; 6:24; 13:21; 22:23; 30:6.

39 Jer 8:14–16, 20; 9:17–21.

40 Jer 9:22–23; 13:18.

41 Jer 14:7.

42 In addition to these, Jeremiah censures the prophets and priests for being profane (Jer 23:11–15), he laments that God has filled him with indignation (15:17), and he reports his weakness in fearing his own death (37:21; 38:15) and in hesitating vis-à-vis the false prophet (28:11). The letter

by the Deuteronomistic Historian. In view also of Thiel's items 3, 5, 6, 7, and 11, which were cited earlier as ideas exclusive to the Deuteronomistic Historian, as well as in the light of (a)–(d) above, we can safely conclude that a meaningful divergence in ideas is established here between Jeremiah's authentic words as identified by Thiel and the Deuteronomistic Historian's redactional passages. There is not sufficient space to delve into how Thiel found each expression in the book of Jeremiah that is similar to Deuteronomy or the Deuteronomistic History and how he classified each redactional passage, but even if one might disagree on the specifics,[43] we have been able to demonstrate the effectiveness of his overall framework in terms of its ideas.

What, then, does the essence of the differences in thought between Jeremiah and the Deuteronomistic Historian boil down to in the final analysis? Based on the above considerations, our next task is to throw further light on the contrast between the two, particularly by comparing their main arguments. In order to do this, however, we must first reinforce the interpretation of a passage over which there has been debate as to whether it is the work of Jeremiah himself or the result of redaction by the Deuteronomistic Historian—a passage that is also the most important and well-known in the entire book of Jeremiah.

4 Interpretation of the "New Covenant" Prophecy: The First Point of Debate

This passage consists of the prophecy in Jeremiah 31:31–34 of a "new covenant," which has also acted as a bridge linking the Old and New Testaments.

> 31:31 Behold, the days are coming when I will make a new covenant with the house of Israel and the house of Judah. This is the oracle of Yahweh. 32 That covenant is not like the covenant that I made on the day when I grasped their fathers' hand and brought them out of the nation of Egypt. They broke that covenant of mine, Even though I was their lord. This is the oracle of Yahweh. 33 This is the covenant that I will make with the house of Israel after the days with them. This is the oracle of Yahweh. I will place my law within them, I will write it in their heart. I will be God to them, they will be a people to me. 34 In that way, people shall no longer teach their neighbor and their brother, saying, "Know Yahweh." Be-

---

to the people in exile (29:1, 3–4a, 5–7) and the words to the people concerned are also thought to be Jeremiah's own (34:3–7, 8b, 9a, 10–11; 35:2–7a, 8–11; 42:1–9; 44:25aßb, 26b, 29–30; 45:3–5). I will not, however, go into these points.

43 For instance, Masao Sekine, *Eremiya-sho Chūkai (Jō) Chosakushū Dai-jūyon Kan* (Commentary on the Book of Jeremiah, Vol. 1; Collected Works, Vol. 14) (Tokyo: Shinchi Shobō, 1981), 17 ff.

cause truly, from the least to the greatest, they shall all know me. This is the oracle of Yahweh. Truly, I will forgive their iniquity, I will not remember their sin again.

As I explained in Chapter 6, the interpretation of this famous passage, which was quoted by Paul (2Cor 3:6) and gave rise to the names of the Old and New Testaments, has been long been debated with regard to two points in particular.

The first point is the question of authorship. We might (1) treat this passage as Jeremiah's original composition; (2) treat it as the work of the Deuteronomistic Historian in a later age; or (3) assert an "essential authenticity" that attributes the essential core to Jeremiah while attributing the formal wording to the Deuteronomistic Historian. Once again Thiel provides a meticulous, redactional analysis of this point. Below, we must first closely examine each of Thiel's arguments, which are based on the second viewpoint, and ascertain the scope and diversity of this issue. In my view, the evidence put forward by Thiel can be summed up in the following six points, which I wish to consider in turn.

1) Thiel argues that "Statements about violations of the covenant appear frequently in texts dating from the period of exile, particularly in the writings of the Deuteronomistic Historian. This makes it more likely that the question being asked and explored at that time was whether the relationship between Yahweh and Israel remained more or less in effect or whether it had been fundamentally abandoned as a result of the judgment of 587 BC (Jer 14:21). Naturally, this question also expresses the ideological background of the texts concerned [31:31–34]."[44] As with many other passages, Thiel attributes this excerpt from Jeremiah 31:31 ff. to the Deuteronomistic Historian. As his primary reasons Thiel cites the fact that relations between Yahweh and Israel had broken down as a result of judgment in the form of Israel's destruction and the fact that the question of whether a "new covenant" was necessary was being asked in the time of the Deuteronomistic Historian (around 550 BCE).

Yet this question would not be odd even if it were in the future tense or posed by Jeremiah himself. This is because it is equally plausible that Jeremiah might ask whether the covenant with Israel, which was on the verge of ruin as a result of its sinful history, must be renewed. Although Thiel cites only Jeremiah 14:21, which he attributes to the Deuteronomistic Historian, Jeremiah's original words prior to that, particularly 14:7–9, are in fact an example of him asking a similar question, even if he does not use the actual word "covenant." In that case, we must conclude that Thiel's first argument

---

44 Thiel, *Die deuteronomistische Redaktion von Jeremia 26–45*, 25.

does not constitute sufficient grounds for attributing the entirety of the passage to the Deuteronomistic Historian and for hence adopting the second viewpoint rather than the third.

2) Thiel goes on to say that although the new covenant (v. 33) and Deuteronomy (Deut 6:6; 11:18; and 30:14) both underscore writing the law in one's heart, they differ in emphasis, with the former stressing this as a "gift from Yahweh" and the latter viewing it as a "demand" on mankind. Hence Thiel regards the former as a redactional passage that was based on the latter but revised it slightly.[45]

Even in such passages as Deuteronomy 30:6, however, the law is considered as a "gift from Yahweh," and Thiel's contrast overlooks the complexity of the matter. In addition, if one were to stress the differences between "gift" and "demand," then the deduction that the new covenant is not the work of the Deuteronomistic Historian should hold equally true.

3) With regard to the formula of the covenant in 33b, Thiel focuses on the fact that throughout the book of Jeremiah this is hardly used anywhere besides Deuteronomistic redactions (Jer 7:23; 11:4; 24:7; 31:1, 33; 32:38) and that it also appears in Deuteronomy and writings by the Deuteronomistic Historian (Deut 26:17, 18; 29:12; 2 Sam 7:24). In particular, Thiel argues that Jeremiah 24:7 is important in how it corresponds not only to the form but also to the mention of "know[ing] Yahweh" that appears in 31:34.

Nevertheless, as pointed out by many scholars who attribute 31:31ff. to Jeremiah,[46] this does not rule out the possibility that chapter 24 is a redactional text based on chapter 31 and that the similarity to Deuteronomistic texts can be explained by the fact that Jeremiah was placed in a Deuteronomistic environment.

4) Thiel's further observation relates to the usage of the Hebrew word *salach* (to forgive): "An investigation of the concept of *salach* reveals that most examples derive from works written during or after the period of exile. Of the thirty-three instances, only four are clearly of pre-exilic origin, and of these only one is by Jeremiah (two instances in 2Kgs 5:18, and one each in Amos 2:7 and Jer 5:7). It is during the period of exile that this concept shows up very frequently (cf. Deut 29:19 and Lam 3:42), and it particularly appears in texts by the Deuteronomistic Historian (Num 14:19, 20; 1Kgs 8:30, 34, 36, 39, 50; Jer 31:34; 36:3). As a result it is

---

45 Ibid.

46 See the passage in question in the commentaries by Thiel, Volz, Rudolph, Bright, and especially McKane (*Jeremiah*, Vol. II, 821) and M. Sekine (*Eremiya-sho Chūkai [Ge]* [Commentary on the Book of Jeremiah, Vol. 2], 41–42).

subsequently concentrated in post-exilic texts and in texts partially influenced by the historian's characteristic wording."[47]

It goes without saying, however, that this is a matter of probability, and as Thiel admits, if there are also occurrences in Jeremiah's authentic passages we cannot conclusively rule out the possibility of attributing the instance in chapter 31 to him. Of course, there is little likelihood of this, so even if we accept that these expressions are redactional passages by the Deuteronomistic Historian, this can support the third theory in favor of "essential authenticity." At any rate, it is not a decisive factor for adopting the second theory along with Thiel.

5) Thiel next focuses on the usage of the Hebrew word *berit* (covenant), stating that "Out of the twenty-four instances of the word *berit*, there is only a single example in a non-prose passage, but this verse (14:21) occurs not in the words of the prophet but in an appeal by the people."[48] Thiel's analysis concludes that, of the twenty-four examples of *berit* in the book of Jeremiah, if we set aside the four examples in Jeremiah 31:31–34, then ten are by the Deuteronomistic Historian, six postdate the Deuteronomistic Historian, and four are probably by Jeremiah.

Yet this, too, is a matter of probability, and because there are four instances attributed to Jeremiah, this argument is weak even in probabilistic terms. Thiel also argues that Jeremiah 14:21 represents an appeal by the people, but here Jeremiah is appealing to God as one of the people, and he cannot be separated out from them so distinctly. In either case, this argument likewise fails to constitute a decisive factor in choosing between theories (2) and (3).

6) Thiel goes on to say, "A look at the occurrences of the form of the covenant leads to a similar conclusion. If we exclude the addition of Jeremiah 30:22, this covenant form occurs only in texts by the Deuteronomistic Historian, and not once in the old tradition."[49]

In sum, however, Thiel is merely saying that this form occurs in five cases in the book of Jeremiah, and apart from the passage in question, 31:33, the Deuteronomistic Historian is responsible for three instances (24:7; 31:1; 32:38), and there is one instance that is not his work. This is statistically inadequate. Naturally, in view of the correspondence with Deuteronomy 29:12, I lean

---

47 Thiel, *Die deuteronomistische Redaktion von Jeremia 26–45*, 26.
48 Ibid., 27.
49 Ibid.

more toward theory (3) than theory (1), but this does not constitute a decisive factor for choosing theory (2).[50]

These six points are Thiel's main grounds for adopting the second theory, which posits the Deuteronomistic Historian as the author of the "new covenant." As demonstrated by the above analysis, however, none of these points constitute sufficient grounds for resolving the question of authorship. Even if it is difficult simply to assert theory (1), which regards Jeremiah as the author,[51] the existence of many Deuteronomistic expressions, such as *salach* and *berit*, means there were no decisive factors for determining whether the most plausible solution is theory (2), which attributes authorship to the historian, or theory (3), which posits essential authenticity. However, when we supplement Thiel's considerations, which were restricted to formal questions of terminology, with a careful examination from the substantive side of content, perhaps a conclusion might naturally emerge as to whether theory (2) or (3) is appropriate. Toward that end, we must continue our considerations and proceed to the second point of debate about the "new covenant" prophecy.

5 Interpretation of the "New Covenant" Prophecy: The Second Point of Debate

The second point of debate concerning the "new covenant" prophecy is based on whether it might be merely speaking of an eschatological utopia that is simply too divorced from reality.

Let us take a critical look at the history of interpretation. First, the commentary by Duhm, the pioneer in modern studies of Jeremiah, took the view that

---

50 Moreover, this form is also common in Exod 6:7, Ezek 14:11, Hos 2:25, Zech 8:8, etc., and it cannot be described as particularly characteristic of the Deuteronomistic Historian.
51 In recent years the leading commentary adopting viewpoint (1) is William L. Holladay, *Jeremiah 2* (Minneapolis: Fortress Press, 1989), 164–65, 197–99. In much of this commentary Holladay consistently regards most of the poetry as genuine writing by Jeremiah, and he attributes the prose to Baruch (in doing so, there is a strong tendency to give weight to the shorter Septuagint text and to regard it as the original). Holladay attempts to explain the expressions that have counterparts in Deuteronomy on the basis of the fact that Jeremiah was in a Deuteronomistic environment. However, it is difficult to explain not only the similarities to Deuteronomy, but also the word-for-word correspondence with the Deuteronomistic Historian revealed by Thiel's systematic study, and even if the nucleus of this passage traces back to Jeremiah, it seems difficult to regard all of it as genuine. In other words, I lean not toward theory (1), but toward theory (3).

grand theological interpretations of this passage need to be deflated. He was of the opinion that, like Deuteronomy 11:18, Deuteronomy 6:6 is merely prophesying the coming of a time when it will no longer be necessary for teachers of the law to sweat over imparting knowledge to slow-learning students.[52] (In recent years Levin[53] has also presented a more detailed interpretation along these lines.) As McKane[54] rightly points out, however, it seems the fact remains that such interpretations also speak of the dreams of teachers of the law, and, as with theological interpretations, they are eschatological and unrealistic.

So what is the connection with Deuteronomy in the first place? H. Schmidt, Volz, Rudolph and others have focused on this point and argued that in his early prophecies Jeremiah gradually became critical of religious reforms based on the Deuteronomic Law of King Josiah, growing convinced that what is more necessary than an external legal system are laws that are engraved on the heart and based on internal harmony and accord, and so Jeremiah prophesied this to northern Israel.[55] If we adopt such a view, then the new covenant can certainly be construed intra-historically to some extent, and perhaps the precipitousness of an eschatological interpretation can be avoided.

Yet is it really true that Deuteronomy is merely an external legal system? Such passages as the one cited earlier from Deuteronomy 30:6—"Moreover, Yahweh your God will circumcise your heart and the heart of your descendants, so that you will love Yahweh your God with all your heart and with all your soul, in order that you may live."—seem already to be stating that the law there is not imposed merely from the outside, but entails an internal change from God (see also Deut 10:16; 30:11–14; etc.). In that case, the suggestion that the early Jeremiah became dissatisfied with reforms based on the external laws of Deuteronomy and thus prophesied an internal "new covenant" in fact stands on shaky grounds.

Is Jeremiah's "new covenant" not "new" at all, then, but merely a rehashing of things already spoken about in Deuteronomy? The conclusion drawn by McKane, the scholar who has discussed this question most exhaustively in recent years, is along those lines. While mentioning the possibility that chapter 31 in the book of Jeremiah "may be a more refined longing for the kingdom of God on

---

52 Bernhard Duhm, *Das Buch Jeremia* (KHCA; Tübingen: J.C.B. Mohr, 1901), 156.

53 Christoph Levin, *Die Verheissung des Neuen Bundes: in ihrem theologiegeschichtlichen Zusammenhang ausgelegt* (FRLANT 137; Göttingen: Vandenhoeck & Ruprecht, 1985), 257–64.

54 McKane, *Jeremiah*, Vol. II, 826.

55 See the relevant sections in each commentary. For instance, Wilhelm Rudolph, *Jeremia* (HAT; 2nd ed.; Tübingen: J.C.B. Mohr, 1958), 184, links this to the prayers for the turning of Ephraim in Jer 31:18, 21, and he regards the "house of Judah" in 31:31 as belonging to v. 33 and deletes it.

earth," based on the various places in Deuteronomy cited above and on Jeremiah 24:7, which is by the Deuteronomistic Historian, as well as on similar prophecies by Ezekiel (e.g., Ezek 11:19 and 36:26), who was Jeremiah's contemporary, McKane suggests the possibility that Jeremiah's prophecies are not novel at all.[56]

If we view the reason for the "newness" of the "new covenant" as residing solely in the fact that God "will place [his] law within … their heart"—i.e., in its internalization—then such a conclusion is no doubt inevitable. Yet this prophecy by Jeremiah is not emphasizing just that point. Verse 32 touches on the history of past sins whereby they broke the covenant, but v. 34 says that Yahweh will "forgive their iniquity." Unless we ignore the fact that the reason for the "newness" of the "new covenant" also lies in these sins and their forgiveness,[57] then surely the originality of Jeremiah's prophecy remains obvious even when compared with the similar passages cited above. In my view, the issue of the unrealistic flight of fancy in this prophecy will also probably disappear when we pay close attention to this fact and reflect back on Jeremiah's prophetic activities up to that point. In the following section I would like to review the main details of his prophetic activities.

6 The Prophetic Content of Jeremiah's Authentic Texts

From the time of his early prophecies, Jeremiah consistently focuses on the sin of the Israelites.[58] He particularly censures wrongdoers who exploit the weak, such

---

56 McKane, *Jeremiah*, Vol. II, 827. McKane is of the opinion that chapters 31–33 can fundamentally be traced to Jeremiah. On the grounds that there is mention of Ephraim in Jer 31:5–6 and 15–20, he does not subscribe to the view that regards all of the references to Judah in chapters 30–31 as secondary (William McKane, "The Composition of Jeremiah 30–31," in *Texts, Temples, and Traditions* [eds. Michael V. Fox, et al.; Winona Lake, Ind.: Eisenbraun, 1996], 187–94). McKane regards chapters 26–29 and chapters 34–35 as a combination of authorship by Baruch and redactions by the Deuteronomistic Historian, but with regard to the other passages in the book of Jeremiah he follows the post-Duhm line of thought in attributing to Jeremiah most of the poetic sections and part of the prose. In relation to the correspondence with Ezekiel, he regards Jer 31–34 as drawing on Jer 36–41 and Ezek 36–37. See the view in Konrad Schmid, *Buchgestalten des Jeremiabuches* (Neukirchen-Vluyn: Neukirchener Verlag, 1996) and the criticism of this in Winfried Thiel, "Das Jeremiabuch als Literatur," *Verkündigung und Forschung* 43/2 (1998): 76–84.

57 One recent article that focuses on this point is Jože Krašovec, "Vergebung und neuer Bund nach Jer. 31, 31–34," *ZAW* 105/3 (1993): 428–44.

58 In relation to the authentic texts by Jeremiah, ever since Sigmund Mowinckel, *Zur Komposition des Buches Jeremia* (Kristiania: Jacob Dybwad, 1914) such issues as the handling of the poetic materials A and the prose materials B and the diachronic development from the early

as orphans and the poor (Jer 5:26–31; 21:12[59]). He also points out the foolishness, impurity, and deceit of the prophets and priests, who are shepherds of the people, as well as that of the scribes and sages (8:8–12; 10:21; 23:11–16, 18–22, 25–31). Nonetheless, the people as a whole generally commit wrongful acts such as murder, adultery, theft, and perjury (7:9; 9:1–5, 7; 23:10). Jeremiah's God pronounces judgment on such sins (2:9, 19, 35; 5:6–9; 6:15; 8:14; 9:10; 13:22, 26; 14:10; 15:6–9; 17:3–4; 18:6, 16; 21:14; 22:6–7), and along with portraying their suffering (4:19–31; 5:15–17; 6:7), he announces misfortune (4:5–18; 5:6, 9; 6:22–26; 7:14; 8:15–17; 14:2–6; 16:4a, 9). Yet neither the people nor the kings incline their ears to God's words of judgment (36:29–30; 45:5a). It is said that their arrogance in despising God in this way is also a form of sin (13:9, 15). Thus the Israelites continue piling up sins, all the while blithely confident that things will be fine (3:4–5; 5:12–13; 21:13). Or perhaps they blindly believe that it is the temple that will be the stronghold of their salvation (7:4). Although true human wisdom should consist of knowing and loving God (9:22–23), they fail to realize this and do not repent of their misdeeds (8:6–7). As for the prophets, who should be guiding the people, they unashamedly declare "peace, peace," though there is no peace (6:4; 8:11; 28:9). Upon being shown the people's desperate state by God (3:23–25; 8:14; 10:19–22; 14:7), Jeremiah continues to censure the people and to lament (4:19–20; 5:1–5; 6:10–11; 8:18–19a, 20–23; 9:16–21; 13:17; 14:7). This often leads to discord not only between Jeremiah and the people to whom he has conveyed unpalatable messages, but also between Jeremiah, who wants to appease the people, and God, who ultimately pronounces judgment. No one else in the Old Testament responds so sensitively to the difficulties of the prophet's position, where friction with God and the people is inevitable, and repeatedly appeals this directly to God. Such appeals are spelled out intricately in the series of "confessions" (12:1–6; 15:10–21; 17:14–18; 18:18–23; 20:7–18), and the passage located at the end of this seems to conclude in a desperation verging on suicidal despair, challenging the God who granted him life (20:14–18; the only comparable passage in the Old Testament is Job 3:1 ff.). Although it is not a confession and it is unclear when it was written, the prayer

period to the later period can be problematic. Here, however, I will omit a detailed philological discussion and restrict myself to a rough synchronic overview. In connection to such matters as the authenticity and historical background of each text, I have included a list in the pertinent notes and commentary in my translation of Jeremiah in *Eremiya-sho* (The Book of Jeremiah) (Tokyo: Iwanami Shoten, 2002). On pp. 340–41 in that book and in note 7, above, I have listed the passages that Thiel attributes to the Deuteronomistic Historian.

59 Together with Thiel, I attribute Jer 7:7 and 22:3, which also mention foreigners and widows, to the Deuteronomistic Historian.

in 10:23 – 24, where Jeremiah becomes aware of his own sin and begs forgiveness, is inferred to be the product of a time when the prophet, who had cockily challenged God, realizes his sins. It conveys the image of Jeremiah bowing his head before God and begging for punishment and compassion.

In this way it becomes clear that sin is not merely censured in relation to Israel alone, but also resides within the prophet himself. And the realization he eventually arrived at in relation to the sins to which all people fall prey was the hopeless one that this multi-layered mechanism of sin derives from the fact that people's hearts are inherently and naturally recalcitrant.

> Can Cushites change their skin, or leopards their spots? Then you, who are accustomed to do evil, can also do good. (Jer 13:23)
>
> Unrighteous above all else is the heart, it is sick. Who can know it? (Jer 17:9)

Jeremiah says that the reason people resist obeying God is that it is human nature and that the source of their rebellion lies in the very fact that they have not been circumcised in their hearts (Jer 6:10; 9:24 – 25[60]). Jeremiah arrived at a hopeless insight into original evil or sin, which governs all of human existence. Yet the ray of hope he left in the end was the salvation, healing of wounds, comfort, joy, and absolution that come from God, which occurs after judgment (10:18; 30:5 – 8,[61] 12 – 24; 31:1 – 14; 46:27 – 28; 50:19 – 20). To put it more plainly, it is the people's change of heart (31:33) based on the "new covenant" from God, which encapsulated the way of hope, and the forgiveness of sin (31:34).[62]

When seen in this light, both issues involving this prophecy of a "new covenant" can be resolved. Far from being a wild and unrealistic fancy or a boon awaited passively by indolent people (the second point of debate), this text is none other than a leap of faith toward salvation through the power of another, as the inevitable corollary of realizing the impossibility of salvation through one's own efforts—a conclusion reached after despairingly recognizing one's

---

60 There is a similar expression in Jer 4:4, but I agree with Thiel that this should be attributed to the Deuteronomistic Historian.

61 Jeremiah 30:10 – 11 also speaks of salvation, but this is absent from the Septuagint, and it is repeated more or less verbatim in 46:27– 28, so I would interpret it as a later redactional passage based on Second Isaiah (Isa 41:8 – 9, 13 – 14; 43:1, 5; etc.).

62 Hisao Miyamoto's essay "Eremiya no Kokuhaku: Atarashii Keiyaku o Nuku Gengo Kūkan" (Jeremiah's Confessions: The Language Space Threading the New Covenant), a gem that offers a rare synthesis of philosophical and philological reflections on Jeremiah's confessions, finds already present in the language space of the confessions themselves the process that leads to the "new covenant." The essay appears in Hisao Miyamoto, *Seisho to Aichi: Kenōshisu o Megutte* (The Bible and Philosophy: Concerning Kenosis) (Tokyo: Shinseisha, 1991), 531– 85.

sins and trying to alter one's ways. Criticizing this as a wild fancy would surely mean having to reject religion itself.

Moreover, the author of this core part must be Jeremiah (the first point of debate). This is because a Jeremian prophecy lacking the new covenant passage would ultimately fall into a quagmire of disgust, judgment, grumbling, and resentment against the people's sins, and it would lack the finishing touch. Conversely, the prophecy only comes to life when the lamp of this hope is lit. It resolves the hopeless awareness of human original sin, which is otherwise an object of disgust and judgment, and leads one to discover the certain and ordered path of salvation, wherein hope rests solely in the "new covenant" from God. The content of Jeremiah's prophecies, then, requires the prophecy of a "new covenant" as their necessary conclusion.

Some, however, might still disagree. After all, Jeremiah's prophecies do adopt a middle-of-the-road position. Would it be so mistaken to think it was the Deuteronomistic Historian who compensated for their deficiencies and added the finishing touch? Logically speaking, there is room for such an argument. Yet was that something of which the Deuteronomistic Historian was ultimately capable? When we finally reexamine the redactions by the Deuteronomistic Historian and, in particular, examine the contours of his thought carefully, do we not reach a conclusion as to whether his ideas have that potential? And does not the final answer to this question about authorship of the "new covenant" also naturally emerge then?

7 A Comparison of the Ideas of the Deuteronomistic Historian and Jeremiah

In Part 2 we compared how the Deuteronomistic Historian and Jeremiah responded to false prophets. After Judah's destruction, the Deuteronomistic Historian speaks in what might be regarded as an assured manner, full of post facto prophetic confidence. By contrast, we noticed that in the turmoil of his times Jeremiah speaks in a self-relativizing manner while struggling somewhat more. This, in fact, seems to be a fairly essential distinction between their ideas.

A major characteristic of the Deuteronomistic Historian's manner of speaking is that he talks categorically of the threat of judgment as a choice between salvation if one obeys the law and judgment if one disobeys. This is evident in idea 11 mentioned in Part 3, which, according to Thiel, is exclusive to the Deuteronomistic Historian, and it is also evident in supplementary points (a), (b), and (c). Let us extract the Deuteronomistic Historian's redactional passages from Jeremiah 11 and 21:

11:3b Let anyone who does not obey the words of this covenant be cursed. … 4b "Listen to and follow my voice, and do everything that I command you. Then you shall be my people, and I will be your God." 5 This was so that I might perform the oath that I swore to your fathers, to give them a land flowing with milk and honey, as at this day. […] 10b The house of Israel and the house of Judah have broken my covenant that I made with their fathers. 11 Therefore, thus says Yahweh. "Behold, I am going to bring misfortune upon them" … 14 Do not pray for this people. Do not lift up a cry or prayer for them. For indeed, I will not listen when they call me in the time of misfortune."

21:8b Thus says Yahweh. "Behold, I am placing before you the way of life and the way of death. 9a The one who stays in this city shall die by the sword, by famine, and by plague. But the one who goes out [of this city] and surrenders to the Chaldeans who are besieging you shall live."

As Thiel points out, the Deuteronomistic Historian's redactional intention of informing the people at the time of exile that their hope of salvation lay in the land of exile can be detected in Jeremiah 21. The Deuteronomistic Historian put these words in the mouth of Jeremiah and, on Jeremiah's authority, announced them to the people of his time. The moralistic thought typical of the Deuteronomistic Historian is also striking in Jeremiah 11. One is saved if one leads a moral life based on Deuteronomic law, but otherwise judgment will fall on one. According to the Deuteronomistic Historian, salvation is achieved by performing righteous deeds through one's own strength. This is the first point of contention that characterizes the thought of the Deuteronomistic Historian.

This leads directly to the second point. In his early period Jeremiah also sought the way of self-salvation through righteous deeds. As stated above, however, he gradually became aware of the depth of original sin that he too shared with others, and he despaired of salvation through his own strength. On the other hand, nowhere in the Deuteronomistic Historian is there any such awareness of his own sin or a realization of the gravity of original sin. Of course, the Deuteronomistic Historian is not entirely without an awareness of sin:

You yourselves have done more evil than your fathers, and behold, each of you has walked according to your stubborn, evil heart, and you have not listened to me. (Jer 16:12; see also 7:26)

Nevertheless, ultimately this is "your" sin, and it does not develop into the deep awareness of original sin entertained by Jeremiah, that "all the house of Israel has not received circumcision at heart" (Jer 9:25b).[63] Instead, the Deuteronomis-

---

63 Admittedly, in Jer 4:4 the Deuteronomistic Historian does speak of being uncircumcised in

tic Historian goes on to say, "Therefore I will cast you out; from this land into a land that you and your fathers have not known" (Jer 16:13a), and he merely proceeds to a theodicean apologetic that Israel's destruction and the Babylonian exile were Yahweh's violation of the covenant. Whether or not intended that way, this must have constituted a defense of the established religious order to which the Deuteronomistic Historian himself belonged.

According to the Deuteronomistic Historian's view of God—this is the third point of debate—in the final analysis Yahweh is a being who steers history through the righteousness of moral retribution, and he is merely a being based on the law of mundane rationality along the lines of a bilateral agreement. Hence, as in the quotation above (Jer 11:14), this God flatly rejects things that run counter to rational laws of retribution, such as intercession by prophets (also see 7:16; 14:11–12; 15:1, which are related to point [d] in Part 3; this was stressed repeatedly because, in the retributive logic of the Deuteronomistic Historian, it was a point that could not be conceded). By contrast, Jeremiah's God was a God who could not be measured by such purely intellectual logic. That is exactly why, as pointed out in (i) in Part 3, Jeremiah does not give up interceding for God to rescind his punishment against the people's sins[64] (15:11; 18:20; see also 37:3). I agree with the observation by a philosopher that "the divine-human relationship [as understood by the Deuteronomistic Historian] is a tie relying solely on a pure, purposeful and intellectual logic ... just as is generally the case with legal contracts ... and it is a stark and dry relationship that totally excludes any irrational, emotional elements."[65] In a view of God where such an intellectual logic and morality reign supreme, the irrational and emotional elements in religious experience would be discarded, and the desperate dialogue with God, the question-

---

the heart, but he goes on to say "remove the foreskins of your heart," and this fails to constitute an awareness of immutable original sin.

64 While struggling, Jeremiah continued to seek salvation from God despite the people's multitude of sins, but there is absolutely no such struggling or appealing to God on the part of the Deuteronomistic Historian. Instead, according to the Historian, people's righteousness or lack thereof automatically leads to salvation or judgment. When compared in this way, it might seem that Thiel's point 3 constitutes counter-evidence, but this is merely because Thiel, in context, discusses only a "reconsideration" of judgment. The Deuteronomistic Historian's expression belongs to the lineage of the moral alternative format whereby if one does good then God "will reconsider the misfortune," but if one does evil he "will reconsider the fortune" (in particular, see Jer 18:7–10, which Thiel describes as a "principle"). Here it is too difficult to dislodge the dogma of retribution whereby good actions lead to good outcomes and bad deeds lead to bad outcomes.

65 Yasuo Yuasa, *Yungu to Kirisuto-kyō* (Jung and Christianity), *Zenshū Dai-san kan* (Collected Works, Vol. 3) (Tokyo: Hakua Shobō, 2002), 189.

ing of God's irrationality, and a lively communion such as in Jeremiah's confessions would be erased. By contrast, among those ideas exclusive to Jeremiah that we noted in Part 3, items such as (iv), (v) and (xii) essentially hint that there fomented within Jeremiah a questioning of whether God truly is steering history through retributive justice.

> ... Let me speak with you concerning justice.
> Why does the way of the wicked prosper,
> And why are all who commit treachery at ease? (Jer 12:1b)

By contrast, such frank doubts are quickly disguised in the Deuteronomistic Historian, and as in the earlier quotation (Jer 16:12–13a), he tends simply to ignore the breakdown of actual retribution, whereby the righteous and the covenant people perish and the evil and heathens prosper. Or he insists on clinging to the framework of the dogma of retribution and covenant logic, arguing that those who perished did so because they violated the covenant, and he tends to give a forced interpretation of the reality (as Thiel, for instance, also mentions [(1) in Part 2 above]; see also Jer 40:2b–3, which is a typical formula by the Deuteronomistic Historian).

Let us sum all this up. According to the Deuteronomistic Historian, first, salvation is achieved by people doing righteous deeds through their own strength. Second, in line with this, people's sins cannot be so grave that they can only be wiped away by clinging to the strength of another. Third, God was understood intellectually and rationally within a framework of moral retribution, not as a being encountered in a faith-struggle with irrational and emotional people, as was the case with Jeremiah. It is virtually inconceivable, therefore, that the "new covenant" prophecy in chapter 31 is the work of the Deuteronomistic Historian. This is because the prophecy proclaims that, regardless of one's own righteous deeds by one's own strength, salvation is granted through the strength of another, and this presupposes grave "sins" and "iniquities" from which one cannot otherwise be saved. Another reason is that this is an irrational, amoral grace that transcends the rational and moral retribution of the God who will "write [the law] in their heart" (see also Thiel's second point introduced in Part 4 and Hisao Miyamoto's essay[66]).

---

[66] Miyamoto's essay introduced in note 62 is unassailable where he addresses this point. "Judah cannot appeal to the Sinai and Davidic covenants, which were transformed into traditional and external matters, but it must become authentically aware of its own infidelity, pledge its heart to God, and become a new humanity once again. This is not, however, something that is possible for powerless humans. It is a mystery within history that occurs only to those people

In that case, the question pending since Part 4 as to the authorship of the "new covenant" prophecy is settled here. This prophecy is too dissimilar to the fundamental ideas of the Deuteronomistic Historian and cannot be his work. Instead, as we saw in Part 6, it must be the verdict reached by Jeremiah after his lifelong struggle with God and after a deepening of his understanding of sin and forgiveness.

8 Revisiting Questions about Authenticity: The Task of Philosophical Interpretation

This brings us back to our starting point, where the Deuteronomistic Historian was no more than a forger purporting to be a true prophet, similar to the forged paintings and antique instruments mentioned at the outset of the chapter. While conducting a historical examination of Thiel's redaction history, I have focused on its theological ideas and developed my argument in the direction of philosophical interpretation. Unlike theological interpretation, however, philosophical interpretation does not presuppose faith to be self-evident, so it can take a decisive step when it reaches the point of expressing value judgments about the validity of the theological ideas. We are already moving toward philosophical reflections on religious experience, so here at the end it is necessary to take this extra step intentionally. This must deal not only with the value judgments that historical criticism has been apt to make in the past. Guided by the yearning for true value that emerges on the other side of criticizing counterfeit value, it must also be accompanied by an examination of their validity.[67]

---

who have had their hard hearts broken by God's grace. Jeremiah gained insight into a universally significant community of hidden and small people who are newly resurrected in the midst of Judah's destruction and establish a covenant with God. It is the very 'new covenant' of which he speaks that threads the rounded horizon of this new people (31:27–34)." See "Eremiya no Kokuhaku" (Jeremiah's Confessions), 80–1.

67 Upon reflection, I realize that Tomonobu Imamichi provided a beacon for my grounding the present work in philosophical interpretation. Tracing all the way back to Homer's *Iliad*, he opened my eyes to the fact that "in classical Greek usage, and therefore in Western culture's orthodox and traditional usage, *critique* reflects an attitude of longing that 'yearns for value and chooses it selectively.' It does not carry the connotation found in Eastern criticism, which connotes a negative judgment or criticism handed down by a person of superior rank. We must not forget that this attitude of *critique* that expects and longs to find value in something is the motivation behind interpretation." Tomonobu Imamichi, "Hihyō to Kuritīku" (Criticism and Critique) in *Bi no Isō to Geijutsu* (Phases of Beauty and the Arts) (Tokyo: University of Tokyo Faculty of Letters, Department of Aesthetics, 1968), 353–34. I wish to express my gratitude to

The Deuteronomistic Historian clung persistently to a notion of God rooted in retributive dogma and tradition, a view that should have been in jeopardy as a result of Israel's destruction. The destruction of the nation and the period of exile should have presented a valuable opportunity to unsettle such a view of God as guiding history and the concept of a personal God constrained by a rational covenant. The appearance in Job 38 ff. of an amoral God who shatters Job's idea of retribution, and the nihilism of Qohelet, who declares "Vanity of vanities, all is vanity," are examples of the dramatic development of such a view of God in the Old Testament,[68] as discussed in Chapter 4. Ultimately, however, the Deuteronomistic Historian never progressed in that direction. Would it be overly harsh to say that instead he falsified past history from the perspective of a traditional, entrenched retribution ideology, thereby preventing modifications to their view of God and reforms of their religion, and that he upheld the conventional religious order exactly as it was?

As seen in the earlier argument by Yoshida, however, the economic issues surrounding forgeries affect religion as well. It is necessary to point out that as long as the Deuteronomistic Historian was on the payroll of a conventional religious order, he was an old-guard ideologue, or at least his views incorporated those aspects. Naturally, to some extent we can and even should argue that in those days there was of course no awareness of matters such as copyright and that people jotted down redactional sentences in the belief that they were a revelation from one and the same God, erasing their own insignificant names in the shadow of the prophet's eminent name. Nevertheless, the Deuteronomistic Historian failed to grasp the true intent of the prophet's religious reforms, and he even became a force opposing them. Hence he is not free from blame for falsifying the prophet's words and ultimately making it difficult to discern the thrust of the reforms leading to the prophet's "new covenant."

These negative criticisms are not the important thing here. Rather, I wish to determine some positive value beyond them. Thiel's comprehensive redaction history shed light on these redactions by the Deuteronomistic Historian, but

---

him. On the contrast between "fact" and "truth," see Tomonobu Imamichi, "Shisō toshite no Kyūyaku Shakugi" (Old Testament Exegesis as Philosophy), in *Shisō* (Thought) (Vol. 855; Tokyo: Iwanami Shoten, 1995), 149.

68 For a more detailed and outstanding observation from a philosophical and psychological perspective concerning Job's moral debate and the appearance of an amoral God who transcended it, see Yuasa, *Yungu to Kirisuto-kyō*, esp. 190. On the relation between that and the Deuteronomistic Historian, see my commentary in Yuasa's Collected Works in "*Yungu to Kirisuto-kyō* to Sono Zengo o Yomu" (Reading *Jung and Christianity* and Works Around Then), 413. With regard to Qohelet, see "Qohelet as a Nihilist," Chapter 2 in my *Transcendency and Symbols in the Old Testament* (trans. Judy Wakabayashi; Berlin: Walter de Gruyter, 1999).

we also need to rescue from obscurity the prophet lingering in his shadow. Until we leave behind the Deuteronomistic contaminants and pursue the message of Jeremiah's authentic words, the work of redaction-historical research is not complete. We will see the greatest fruit when we shine light on this point.

In reality, for the prophet and the people to encounter the living God, they would have had to abandon dogma that sought to parse matters at the intellectual level through moral judgments and legal logic. Because human beings' experience of God is a transcendental one that rises above the intellect and is felt in the heart, this experience should far transcend the objective workings of God in history that are logically foreseeable through the dogma of moral retribution and the bilateral covenant. Admittedly, perhaps "it is not impossible to discern the workings of an absolute being in the mysteries of physical space and the large movements of history,"[69] but before conjecturing about the existence of God in such a dimension, we should realize that "We must ask about the relationship with God in the world inside our own hearts. In other words, the passage of internal psychological experience is a narrow entrance leading to the world of religious experience."[70] God's statement in Jeremiah's "new covenant" that "I will place my law within them, I will write it in their heart" (31:33) proclaims the attainment of awareness on the part of the prophet who, after numerous vicissitudes, was shown where such a "narrow entrance" is hidden after all.

Moreover, the passage from this entrance was opened up through an awareness of the sin of breaking "the covenant that I made" (Jer 31:32) and through forgiveness by the God who "will forgive their iniquity, [and] … will not remember their sin again" (31:34). And that is not all. It is not just that "their" sins and iniquities are abhorred and condemned; this corresponds with the realization of sin on the part of the prophet, who passed judgment on himself, saying, "Discipline me, O Yahweh" (10:24), and also with a consciousness of fundamental evil whereby "unrighteous above all else is the heart, it is sick" (17:9). Here the prophet discovered the narrow path leading to God.

Philosophical interpretation intentionally adheres to, and raises questions from, the horizon of the interpreter. Upon reading through the book of Jeremiah, many interpreters wonder how to understand the differences between sections that give off a faint whiff of dogmatism and sections that speak directly to our hearts. The more readers share this concern, the more likely it is that philosophical interpretation will be viewed as a valid approach, but it is impossible to estimate the number of such readers in advance. Philosophical interpretation sim-

---

69 Yuasa, *Yungu to Kirisuto-kyō* (Jung and Christianity), 190.
70 Ibid.

ply issues the following challenge. Only when we have identified the authentic texts by taking advantage of redaction-historical research can we leave behind questions about true and false views of the prophet, or the contradictions between authentic and counterfeit texts attributed to him. And only then can we encounter the original spirit found throughout the text and open up a way to hear the subtle pulse and breathing of the spirit of this prophet who transcended ossified dogma.

In this chapter, I have added my own critical analysis to the redaction-historical work of Thiel and McKane, who adorned the end of the last century with their research. In doing so, I have argued for the need for critical discussion not only of the oft-praised positive aspects of redaction, which comprises a theodicy based on a grand historical view, but also of its negative aspects as a counterfeit. Moreover, I propose that removing the counterfeit parts makes it especially important to seek a direction for new readings obtained by encountering Jeremiah's authentic passages, which emerge in pure form. By accumulating these readings, I wish to find the core treasure from this inscrutable text that has acquired many layers of history's deposits. Dissatisfied with both the traditional determination of historical facts and the disparagement of its critical value, philosophical interpretation will at least continue to proclaim the necessity of such research. The present chapter is but one small attempt to speak of these prospects and hopes and to offer a tentative, foundational outline toward that end.

I wish to add this note in conclusion. According to Hideo Kobayashi, whom I cited above, in order to distinguish between authentic and counterfeit works one must be trained through contact only with authentic works. In one of her short stories, however, Kuniko Mukōda makes a different point about the criterion for distinguishing between authentic and counterfeit works—"whether there is warmth or not."[71] This is absolutely correct. My verdict is that there is certainly warmth in Jeremiah, but not in the Deuteronomistic Historian. I leave it up to the reader to determine whether there is warmth in this verdict of mine.

---

71 Kuniko Mukōda, *Nemuru Sakazuki* (The Sleeping Cup) (Tokyo: Kodansha Bunko, 1982), 191.

Part IV **Old Testament Studies in Japan**

Chapter 8 Old Testament Studies in Japan: A Retrospect and Prospects

Introduction

The Society for Old Testament Study in Japan, established in 1933, has the longest history among Japan's academic societies related to Christianity. It turned 77 in 2010. In terms of human age, in Japan one's 77th year is a special cause for celebration known as *kiju*. It had been 22 years since the Society compiled its *55-Year History of the Society for Old Testament Study in Japan* in 1988, so it seemed fitting to commemorate the Society's 77th year by reflecting on its past and future. With that in mind, in 2009 the Society's steering committee planned a symposium on "Old Testament Studies in Japan," and this was also chosen as the theme of the new president's address.

I shall divide this lecture into two parts. In the first part I shall reflect on the history of Old Testament academic societies and scholarship in Japan, with a special emphasis on the latter—that is, Old Testament scholarship. Based upon this, in the second two I wish to suggest some future directions for Old Testament scholarship and, in particular, the Society's future. The aim of addressing both these aspects is for us to reconsider the past and future of "Old Testament studies in Japan."

1 A Retrospect

1.1 A Brief History of the Society for Old Testament Study in Japan and the Japanese Biblical Institute

The Society for Old Testament Study in Japan has been ecumenical ever since its establishment in 1933. The foundation of Old Testament studies in Japan was laid in the following way. In the beginning, around 20 Old Testament scholars gathered together for monthly meetings. During World War II these regular meetings were frequently interrupted because many of the members were engaged in translating and editing the Japanese Colloquial Bible (*Kōgoyaku Seisho*), which would replace the Classical Japanese Bible (*Bungoyaku Seisho*), and they were also called to serve in the military. Regular meetings resumed after the war, and the Society continued meeting monthly until 1965. It then switched to meeting twice a year, and it has continued doing so down to the present day. The Society is active. It currently has around 150 members, and it has published *Kyūya-*

kugaku Kenkyū (*Old Testament Studies*), the Society's academic journal, since 2004. It has had the following presidents: Zenta Watanabe, Senji Tsuru, Giichirō Tezuka, Jun'ichi Asano, Yoshishige Sakon, Masao Sekine, Kōki Nakazawa, Kiyoshi Sakon, Ken'ichi Kida, Toshiaki Nishimura, Kōichi Namiki, Akio Tsukimoto, and Seizō Sekine.

Kiyoshi Sakon has divided the history of the Society for Old Testament Study in Japan through 1988 into four periods: (1) the cradle period, 1933–50; (2) the formative period, 1950–67; (3) the developmental period, 1967–79; and (4) the reconstitution period, 1979–88. If we accept this periodization, we can now add (5) the redevelopment period, 1988–2000; and (6) the stable period, 2000–.[1]

I shall now add a few words about the Japanese Biblical Institute, a related organization. The Institute was founded in 1950, seventeen years after the Society for Old Testament Study, and ever since then it has held regular monthly meetings at which an Old Testament scholar and a New Testament scholar each give a research presentation. Namiki points out that whereas the Society for Old Testament Study provides a venue for research exchange among people who are interested in the Old Testament and also engaged in local pastoral work, the Institute is centered in Tokyo and aims to promote research in biblical studies that is more academic in nature (Namiki's statement is correct).[2] The Institute has published *Seishogaku Ronshū* (*Anthology of Biblical Studies*) annually since 1962 (with a few exceptions) and, with the aim of presenting the results of Japanese biblical scholarship to a global audience, it has published the *Annual of the Japanese Biblical Institute* (AJBI) every year since 1975. As a result, Japanese biblical scholarship has received some degree of international recognition. The Institute has also stimulated interest in the Bible within Japan through its translation and publication of the Dead Sea Scrolls (1963, first edition) and the Apocrypha and Pseudepigrapha (1975–82, 7 volumes and 2 supplemental editions).[3] It has had the following presidents (or directors): Tsutomu Oshio, Masao Sekine, Sasagu Arai, Ken'ichi Kida, Takashi Ōnuki, and Akio Tsukimoto. Currently, it has about seventy fellows and ninety members.

---

1 Kiyoshi Sakon, "Nihon no Kyūyaku Gakkai Ryakushi: Daini-ki, 1950–1988" (A Brief History of the Society for Old Testament Study in Japan: The Second Period, 1950–1988), in *Nihon Kyūyaku Gakkai 55 Nenshi* (A 55-Year History of the Society for Old Testament Study in Japan) (1989): 28.
2 Kiyoshi Tsuchido, Kōichi Namiki, Wataru Mizugaki, Yoshinobu Tōbō, Yasuo Furuya, Seiichi Yagi, "Zadankai: Gakkai no Kako to Gakkai no Mirai" (Round-table Talk: The Past of Academic Studies and the Future of the Society), in *Nihon no Shingaku* 41 (*Theological Studies in Japan* 41) (2002): 245.
3 *Shikai Monjo: Tekisuto no Hon'yaku to Kaisetsu* (The Dead Sea Scrolls: Translation and Commentary) (Tokyo: Yamamoto Shoten 1963); *Seisho Gaiten Giten* (Biblical Apocrypha and Pseudepigrapha) (Tokyo: Kyōbunkan 1975–82).

1.2 Brief Overview of International Research Achievements

In order to look back on Japanese Old Testament scholarship, we must now review the achievements of numerous individuals. This is a delicate task. One might wonder why I discuss certain achievements and overlook others. To avoid personal arbitrariness and bias, I shall follow an objective standard regarding which achievements to mention. First, let us distinguish between achievements in European languages and achievements in Japanese. The reason for this stems from my concurrent preparations for this address and the essay, "Hebrew Bible / Old Testament Studies in Asia," which was commissioned by Vandenhoeck and Ruprecht for inclusion in the final volume of their *Hebrew Bible / Old Testament* series. I have no special reason other than that. It is for the sake of convenience that I have distinguished between works made accessible for readers of European languages only and works in Japanese. I do think, however, that this distinction might also be somewhat valid for members of the Society for Old Testament Study in Japan.

For achievements published in European languages, I shall restrict myself to the lectures and works of Japanese scholars who have given invitational addresses to the International Organization for the Study of the Old Testament (IOSOT). For Japanese-language achievements, I wish to focus on major works by past presidents of the Society for Old Testament Study. I shall limit myself to the above for introducing the content of various works. Because this approach would result, however, in only a very small number of works, I also wish to mention some additional authors and their publications. Following these criteria, I present below an overview of the research achievements of which I am aware. This essay needs to be supplemented in the future. I hope to receive and examine corrections of my limited overview and, if given the opportunity at some later point, to revise and expand it.

The first Japanese to be invited to the International Organization for the Study of the Old Testament was Masao Sekine. In 1944 he submitted his doctoral dissertation, "Die Einzigkeit Gottes im Alten Testament," and received his Th.D. at Halle University, but his dissertation was not published in German. Sekine's magnum opuses are *Isuraeru Shūkyō Bunka-shi* (Religious Cultural History of Israel), published by Iwanami Shoten in 1951, and *Kyūyaku Seisho Bungaku-shi: Jōge* (History of Old Testament Literature: Volumes 1 and 2), published by Iwanami Shoten in 1978 and 1980. Unfortunately, these have not been translated into any European languages. In 1977, however, at the IOSOT meeting in Göttingen,

Sekine presented his ideas for the latter work in a paper titled "Wie ist eine israelitische Literaturgeschichte möglich?",[4] so I shall introduce its contents.

In his history of Israelite literature, Sekine incorporates the results of introduction studies, and he begins by pointing out his use of literary research. He
states that views on the Pentateuch or Hexateuch are in a state of flux today,
but that he would follow the traditional line of introduction studies. He argues
that, though one can no longer say it is sufficient to construct a literary history as
a history of biblical genres, as Gunkel did, he would also part ways with literary
research. The reason, he says, is that a history of literature must be a historical
narrative. However, states Sekine, one must recognize that "literature" should
not be understood in the narrow sense of modern European literature and
that the literature of ancient peoples cannot be divorced from religion. For example, in ancient Japanese literature there is the fundamental theme of traveling
across the divine sea to visit the Japanese archipelago and then returning to
the other side of the sea after a period of time. In the literature of Israel in the
desert, there is the theme of a divine being suddenly assailing a human (Gen
32:23–33; Exod 4:24–26). In those life-or-death instances, the human's fate is determined by blessings and curses spoken in rhythmical literary language by God
or human. Sekine concludes that the question of life and death forms the fundamental theme in the history of Israelite literature. And for this reason, he argues,
the law, which protects the shalom of the individual and the community, can also
fall within the purview of a literary history.

Sekine thinks that the Israelites perceived beauty in literature within the crisis of struggling with life and death before God (Gen 22; Isa 6). While death, for
the Israelites, meant separation from God, this beauty in crisis pointed to a situation wherein coexistence with God is restored through salvation from death
and separation (Isa 53).

Furthermore, in order to construct a narrative history of literature, Sekine incorporates the rules of experience through Weberian sociology's "nomological
knowledge" and attempts to fill the gaps in the limited sources. As a sociological
working hypothesis, he then envisages the periods of each familial, tribal, feder-
ate tribal, national, and religious community. He argues that each period has its
own fundamental literary spirit (for example, "dependence" in the patriarchal
period, "austerity" for tribal communities). Sekine also observes that the distinc-
tiveness of biblical language lies in how it doubly portrays the human world
from the original fact of God (for example, the epic battle song of Deborah

---

4 Masao Sekine, "Wie ist eine israelitische Literaturgeschichte möglich?" in *Congress Volume
Göttingen 1977* (Supplements to Vetus Testamentum 29; Leiden: Brill, 1978), 285–97.

and the history of God; the lyricality of David's song of the bow and God's hidd-
enness; the created and evil nature of the Yahwist's serpent; the words of judgment and words of salvation by the writing prophets). Sekine constructs a history of Israelite literature that draws together these various perspectives.

Masao Sekine served as director of the Biblical Institute from 1958 to 1988
and as president of the Society for Old Testament Study from 1970 to 1979. He
was a driving force within Old Testament studies in Japan, and he left behind
a large body of research in twenty volumes—including scholarly papers and commentaries about the Old Testament and his thoughts on Christian evangelism—
as well as his own translation of the entire Old Testament.

The next Japanese to be invited to give a lecture at IOSOT was Tomoo Ishida.
Ishida's doctoral dissertation at Hebrew University, "The Royal Dynasties in Ancient Israel: A Study on the Formation and Development of Royal-Dynastic Ideology," was the first volume by a Japanese scholar to be published in the BZAW
series,[5] one of the most prestigious series in the international field of Old Testament studies. Another English publication by Ishida is *Studies in the History and
Culture of the Ancient Near East.*[6] Here I would like to give an overview of the
former work.

By way of introduction, in Chapter One Ishida examines Albrecht Alt's thesis
that in Israel's establishment of royal dynasties there existed a charismatic ideal
that was at odds with the principle of hereditary succession. Because the Israelites requested "a king to govern us, like other nations" (1Sam 8:5), in Chapter
Two, "The Dynastic Principle in the Monarchies in the Ancient Near East," Ishida
examines the monarchies in Mesopotamia, Egypt, and the nations of Syria-Pal-
estine, and he concludes that the dynastic principle of hereditary succession was
everywhere predominant. In Chapter Three, "The Ideological Problems in the Establishment of the Monarchy in Israel," Ishida begins by treating the problem of
conflict between the prophet Samuel and King Saul, and he finds there vestiges
of anti-monarchical sentiments at the time of the monarchy's establishment. Yet
he argues that these sentiments were swiftly suppressed and that the monarchi-
cal system of government was approved. Chapter Four, "The Legitimation of the
Kingship of David," confirms the process by which David, in order to meet the
requirements of dynastic succession, marries Saul's daughter Michal (1Sam
18:27) and thus secures the right of royal succession as the king's son (1Sam
24; 26). In Chapter Five, "The Royal-Dynastic Ideology of the House of David,"

---

5 Tomoo Ishida, *The Royal Dynasties in Ancient Israel: A Study on the Formation and Development of Royal-Dynastic Ideology* (Beihefte zur Zeitschrift für die alttestamentliche Wissenschaft 142; Berlin: W. de Gruyter, 1977).
6 Tomoo Ishida, *Studies in the History and Culture of the Ancient Near East* (Leiden: Brill, 1999).

and in Chapter Six, "The House of David and Jerusalem," Ishida further argues that events such as Nathan's prophecy, the capture of Jerusalem, and the carrying of the ark of God to Jerusalem were part of the religio-political process necessary for David to be recognized by northern Israel. In Chapter Seven, "The Problem at the Passing of the Royal Throne," and Chapter Eight, "Conclusions," Ishida argues that the principle of primogeniture long continued to function in southern Judah, but that hereditary succession was unstable in northern Israel. He concludes, however, that this owed largely to geopolitical factors and that there was no fundamental difference between Judah and Israel on the principle of dynastic succession.

The third Japanese to be invited to deliver an IOSOT lecture was Seizō Sekine. His doctoral dissertation at the University of Munich, "Die Tritojesajanische Sammlung (Jes 56–66) redaktionsgeschichtlich untersucht," was also published in the BZAW series.[7] Sekine has published one more monograph in the BZAW series—*Transcendency and Symbols in the Old Testament: A Genealogy of the Hermeneutical Experiences*[8]—and he has also published *A Comparative Study of the Origins of Ethical Thought: Hellenism and Hebraism* with Rowman & Littlefield Publishers.[9] Here I shall briefly introduce the contents of *Transcendency and Symbols in the Old Testament.*

The subject of this monograph is aspects of, and a solution to, a fundamental problem of the "Old Testament"—namely, where does one encounter "transcendency." Sekine approaches this through reading the Old Testament text as "symbol." As the subtitle "A Genealogy of the Hermeneutical Experiences" indicates, this reading is developed by confronting the extensive body of traditional historical and objective Old Testament research with the philosophical and subjective hermeneutical approaches of Gadamer and Ricœur, among others.

Chapter One ("The Ten Commandments: An Old Testament-Based Exegesis and their Ethical Grounds") critically assesses the possibilities presented by the history of interpretation of the Decalogue in the field of Old Testament studies and by the substantiation of the ethical imperative from Kant to Tetsurō Watsuji. This identifies a fundamental problem as to when and where the hidden God becomes manifest. Chapter Two ("Qohelet as a Nihilist") identifies Qohelet as a nihil-

---

7 Seizō Sekine, *Die Tritojesajanische Sammlung (Jes 56–66) redaktionsgeschichtlich untersucht* (Beihefte zur Zeitschrift für die alttestamentliche Wissenschaft 175; Berlin: W. de Gruyter, 1989).
8 Seizō Sekine, *Transcendency and Symbols in the Old Testament: A Genealogy of the Hermeneutical Experiences* (trans. Judy Wakabayashi; Beihefte zur Zeitschrift für die alttestamentliche Wissenschaft 275; Berlin: W. de Gruyter, 1999).
9 Seizō Sekine, *A Comparative Study of the Origins of Ethical Thought: Hellenism and Hebraism* (trans. Judy Wakabayashi; Lanham, Md.: Rowman & Littlefield Publishers, 2005).

ist according to the definitions of Nietzsche and Heidegger, and it examines this enigmatic text in minute detail from that perspective. Having identified Qohelet's argument as to how to overcome nihilism, as well as its limitations, Chapter Three ("Sin, forgiveness and atonement in David: Focusing specifically on 2 Samuel 12 and Psalm 51") moves beyond this through a consideration of sin, forgiveness, and atonement in David's commission of adultery and murder, while engaging with arguments presented by R. G. Collingwood, S. Hatano, and M. Goulder. Chapter Four ("A Symbolism-based Interpretation of the Adamic Myth") considers the origin of human sin in dialogue with P. Ricœur, P. Tillich, and others concerning symbolic interpretations of the Adamic myth. Finally, Chapter Five ("The Concept of Redemption in Second Isaiah") considers the formation of redemptive thought in Second Isaiah while critically examining the redaction-historical research by Dion and others and also challenging Weber's theory of theodicy. Second Isaiah understood the redemptive servant as the future Messiah, but one of his disciples, a redactor, identified the servant as the suffering righteous one who had actually already appeared. Through this shift in thinking, it once again became possible to receive forgiveness of sins from both humans and God. It is precisely this shift that is the sole essential point inherited in the New Testament's understanding of redemption, and it is the author's contention that this should provide a sufficient solution to the criticisms of redemption raised by Kant and the young Hegel, as well as to the questions concerning redemption that remained unresolved in the third and fourth chapters.[10]

---

10 In the lecture, I limited the introduction of my work to the above. However, because Toshiaki Nishimura, Shinya Nomoto, and Akio Tsukimoto (who participated in written form) presented their work in detail at the symposium, it is necessary to balance this with a little more detail about my work. In my research from *Chōetsu to Shōchō* (*Transcendency and Symbols*) up to my recent *Kyūyaku Seisho to Tetsugaku* (The Old Testament and Philosophy) (Tokyo: Iwanami Shoten, 2008), I have aimed to integrate objective readings of the text through traditional historical methods with philosophically subjective readings. "These two hermeneutical directions are not necessarily opposed to one another. Rather, they stand in a complementary relationship. Without incorporating the fruits of objective, historical hermeneutics as much as possible, philosophical hermeneutics might fall into dogma and bias through arbitrary eisegesis. On the other hand, without adding philosophical hermeneutics and scrutinizing the subjective horizon of the interpreter, there is a risk that historical hermeneutics might lack ideological reflexivity and accountability concerning the significance of the research. Modern interpreters face the necessary task of comprehensively inquiring into specific ways through which these two hermeneutical approaches can strike a mutually beneficial balance. The days when scholars could remain holed up in their ivory towers and simply follow their intellectual curiosity while neglecting the world around them under the dignified name of Weberian 'asceticism' are coming to an end. We live in a complex yet fascinating era. While I acknowledge this hermeneutical situation in today's world, the primary task of this book is consciously to pursue possibilities for a philosophical interpretation of the Old Testament. This is especially needed today because historical hermeneutics have been overwhelmingly dominant in Old Testament studies, and there is poor understanding of philosophical hermeneutics. This implies, then, an integrative approach—not one that ignores historical hermeneutics, but one that also emphasizes philosophical hermeneutics" (see pp. 13–14 in the Introduction, above). At least one review of my efforts has completely failed to understand these philosophical and intellectual concerns and has utterly missed the point (*Shūkyō Kenkyū* 361 [Religious Studies 361] [2009]: 409 ff.). And there has been an emotional response to debate over these matters (*Kyūyaku-gaku Kenkyū* 3 [Old Testament Studies 3] [2006]: 77). Nevertheless, I have been gratified to receive positive comments from more than a few researchers. The following are from *Hon no Hiroba Zōkan-gō 2009* (Book Square Special Issue 2009): "Each section shows the tracks of the author's research, and the reader is led on a grand, Odyssean adventure by following those tracks" (Akio Moriya); "The author adds a new dimension to methods of interpreting the Bible" (Tetsuo Sasaki); "As a scholar of antiquity, I was fascinated by the arguments, which intentionally move beyond the fields of historical and philological research and approach the Old Testament text philosophically" (Kenji Doi). The most detailed review was by Satoru Ōtomo (*Nihon no Shingaku* 48 [Theological Studies in Japan 48] [2009]: 101 ff.). He writes: "There have been very few statements from Old Testament studies about the serious issues facing modern people. There is a sense that Old Testament scholars, secluded in their ivory towers, have until now concentrated only on interpreting texts that are troubling at the historical or theological level. For instance, Old Testament monotheism has been the object of severe criticism by people on the street, but how persuasively have Old Testament scholars been able to respond? Adhering to the Old Testament text, the author earnestly attempts to answer contemporary questions such as these through philosophical interpretation. ... His interpretation of the Old Testament text through such a methodological self-awareness overcomes the limitations of conventional historical interpretation of the Old Testament and invites the reader into a masterful problem-solving study" (101, 105). In conclusion, Ōtomo poses three challenges. I wish to attempt a response here and, in doing so, confirm the distinguishing features and direction of my research. First, Ōtomo asks whether I might also consider theological interpretation alongside philosophical interpretation. Although I do not reject that possibility, the mode of argumentation will differ according to whether or not one presupposes faith and whether one focuses on the Old Testament's universality or particularity. In this book, I have attempted to speak universally to the vast majority of modern people who do not presuppose faith. Secondly, Ōtomo expresses the following concern: "The philosophical interpretation of the story of the sacrifice of Isaac is brilliant ... but the historical context vanishes through the fusion of horizons" (106). However, I have already considered this possible challenge and presented a response on pages 41–42 in the book. My aim was to draw attention once again to the fact that historical interpretation until now has overly favored explanations that justify the people of God or God himself. By focusing too much on the people of Israel, this line of argument has neglected Abraham's individual struggle, which is full of visceral power. As far as the rehabilitation of salvation history is concerned, though, I cannot deny that at present I am quite negative. "The third point," says Ōtomo, "concerns the question of Jeremian authorship in the prophecy of the 'new covenant.' The author's solution to the riddle of what is authentic to Jeremiah is eye-opening. The conclusion that Jeremiah must have been the author is presented in a highly lucid fashion, and it is sure to make a deep

In summer 2010 Tetsuo Yamaga became the fourth Japanese invited to give a lecture at IOSOT. Yamaga's most important work at this point is perhaps *Seisho Jidai-shi: Kyūyaku-hen* (History of the Biblical Era: The Old Testament),[11] but he has been tireless in translating many Western scholarly works on the Old Testament into Japanese, and his contribution to the Japanese academy through these achievements merits special mention. Here I shall introduce his invitational lecture at IOSOT in Helsinki.

In this lecture, titled "Treaty and Covenant in Chronicles,"[12] Yamaga focuses on the stance of Chronicles against treaties with other nations. This is a feature in Chronicles that is deeply interesting and yet frequently ignored. The alliance policies of Kings Asa (2Chr 16:7–9), Jehoshaphat (2Chr 19:2–3; 20:37), and Amaziah (2Chr 25:7–9) are all criticized. Chronicles basically evaluates Jehoshaphat highly (2Chr 17:3–6), but it intentionally does not refer to the joint campaign with Israel and Edom against Moab, and the failure there, which are reported in 2 Kings 3:4–27. It appears, rather, that 2 Chronicles 20 falsifies history by reporting that Judah is saved when it stands, as a non-aligned nation, against the triple alliance of Moab, Ammon, and the Meunites (Edom) and Jehoshaphat admonishes the people, "Trust Yahweh and you will be established." Second

---

impression on readers. Nevertheless, the extraction of Jeremiah's own particular thought is still, in the long run, from the book of Jeremiah. Is there not a potential problem in how the interpreter is extracting Jeremiah's thought in accordance with the interpreter's own conceptual image of Jeremiah?" (ibid.). This is an astute point, yet because we have no other reliable documents on the prophet, we cannot avoid a certain degree of such circularity. In order to minimize this circularity, however, I have relied upon and critically examined arguments that distinguish between Jeremiah's authentic sections and Deuteronomistic additions, based on style and terms as identified by Thiel, and I have incorporated various redaction-critical considerations. Thiel's distinctions help to explain why, upon reading the book of Jeremiah, we detect a sense of incongruity—a sense that there are two contradictory levels. One is the retributive and dogmatic concept of God guiding history, and the other is a fresh breath coming from a living experience of God that destabilizes the former concept. Apart from consistently constructing an interpretation by drawing on these clues, I do not think we have any other methods for interpreting Jeremiah. Ōtomo's point sharply demonstrates the limitations of merely hypothetical interpretations, but I think that constructing new interpretations—ones that are more comprehensive and consistent than previous interpretations—as provisional truth is the task of scholarship in every age. Is my personal view too philosophical, after all? I am thankful to Ōtomo for his important challenges, and I intend to continue thinking about them, but I also wanted to give my provisional answer here.

11 Tetsuo Yamaga, *Seisho Jidai-shi: Kyūyaku-hen* (History of the Biblical Era: The Old Testament) (Tokyo: Iwanami Gendai Bunko, 2003).
12 Published as Tetsuo Yamaga, "Anti-Treaty Theology of the Chronicler and His View of History," in *Congress Volume Helsinki 2010* (Supplements to Vetus Testamentum 148; Leiden: Brill, 2012), 277–306.

Chronicles 20 is a mirror image or inverted image of 2 Kings 3. Jehoshaphat's admonition here shows obvious awareness of the prophet Isaiah's words to Ahaz during the Syro-Ephraimite War (Isa 7:9b). However, the Syro-Ephraimite War represented a clash of two treaty policies when, according to 2 Kings 16, the Aram–Israel coalition army attacked Judah's King Ahaz to force him to join the anti-Assyrian alliance, but Ahaz came under Assyria's suzerainty and thereby escaped the crisis. By contrast, the discussion of Ahaz in 2 Chronicles 28 mentions not even a single treaty policy. Nor does the Chronicler acknowledge at all that Judah was under Assyria's suzerainty during the reigns of the later Kings Hezekiah, Manasseh, and Josiah, because for the Chronicler it would have been problematic for a treaty policy with any foreign nation to have been successful.

Regarding the post-Assyrian period, however, the Chronicler accepts that Judah did in fact come under the suzerainty of Egypt and Babylon. Even the Chronicler could not deny the historical fact that the anti-Egyptian and anti-Babylonian policies led to the destruction of Judah. Instead, Yamaga conjectures, the Chronicler interpreted this as the reasonable cause of the catastrophe.

Based on these observations, Yamaga concludes that the Chronicler's anti-treaty attitude stems from the pre-exilic prophets' criticisms of treaty policies (Hos 5:13; 7:11; Isa 7:4–9; 30:1–5; 31:1–3). The Chronicler is an heir of the prophetic spirit. Yamaga concludes his lecture with the speculation that, whereas Chronicles is generally thought to have been composed in the late Persian Period (before 332 BCE) or in the early Hellenistic Period (after 332 BCE), the latter possibility is more likely.

In the BZAW series, one can also find Fujiko Kohata's source-critical analysis of Exodus 3–14, *Jahwist und Priesterschrift in Exodus 3–14*.[13] The following dissertations published in research series in the West should also be mentioned: Akio Tsukimoto's *Untersuchungen zur Totenpflege (kispum) im alten Mesopotamien*;[14] Tarō Odashima's *Heilsworte im Jeremiabuch*;[15] and Yūichi Ōsumi's *Die Kompositionsgeschichte des Bundesbuches Exodus 20,22b–23,33*.[16]

---

13 Fujiko Kohata, *Jahwist und Priesterschrift in Exodus 3–14* (Beihefte zur Zeitschrift für die alttestamentliche Wissenschaft 166; Berlin: W. de Gruyter, 1986).
14 Akio Tsukimoto, *Untersuchungen zur Totenpflege (kispum) im alten Mesopotamien* (Alter Orient und Altes Testament 216; Neukirchen-Vluyn: Neukirchner Verlag, 1985).
15 Tarō Odashima, *Heilsworte im Jeremiabuch: Untersuchungen zu ihrer vordeuteronomistischen Bearbeitung* (Beiträge zur Wissenschaft vom Alten und Neuen Testament 125; Stuttgart/Berlin/Cologne/Mainz: Kohlhammer, 1989).
16 Yūichi Ōsumi, *Die Kompositionsgeschichte des Bundesbuches Exodus 20,22b–23,33* (Orbis Biblicus et Orientalis 105; Göttingen: Vandenhoeck & Ruprecht, 1991).

Many other Japanese have submitted doctoral dissertations and laid their own foundations as Old Testament scholars outside of Japan, including Yutaka Ikeda (Hebrew University), Toshio Tsumura (Brandeis University), Akio Moriya (Hebrew Union College), Satoru Ōtomo (Kirchliche Hochschule Wuppertal/Bethel), and Ritsu Ishikawa (University of Munich). Particularly notable is Takamitsu Muraoka's work at Western universities as a leading scholar in ancient translations of the Old Testament and Semitic linguistics, as represented in his *A Grammar of Biblical Hebrew* and *A Greek-English Lexicon of the Septuagint.*[17]

I shall limit my overview of international achievements to the above.

1.3 Brief Overview of Domestic Research Achievements

Next I wish to reflect in particular on the work of four past presidents of the Society for Old Testament Study: Kōki Nakazawa, Kiyoshi Sakon, Ken'ichi Kida, and Kōichi Namiki. Regardless of whether or not they studied abroad, their contribution as Old Testament scholars has primarily been through Japanese publications. Nishimura and Tsukimoto were themselves to present on their major works at the next symposium, so I have excluded them from my consideration.

Nakazawa has closely followed and continually introduced within Japan the history of Western research on the interpretation of Deutero-Isaiah's songs of the suffering servant.[18] Furthermore, he has made a sincere contribution to Deutero-Isaiah studies with his own philological interpretation in his monograph on the whole of Deutero-Isaiah.[19] Sakon, who died suddenly at around the age of 60, published several collections of essays probing the modern message of the Old Testament, as well as precise philological research on the Psalms, among other biblical texts. His publications and sermons have been collected in a six-volume anthology.[20]

Kida has published three essay collections: *Kyūyaku Seisho no Chūshin* (The Heart of the Old Testament), *Heiwa no Mokushi* (Revelation of Peace), and *Kyūyaku*

---

17 Paul Joüon / Takamitsu Muraoka, *A Grammar of Biblical Hebrew* (Subsidia Biblica 27; Roma: Pontificio Istituto Biblico, 1991, 2006); Takamitsu Muraoka, *A Greek-English Lexicon of the Septuagint* (Leuven: Peeters, 2009).

18 Kōki Nakazawa, *Kunan no Shimobe: Izaya-sho 53-shō no Kenkyū* (The Suffering Servant: Research on Isaiah 53) (Tokyo: Yamamoto Shoten, 1975).

19 Kōki Nakazawa, *Dai-ni Izaya Kenkyū* (Deutero-Isaiah Studies) (Tokyo: Yamamoto Shoten, 1962).

20 Kiyoshi Sakon, *Sakon Kiyoshi Chosaku-shū* (Kiyoshi Sakon Anthology) (Five Volumes plus one Additional Volume; Tokyo: Kyo Bun Kwan, 1992–93, 1998).

Seisho no Yogen to Mokushi (Prophecy and Revelation in the Old Testament).[21] The latter work consists of three parts. Part One is an introduction to the essence and historical development of prophecy and revelation in the Old Testament. Part Two discusses these four subjects—namely, the essence and historical development of prophecy, and the essence and historical development of revelation—in detail. Part Three presents three essays on practical issues facing modern Christians. Kida views the religion of the Old Testament as "prophetic." He defines prophets as "individuals who, as 'founders' of a religion with a universal character that is generally termed 'founded religion' or 'revealed religion,' reveal a new religious realm while questioning anew the fundamental problems of the world from a transcendental standpoint." Although we must reject religious studies that propose simplistic objective comparisons of various religions, we cannot accept theology that absolutizes subjective Christian faith. On this issue Kida stresses the position of Gustav Mensching's "religious studies of understanding," which sublated both of these. This is none other than "the position of understanding while respecting the character of 'revelation' that possesses some manifestation of 'the holy' in each religion." Criticizing scholars from Wellhausen to Gunkel, Noth, and von Rad, Kida argues that prophets research in modern Old Testament studies has not sufficiently reflected on this sort of standpoint. In the course of considering the Jewish positions expressed by Buber and others, Kida seeks an integration of "religious studies of understanding" and theology.

Kida contends that "the holy" is a phenomenon that can be found throughout the history of human religion and that "the holy" in "ancient religion" and the systems constructed around it supported the structures of ruling powers. The fundamental feature of "prophetically founded religion" is that it created an egalitarian "covenantal community" and opened up a path to a direct relationship between the transcendent being and humans by rejecting outright the ruling powers' authority structures. Kida sees in this criticism of power the essence of prophetic religion, and the fundamental claim running through his book is the view that this is the ideal form of Old Testament religion in general, as well as of religion today.

Namiki, whose previous work includes essay collections such as *Kodai Isuraeru to Sono Shūhen* (Ancient Israel and its Environs) and *Heburaizumu no Ningen Kankaku* (Sense of Humanity in Hebraic Thought), has in recent years presented his translation of, and research papers on, the book of Job, leading to

---

21 Ken'ichi Kida, *Kyūyaku Seisho no Chūshin* (The Heart of the Old Testament) (Tokyo: Shinkyo Publishing, 1987); *Heiwa no Mokushi* (Revelation of Peace) (Tokyo: Shinkyo Publishing, 1991); and *Kyūyaku Seisho no Yogen to Mokushi* (Prophecy and Revelation in the Old Testament) (Tokyo: Shinkyo Publishing, 1996).

the publication of *Yobu-ki Ronshūsei* (Studies on the Book of Job).[22] In this monograph Namiki considers the uniqueness of the book of Job, which continues to inspire new writings even today, and he examines the conditions for its interpretation. Seven essays discuss the ways of thinking reflected in the book of Job, its literary nature, theodicy as a question, intertextual interpretation, the justice of God and humans, interpretation of Job in the Jewish world, and problems raised by the Jewish thinker Margarete Susman in her *Das Buch Hiob und das Schicksal des jüdischen Volkes*.[23] Namiki—who views the main body of the book of Job as dramatic poetry wherein Job, Job's friends, and God exchange sharp words—argues that behind this dimension of dramatic poetry lie the problems of evil in the world, God's sovereignty and human dignity and freedom, the individual and the ethnic group, and the humanity of atypical people. In Namiki's view, the book of Job throws into question readers' attitudes toward each of these problems. For that reason, the book of Job is extremely difficult to interpret, and it is impossible for readers to avoid reading into the text their own personal historical and human historical experiences. Since Auschwitz, in particular, many Jews have read the book of Job not as an account of individual suffering, but as a book about the suffering of the people. This is in sharp contrast to Christological eisegesis within Christianity. Along these lines, Namiki presents Job as a book that causes its readers to discover the meanings of self and the world.

Finally, in addition to the above overview, I also wish to mention works by several others who have strengthened the foundation of Old Testament studies in Japan. Among a steady flow of philological research, Yoshihide Suzuki's dissertation at Claremont Graduate University in the U.S. was published in Japanese as *Shinmeiki no Bunkengaku-teki Kenkyū* (Philological Studies of Deuteronomy).[24] Hisao Miyamoto's research includes a series of studies on Hebraic philosophical interpretations of Jeremiah's confessions and the story of Abraham's sacrifice of Isaac. And while Tetsuo Yamaga produced translations of German Old Testament research, as noted above, Toshiaki Nishimura continued to produce Japanese translations of French Old Testament research.

22 Kōichi Namiki, *Kodai Isuraeru to Sono Shūhen* (Ancient Israel and its Environs) (Tokyo: Shinchi Shobo, 1979, 1988 [two printings]); *Heburaizumu no Ningen Kankaku* (Sense of Humanity in Hebraic Thought) (Tokyo: Shinkyo Publishing, 1997); *Yobu-ki Ronshūsei* (Studies on the Book of Job) (Tokyo: Kyo Bun Kwan, 2003).
23 Margarete Susman, *Das Buch Hiob und das Schicksal des jüdischen Volkes* (Zürich: Steinberg Verlag, 1946).
24 Yoshihide Suzuki, *Shinmeiki no Bunkengaku-teki Kenkyū* (Philological Studies of Deuteronomy) (Tokyo: The Board of Publications The United Church of Christ in Japan, 1987).

In the area of Bible translation before and after Masao Sekine's individual translation,[25] it is also worth mentioning the publication of the ecumenical New Interconfessional Translation (Japan Bible Society, 1987) and the scholarly annotated Iwanami Translation by Iwanami Shoten (the New Testament in 1995–96 and the Old Testament in 1997–2004).

2 Prospects

2.1 Old Testament Studies in Japan: Reflections and Prospects

In the short history of Old Testament studies in Japan, Japanese scholars have learned from Western Old Testament studies, and in their responses to it, the historical-critical approach has predominated. Take the symposium themes of the fall conference of the Society for Old Testament Study in Japan in recent years: "The Final Form of the Old Testament Text" (2003); "Problems Surrounding Deuteronomism" (2004); "The Old Testament and Monotheism" (2005); "Problems Surrounding the Dead Sea Scrolls" (2007); and "The Status Quaestionis of Prophets Research" (2009). To the extent that the Society for Old Testament Study takes on the task of following international academic standards and introducing Western research, these have been important efforts. On the other hand, as we learn from and follow behind Western Old Testament studies and offer piecemeal criticisms in our local language Japanese, which is unintelligible to Westerners, we must reflect on the occasional tendency to fall into debates that fail to make an international contribution or stand accountable internationally.

As pointed out by Namiki,[26] who served as president of the Society for Old Testament Study for over a decade around the turn of the twenty-first century, it is fine to establish a philological foundation through a doctoral dissertation, but after that one must not muddle along only doing philological commentary on ancient texts. In fact, in the research achievements introduced in 1.3, above, Namiki, Kida, and Sekine, while grounded in philological issues, all made explicit claims beyond these issues. Every single word and phrase in the Old Testament is underpinned by specific historical, social, political, ethical, philosophical, ideological, and tradition-historical settings. The discourse is bound to reflect these particular types of thought. But that is not all. It is impossible for an interpreter to be thoroughly and entirely objective. If Japanese, the interpreter cannot

---

25 *Kyūyaku Seisho* (The Old Testament) (trans. Masao Sekine; Tokyo: Kyo Bun Kwan, 1997).
26 Namiki, et al., "Zadankai" (Round-table Talk), 247, 249.

avoid the fusion of horizons between the text and the subjectivity of a Japanese. Japanese interpreters, therefore, must make the Japanese horizon transparently clear to self and others, and, alongside the work of objective exegesis, proceed to read into the text the subjective perspectives of modern Japanese. Otherwise, they will be unable to achieve truly responsible academic inquiries.

A number of scholars have self-consciously pursued their research in this way. For instance, consider M. Sekine's attention to negative intermediation in his early years; his semantic theory based upon self-thinking thought in his middle years; his reference to the *marebito* tradition (about the stranger from the outside) in his above-mentioned Göttingen lecture; and his attention to the presence of "breaks" in Hebrew poetry in his later years. Consider, too, the work of S. Sekine, who, influenced by M. Sekine, attended to Kitarō Nishida's philosophy of the self-identity of absolute contradiction, which can be found at the root of Eastern and Western religion, and examined Tetsurō Watsuji's interpretation of the Decalogue based on Watsuji's ethics of the whole and the part. Then there is the work of Yutaka Ikeda, who drew attention to a point of contact between Hebraic and Japanese aesthetics found in the Song of Songs' observations and depictions of nature. We might also consider the work of Miyamoto, who confronted Western European ontology and theology proper since Auschwitz and Hiroshima with his proposal of "Hayatology" (Hebraic Ontology). These works merit attention as scholarship that suggests possibilities for Old Testament interpretation by Japanese as Japanese.

In today's intellectual currents, the Jewish and Christian faiths are themselves facing severe criticisms because of, among other reasons, ongoing disputes among monotheistic faiths and skepticism about faith in a personal God, which clashes with scientific knowledge. In the area of Old Testament studies we are seeing some appeals for the necessity of philosophical and subjective hermeneutics in response to historical-critical scholarship, which stands as a rough analogy to natural science in its advocacy of objectivity. Western Old Testament studies is facing fundamental questions in the face of these challenges, and it cannot avoid conflict and dialogue with diverse values. In response to these challenges, or standing together with others in the midst of these challenges, it will be increasingly necessary from this point forward to consider the possibilities of distinctive contributions and counter-arguments presented by Japanese scholars.

2.2 Looking to the Future of the Society for Old Testament Study in Japan

Namiki has made the important point that although the Society for Old Testament Study has provided a forum for collaborative exchange among pastors and researchers, the Japanese Biblical Institute has been set apart as a forum for research (and, I should note, especially for the training of young researchers in recent years). A look at the Society for Old Testament Study's recent symposium themes, however, suggests that it is mostly pursuing topics that figure prominently in Western Old Testament studies and that collaboration at the pastoral level has decreased significantly. Most paper presentations are by university professors and graduate students, and too few are given by pastors. It is time now, I think, for us to return to our roots and seek several new directions for the Society.

2.2.1

We could return to the Society's starting point as a place for collaboration with local pastors by having active local pastors and those in academia present issues arising from within their own areas and then holding symposia for dialogue on these issues. For instance, there would be many fruits and benefits for both sides if we were to have dialogue on themes such as "Old Testament studies and pastoral ministry," "academic biblical hermeneutics and preaching," and "historical facts and faith-based truth."

2.2.2

Of course, because we are an academic society we must maintain certain scholarly standards. It would be good to continue holding symposia at least every other year so as to pursue matters being debated in Western academic circles, and there is no reason to do away with independent research presentations that critically engage with those topics. Indeed, such activities will undoubtedly continue to be the foundation of the Society and to constitute its mainstream.

2.2.3

I would like to reconsider, however, what people mean when they say "scholarly" standards. In particular, what is "scholarship"? By this, do we not mean "scholarship" that has traditionally slanted toward the historical science of the West? Of course, the above-mentioned high-level research on the historical books by Ishida and Yamaga is historical study in the true sense, but there has been a tendency for scholars to produce historical expositions and conjectures without deepening their exegeses through attention to ideological and literary interpretation. Yet if there has been a tendency to bar presentations that are regarded as failing to meet academic standards because they do not take the accumulated scholarship into account, or if many people have been hesitant to present, is that not oppression in the name of scholarship? If that wording is too strong of a way, I could restate it this way. The Society for Old Testament Study is different from a typical academic society. It shares similarities with medical associations, for instance. Old Testament scholars are like medical scholars who, through medical associations, collaborate with clinicians working in local medical practices. Old Testament scholars must not forget the need to collaborate with local pastors. Our society must be an "Old Testament" society, not a gathering for "Old Testament scholarship" as defined by the West. If, out of love for and interest in the "Old Testament," one were to propose interpretations in order to find messages that speak to the modern world based on one's own experience and thought, without even considering any Western scholarly traditions, should that not be regarded as scholarship?

2.2.4

Let us return to the question of whether Western Old Testament studies deserves such a faithful following. After World War II nearly every major theory was overturned, beginning with the documentary hypothesis of the Pentateuch. In response, Levin, for instance, posited the existence of a single author or editor—the "Yahwist"—during the exilic period, but this is not sufficiently persuasive. In fact, anyone can put forward such hypotheses. But instead of saying new things about the text based on such hypotheses (in the case of Levin, it has to do with matters such as Deuteronomistic unification of the place of worship; the thought of the Yahwist from the perspective of the diaspora, which intentionally opposed centralization of the cult), is it not possible to deepen our reading and exegeses based on the text itself as it has been transmitted to us today? In fact, I think the time is ripe for detachedly asking essential questions about the current state of affairs—namely, whether scholarship has drifted toward non-essential, intellectual games of batting around indeterminable hypotheses concerning historical theses and antitheses. The essential task of hermeneutical scholarship is to deepen our reading of the text, and scholarship that contributes nothing to this has lost its way. Perhaps the current state of Western research exposes the dead-end of historical research methods that tend to run in circles while bouncing around such theses. Perhaps it is also necessary to acknowledge this frankly and to hold a symposium on "criticisms and an evaluation of Old Testament studies in the West."

2.2.5

The Old Testament is a book that speaks about the value of human religious life, so methods that criticize the historical or formulate historical hypotheses to explain it are an unfortunate mismatch and somehow miss the point. Even if these methods produce facts and hypotheses, truth simply falls through the cracks. On the other hand, as Kida points out, a theological approach presuposing a set faith leaves regrets that one has been unable to gather the Old Testament's universal value. I think that philosophical approaches that raise questions of value without presupposing a set faith are best suited for treating the Old Testament, and I would advocate them above Kida's religious studies of understanding. Yet if many people prefer to take a fresh look at faith values from theological perspectives without jumping ahead to philosophy, I am willing to concede that this is fine for now. The change in direction that is urgently needed in Old Testament studies in Japan and elsewhere is to delve deeper to debate not only historical facts but also faith-based truth. It is in this sense, I suggest, that symposia such as those proposed in 2.2.1 are sure to be highly beneficial not only at the pastoral level but also the scholarly level.

2.2.6

If the Society for Old Testament Study were to move in this direction, our eyes would undoubtedly be opened to possibilities of collaboration with people in other fields. The Society would turn to the fields of Christian studies, theology, philosophy, Judaic studies, ancient Near Eastern studies, Islamic studies, Western classical studies, Buddhist studies, and so on. This would require taking our research exchanges to the next level.[27]

2.2.7

We must also consider the extent to which we can, or cannot, offer wisdom and insights from an Old Testament perspective concerning the issues actually being debated in Japan today, such as environmental ethics, life sciences, and the collapse of morals. The Society for Old Testament Study should be aware that one of its tasks is the active communication of certain messages to modern Japanese society. By willingly taking up this task, we will have the chance to breathe fresh air into the confines of scholarship that professes objectivity.

---

27 See Yoshinobu Tōbō's statement in "Zadankai" (Round-table Talk), 252. I have added to this point based on Izaya Teshima's remarks at the symposium. I wish to express my thanks to him.

2.2.8

In the retrospect of Old Testament studies in Japan, there were certain points where Japanese have contributed to scholarship. What did these consist of? Over-reaching so as to present self-serving Old Testament interpretations from a unique Japanese perspective makes no contribution to scholarship and lacks persuasive power. If instead we consider the neighboring field of bioethics, we ought to be able to recognize a distinctive Japanese view of life. What if we start there? And for inter-religious dialogue, we have a familiarity with the Buddhist tradition. What can we say from that viewpoint? Perspectives for criticizing the absoluteness of the Old Testament and, by extension, Judaism and Christianity, naturally emerge, and perhaps we can obtain glimpses of a freedom that transcends faith, based on insights into philosophical and universal truths that are common to the various religions. When the Society for Old Testament Study opens itself to these possibilities and begins a new journey, it will be possible for the Society's history to move beyond Sakon's "stable period" and enter a "new redevelopment period."

2.2.9

Finally, I wish to comment on the significance of holding the Society for Old Testament Study meeting in Kansai, thanks to Doshisha University's hosting. Until now, most meetings have been held in Tokyo, and quite a few members have found it difficult to attend because of travel expenses and other issues.[28] Moving forward, if the Society alternates its meetings every year between Tokyo and a regional city, or between Kanto and Kansai, we can have energetic presentations by young researchers from the host schools, as happened this time. We should also consider the possibility of selecting church sites, not just universities, for our meetings. It would be beneficial, then, to plan public lectures or symposia open to local congregation members. The number of participants would increase, and my proposal in 2.2.1 regarding research and pastoral collaboration might materialize more readily. Doshisha's hosting of this meeting was a highly significant initiative in that direction as well. I wish to take this opportunity to express my gratitude for your dedicated work.

---

28 See Kiyoshi Tsuchido, "Zadankai" (Round-table Talk), 276.

Conclusion

It should go without saying that a retrospect of scholarship should not simply end in nostalgia; we must also consider prospects for the future. No doubt it is true that each member has a different vision, and this very diversity invigorates our Society. Nevertheless—or precisely because of this—I felt it necessary to reconfirm the prospects of the Society for Old Testament Study as a whole, rather than each individual's vision, and to offer a number of proposals for moving together in a new direction. Perhaps I have focused too much on dreams reflecting my own biases as the new president. I hope you will understand my true intentions and, in the symposium to follow, use this as a springboard for candidly sharing your criticisms and constructive opinions.[29]

---

29 I wish to note here the key points raised during the question and answer session at the symposium. First, Susumu Higuchi expressed basic agreement on the various proposals especially in 2.2. I expressed my desire for Higuchi, symposium panelists Toshiaki Nishimura and Shinya Nomoto, and other society members who have worked bi-vocationally in research and pastoral ministry to take the lead, as well as my wish to create more presentation opportunities for our members who work primarily in pastoral ministry and tend to miss our Society gatherings. Johannes Unsok Ro stated his hope that we will hold an international symposium that moves beyond Japan to bring Asia into view, and he suggested that there might be some contradiction between my emphases on philosophy and pastoral ministry. I answered that I have written the above-mentioned HBOT essay on "Hebrew Bible / Old Testament Studies in Asia" but that it is inadequate because I do not understand the Korean and Chinese languages. I hope, therefore, that researchers such as Ro will become bridge-people so that we can include in our vision cooperation with other Asian Old Testament scholars and societies. Regarding Ro's suggestion, I noted that the Old Testament has both universalistic and particularistic aspects. A philosophical emphasis suits the former, but it is theology's task to grapple with the latter. I confirmed my desire, therefore, to move at least to the level where Old Testament studies includes arguments concerning faith "values." Hiroshi Kita said that in his experience the Japanese Biblical Institute has become empathetic to pastoral concerns through informal times of fellowship and that the Society for Old Testament Study has focused more on scholarship proper. In the future, when we hold society meetings in regional cities, our meetings will go for two days and one night, as was the case last year at Hokusei Gakuen University. I expressed my hope, therefore, that opportunities for fellowship will increase in the natural course of things. Finally, Chikara Ōshima expressed his hope that we can publish biblical exegeses through the collaborative work of scholars and pastors. Indeed, we should see many fruits if, as a preliminary step, we propose and debate exegeses of the same texts from both sides at Society symposia. I thanked the participants for their many ideas, and the symposium came to a close.

Subject Index

Aaron 121, 125

'abad 103

Abraham 1, 19–72, 122, 132–33, 145, 218, 223
– agony of 28–29, 31, 34, 45
– blessing of 28–29, 32–34, 40, 51, 55, 61–62, 64–65, 69
– death of 28–29, 34
– descendants of 36–40, 49, 51, 54, 59, 61, 66, 68–69, 78
– faith of 19–22, 30, 35, 49–52, 55–56, 59–60
– journey of 28–29, 45, 48, 52
– kenosis of 29, 32–33, 53
– knight of faith 20, 30, 35, 50, 52
– knight of infinite resignation 20, 30
– logic of 47–53
– obedience of 22, 24–25, 40, 49, 55, 66, 69
– praise of 20–21, 35, 37, 50
– self-denial of 53, 58
– self-negation of 55, 63, 69
– sin of 32, 50, 53, 59–60, 66, 68–69
– struggle of 29, 63, 218
absoluteness 28, 69, 104–5, 229
Adamic myth 109, 217
adultery 10, 97, 122, 142, 173, 187, 199, 217
aesthetics
– Hebraic and Japanese 225
afterlife 78, 81, 84, 214
Ahaz 95, 167, 220
aidagara 134
Akedah 19–72
– accretions to 35–41, 44, 61, 65, 67, 70
– irrationality of 34–35, 43, 68
– style of 37, 38, 41, 48, 52, 67
– also see sacrifice, of Isaac
Alexandrian Manuscript 174
alogos 82
Amaziah 219
Amida Buddha 86–89, 112, 146
Amorites 39, 42
Amos 76, 102, 104
Ananiah 184

anarchy 147

anger 49, 103, 127, 136–37, 151

angst 31

Annual of the Japanese Biblical Institute 212

Anthropic Cosmological Principle 149–50

anthropocentrism 149

anthropodicy 77–78

aphasia 137–38

Apocrypha 212

apologetics 3, 62, 70

aporia 26, 28

apotheoses 76

Aramaic 166, 169

archaeology 101, 126

Aristotle 1, 64, 73, 81–84, 86, 109–10, 115, 148, 156

arrogance 128, 173, 199

arts, the 155–56, 160, 182

Asahi Shimbun 90, 92

asceticism 14, 71, 86–87, 217

Asherah 97, 102

Asia 154, 213, 230

Assyria 95, 102–3, 165, 167, 220

atheism 31, 115

Athens 80, 83, 147

atonement 14, 32, 52, 57, 69, 75–80, 86–87, 89, 109–15, 125, 127–29, 131–32, 156, 170–71, 176, 180, 191, 217; also see righteous servant(s), redemptive work of

Aum Shinrikyo 135–36

Auschwitz 223, 225

authenticity 145, 181–83, 186, 193, 195–96, 199, 205

authority 14, 34, 55, 98–99, 126, 147, 202, 222

authorship 178, 193, 196, 198, 201, 205, 218

awe 29, 129, 140, 145, 150

Baalism 97, 101, 173

Babylonia 93, 95, 106

barbarism 92, 147

Baruch 196, 198

beauty 80 – 81, 83 – 85, 87, 110 – 12, 150, 155, 214
Beersheba 40
being
– absolute 57, 60, 62, 69, 71, 108, 112, 119, 207
– relative 57, 60, 69, 71, 108, 119
berit 179, 195 – 96
Bible Versions 5, 7 – 9, 163
– BBE 7, 170
– Classical Japanese Bible 211
– DRB 7, 65
– EIN 8, 169, 174
– ELB 8, 169 – 70
– ELO 8, 169
– Iwanami Bible 163, 181, 224
– Japanese Colloquial Version 65, 164, 168 – 69, 211
– KJV 8, 164
– LSG 8, 65, 164, 169
– LUT 8, 164, 169 – 70
– Masao Sekine Version 65, 164, 168 – 70, 224
– NAB 8, 65, 169
– NEG 8, 65, 164, 169
– New Interconfessional Translation 65, 164, 168 – 70, 224
– New Japanese Bible 65, 164, 168 – 70, 175
– NKJ 8, 164, 168, 172 – 73
– NRS 8, 38, 54, 64 – 65, 164, 169 – 70
– Peshitta 36, 42, 65, 78
– RWB 8, 170
– Samaritan Pentateuch 36
– SCH 8, 65, 169
– Septuagint 5, 8, 36, 42, 78, 164, 169, 173 – 74, 184 – 85, 196, 200, 221
– Symmachus 42
– Targum 5, 173
– TEV 8, 175
– Vulgate 5, 36, 42, 65, 78, 169 – 70
Biblical Sources 21, 23, 55 – 56, 126, 214
– D (Deuteronomist) 23
– E (Elohist) 23 – 24, 38, 56, 71
– J (Yahwist) 126, 215, 227
– JE (Yahwist and Elohist) 23 – 24, 55 – 56
– Jehovist 23, 126
– P (Priestly) 56

biblical studies 3, 12, 212
bioethics 229
blasphemy 119, 122
blessing 81, 87, 172, 214; also see Abraham, blessing of
boredom 150
Buddhism 57, 86, 89, 92, 145 – 46, 228

Cairo Genizah 173
Canaanites 39, 93
capitalism 91 – 92, 137
categorical imperative 20, 23, 56, 216
catharsis 156
Christianity 14, 54 – 55, 57, 64, 68, 73, 84, 89, 91 – 92, 100, 107, 109 – 10, 113 – 15, 122, 145, 178, 211, 223, 229
Chronicler 95, 219 – 20
civilization 92, 129, 154
clones 133, 141
coexistence 134 – 36, 138, 142, 144, 152, 156 – 60, 214
colonization 91 – 92
compassion 127, 190, 200
conflict 3, 11 – 12, 14, 32, 38, 62, 66, 114, 127, 139 – 40, 215, 225
conversion 86, 95, 97, 111
cosmological principle 141, 149 – 50
counterfeit 130, 182, 205, 208
covenant 38 – 39, 54, 76, 167, 175 – 76, 178 – 80, 190, 192 – 98, 200 – 7, 218 – 19
– Abrahamic 38 – 39, 54
– Davidic 175, 204
– formula 178 – 79, 194, 204
– New 167, 176, 178 – 80, 192 – 94, 196 – 98, 200 – 1, 204 – 7, 218
– Sinaitic 174
– violation of 76, 193, 203 – 4
creation 11, 60 – 62, 69, 107 – 9, 128, 139 – 40, 149, 167
crime and criminals 55, 135 – 36, 151 – 52
criticism
– ethical criticism 2, 3, 104
– form criticism 9 – 11
– historical criticism 3, 22, 205, 224 – 25
– literary criticism 21, 214, 226
– postmodern criticism 2 – 3, 137 – 38, 143, 146

– redaction criticism   2, 9, 11, 21, 182–83, 185–86, 205–8, 217, 219
– source criticism   2, 9, 220
– text criticism   9–10, 36, 174, 182
– tradition-historical criticism   9–11, 24, 56, 71, 224
Crusades   92
curses   38, 190, 202, 214
Cushites   180, 200
Cyrus   104–5, 114
Cyrus Cylinder   105

daimonion   80–81
David   93, 122, 165–67, 175–76, 204, 215–17
– scion of   166–67
Dead Sea Scrolls   78, 114, 165, 212, 224
death   62, 66, 75–79, 81, 83–86, 88, 110–11, 113, 127, 132, 136, 156, 165, 170–72, 178, 191, 202, 214
– gift of   26–27
– also see Abraham, death of; God, death of; Isaac, death of
death penalty   11, 151
Deborah   214
Decalogue   10–13, 99–100, 121, 126, 139, 142, 145, 188, 216, 225
democracy   137, 146–48
demythologization   128–29, 143, 159
desire   82–83, 85, 87, 124, 128, 144, 146–47, 173, 230
despair   77–78, 80, 84–86, 125, 199–200, 202
deus ex machine   139
Deuteronomism   2, 181, 224
Deuteronomistic Historian   3, 95, 172–80, 183–90, 192–96, 198–206, 208
Deuteronomistic History   184–85, 192
Deuteronomistic redaction   122, 186, 190, 194
devotion   85–87, 111–12
diaspora   227
dignity   223
disease   46, 48, 88, 131, 141
dishonor   111
documentary hypothesis   227

dogma, dogmatism   13, 64, 174, 203–4, 206–8, 217, 219
dominion   114, 119, 130, 132, 165
dōri (order, reason)   134
doubt   1, 11, 14, 53–54, 57, 86, 90, 95–96, 119–20, 122–26, 128–30, 143, 204
Draconianism   136–37, 151
dynastic succession   215–16

'*ebed*   103
economics   13, 96, 113, 182, 206
education   see ethics, ethical education
egoism   80, 82, 84–89, 91–92, 96, 109–15
– abandonment of   84–86, 111, 113
– abolition of   113–14
egoist, egoistic   82–84, 86, 91–92, 113, 124, 130, 143
Egypt   10, 39, 93, 99, 102, 127, 142, 176–78, 187–88, 192, 215, 220
eisegesis   13, 185, 217, 223
Eliezer   27
Elijah   97
'*Elohim*   29
emotionalism   137–38, 151–52
enemies   33, 36–39, 61–62, 64–65, 69, 93, 95, 102, 187–88
enlightenment rationality   60
enthronement   166
environment   13, 134, 141, 149, 158, 228
equality   94, 144
eschatology   166–67, 176, 179, 196–97
ethics   2, 13–14, 25, 27, 31–32, 35, 55–56, 81, 96, 112, 115, 128, 131, 134–39, 142–44, 146–50, 156–60, 181, 225, 228
– Christian   2, 13–14, 32
– environmental   134, 141, 149, 228
– ethical education   134, 136–38, 148, 150, 152, 157
– in Japan   2, 134–35, 146, 152, 154, 157, 225, 228–29
– Israelite   14, 23, 55–56, 96, 104, 126, 128–29, 173, 188
ēthos   134
evangelism   19, 88, 115, 215
evil   13, 56, 58–60, 64, 66, 69, 84, 92, 119–20, 123, 128, 172, 175, 177, 180, 200, 202–4, 207, 215, 223

evolution 139–40, 149

exaltation 169, 171

exclusivism 100

exile, exilic period 13, 56, 74–75, 95, 104, 114, 143, 155, 175, 183–87, 189, 192–94, 202–3, 206, 227

existence 34, 63, 66, 88, 96, 99, 101, 107, 109, 114, 129, 132–33, 140–41, 143–46, 148, 150–51, 160, 180, 200, 207

– givenness of 132–33, 140–41, 144–46, 148, 150–51, 158–60

exodus 10, 99, 124, 127, 143, 145, 177, 187–88

faith 1, 3, 19–24, 30, 35, 49–52, 55–56, 59–60, 71, 77, 84, 86–89, 101, 103, 106, 109, 111, 113, 115, 123, 128, 174, 179, 200, 204–5, 218, 222, 225, 228–30

– paradox of 20, 88–89

faith-based scholarship 3, 226, 228

faithful, faithfulness 96, 99–100, 168, 173, 178, 187

fakes, forgery 181–82, 205–6

family 121, 136, 157, 214

fear 44, 47, 53, 56, 59, 68, 126–27, 136, 138, 141, 145, 147, 151, 166–67, 191

filicide 1, 20, 22, 25, 56, 59–60, 68–69

forgive, forgiveness 88, 127, 131, 178–80, 191, 193–94, 198, 200, 205, 207, 217

fornication 97

freedom 146–47, 150, 158, 223, 229

Freudian work of mourning 86, 171

friends, friendship 64, 80, 82–83, 121, 124, 158, 223

fundamentalism 12, 139–40

fusion of horizons 11–12, 218, 225

Gaia Hypothesis 141

Gethsemane 85

gift(s) 26–27, 31–32, 51–52, 55, 60–61, 66, 68–69, 96, 123–24, 132–33, 141, 157–59, 194

God 1–2, 11, 14, 20–35, 37–64, 66–69, 71, 73–80, 84–86, 91, 93–115, 119–33, 139–43, 145, 151, 165, 167, 172, 174–80, 188, 191–92, 195, 197–207, 214–19, 223, 225

– as a fool 121–23

– as absolute 21, 25–27, 47, 57–62, 69, 91, 104–9, 112, 115, 119, 141, 207

– as creator 11, 60–61, 69, 105, 107–9, 121, 128, 139–41

– as cruel 43, 122

– as ethnic deity 61–63, 69, 102, 104, 143

– as good 55, 58–59, 62–63, 66, 69

– as hidden 66, 78, 128, 216

– as immanent 66, 125, 128

– as irrational 14, 30, 35, 55, 61–62, 68, 121, 204

– as personal 2, 14, 57, 68, 71, 115, 122, 124, 130–31, 139, 141, 143, 206, 225

– as relative 57–58, 60–61, 68–69, 71, 107–8, 119

– as revealed 78, 109, 113, 124, 128, 188

– as transcendent 58–59, 66, 104–7, 109, 121, 123–25, 128–33, 141, 145, 207, 222

– as unethical 1, 25, 55–56, 61, 68–69

– as universal 61, 63–64, 69, 104–6

– as wholly other 26–27

– authority of 14, 55, 98–99

– command(s) of 22, 25, 27, 31–32, 35, 42–43, 49–53, 55–56, 59–62, 68, 122, 176–77, 202; also see Decalogue

– death of 14, 123–24, 130

– descent into evil 58–60, 63–64, 66, 69

– fear of 52–53, 68, 145, 167

– justice or righteousness of 56, 75–78, 95, 119, 121, 126–27, 129, 165, 175–76, 203–4, 223

– love of, as loving 56, 59–60, 63, 69, 104, 109, 126–27, 129–30, 142–43, 145

– mercy of 124, 127

– omnipotence of 58, 125

– omnipresence of 105, 120

– omniscience of 58

– promise(s) of 28, 37–39, 49–52, 55–56, 59, 61, 68, 167

– redemptive work of 84, 111, 122, 131; also see righteous servant, redemptive work of

– retributive 61, 96, 120, 123–28, 179, 188, 191, 203–4, 206–7, 219

– self-denial of 53–66, 111, 113–14

– self-negation of 57 – 63, 69, 108 – 9, 113, 115
– sovereignty of 121, 223
– symbolic representation of 58, 106, 108, 113, 115, 126, 129 – 30, 140; also see symbols, symbolism
– traditional views of 65 – 66, 68, 95 – 96, 101, 107, 119 – 20, 123 – 24, 172, 206
– trust in 67, 85, 95, 104, 219
gods 61, 80 – 81, 97, 99 – 101, 104 – 6, 108, 110, 126, 130, 173, 187, 190
government 151, 153, 215
grace 204 – 5
gratitude 141, 154, 158
guidance, divine 75, 93, 95 – 96, 102, 206, 219

Hananiah 184 – 86
happiness 157, 159, 176
hardships 19, 73 – 74, 76 – 77, 128
hate 64 – 65
hayatology 27, 225
Hebraic thought 73, 84, 89, 110, 222 – 23
Hegelian Thought 57 – 58, 91
Hellenistic Period 95, 119, 220
herem 93
hermeneutics 9 – 14, 55, 72, 128, 144, 146, 216 – 18, 225 – 27
hexateuch 214
Hezekiah 166 – 67, 220
Hingabe 85, 89, 111; also see *Selbsthingabe*
hinne, hinneni 45, 48, 51
holiness 98
Holy Spirit 87
holy, the 222
Homeric literature 41, 205
honor 47, 82 – 83, 110, 172
hope 20, 30 – 31, 35, 49, 50, 52 – 53, 59, 69, 78, 80 – 81, 83 – 84, 103, 111, 114, 141, 155 – 56, 165, 180, 186, 189, 200 – 2
hopeless(ness) 30, 50, 84, 110 – 11, 165, 180, 200 – 1
Hosea 76, 95, 97
humanism 14, 130
humility 113, 153 – 54, 157

identity 28, 33 – 34, 74, 115
– self-identity 3, 57 – 59, 61, 108 – 9, 225
idols, idolatry 98, 101, 105 – 6, 120 – 21, 125 – 28
ignorance 13, 80, 88, 105, 174
Iliad 205
imagination 41, 44
imperialism 92
inalienable rights 149
indifference 13, 83, 110
infidelity 75, 204
infinite, the 20, 24, 31, 120, 129
ingratitude 60
iniquity 75, 126, 178, 193, 198, 204, 207; also see sin(s)
injustice 77 – 78, 80 – 81, 132
inspiration, divine 140
integrity 149
inter-religious dialogue 229
intercession 127, 132, 170 – 72, 179, 190, 203
internalization 136, 198
interpretive methods 3, 10, 12, 15, 146, 185, 217 – 19, 227 – 28; also see criticism
IOSOT 19, 213, 215 – 16, 219
iPS 140
Isaac 1, 3, 19 – 22, 26 – 31, 33 – 34, 36, 38 – 56, 58, 60 – 61, 63, 66 – 69, 218, 223
– age of 45 – 46
– as beloved son 1, 27 – 28, 38, 42, 44, 47, 51, 56, 67 – 68
– binding of 19, 46
– death of 26 – 29, 45, 66
– obedience of 45 – 46, 55, 66, 69
– perspective of 19, 44 – 47
– self-denial of 53
– self-negation of 55, 63, 66 – 69
– self-sacrifice of 45 – 46, 67
– trauma of 34
– also see sacrifice, of Isaac
Isaiah 95, 103, 163 – 68, 176, 178 – 80, 220; also see Second Isaiah
Ishmael 39, 52
Islam 92, 100, 114, 228
Israel 23, 37 – 38, 55, 62, 73 – 74, 76, 78 – 80, 84, 93 – 95, 98, 101 – 2, 104 – 7, 110 – 11, 119, 142 – 45, 165 – 66, 170 – 73, 175 –

80, 183 – 84, 187 – 89, 191 – 93, 197,
200, 202 – 3, 206, 213 – 16, 218 – 20,
222 – 23
– cult of   23, 37, 42, 177, 188, 227
– destruction of   74, 103, 183 – 85, 188, 193,
201, 203, 205 – 6, 220
– salvation of   62, 65, 142 – 43, 163, 179,
183, 191, 199, 203, 214
– sins of   76, 78, 95, 170 – 71, 178 – 80, 187 –
88, 191, 193, 198 – 99, 202

Japan   1 – 3, 19, 35, 90, 92, 134 – 35, 143,
146, 152, 154, 157 – 58, 211 – 15, 221,
223 – 25, 228 – 30
– crime   135 – 36, 152
– ethics   see ethics, in Japan
– Juvenile Act   152
– media   157
– religion   92, 111, 113, 145 – 46, 225, 229
– youth   152
Japanese Biblical Institute   211 – 12, 215,
226, 230
Jehoshaphat   219 – 20
Jeremiah   76 – 77, 95, 97, 103 – 5, 167, 172 –
80, 183 – 205, 207 – 8, 218 – 19, 223
– Confessions of   174, 199 – 200, 204 – 5,
223
Jerusalem   42, 98, 174, 191, 216
Jesse   166 – 67, 176
Jesus   13, 27, 63 – 64, 73, 79 – 80, 84 – 87,
110, 112, 156, 178
– cross of   57, 73, 79, 86 – 87, 110, 113, 156
jiriki   89
Job   39, 53, 73, 77, 104, 121 – 22, 128 – 29,
206, 222 – 23
Jōdo Shinshū   86, 87, 145
Josephus   41, 43 – 48, 52, 60, 68
Josianic Period   37
Judah   98, 101, 103, 175, 178, 183 – 85, 188,
192, 197 – 98, 201 – 2, 204 – 5, 216, 219 –
20
Judaism   54, 68, 76, 89, 91, 100, 106, 109 –
10, 114, 145, 166, 229
judgment   95, 102, 104, 127, 180, 186 – 90,
193, 199 – 203, 207, 215
justice   25, 56, 75 – 78, 92, 94 – 96, 119, 126,
165, 171, 175, 204, 223

kenosis   see Abraham, kenosis of
ketib   173
knowledge   80, 105, 121, 128, 148, 152,
166 – 67, 179, 197, 214, 225
ktisiology   139, 142, 144 – 45

lament(s)   132, 138, 157, 191, 199
law   11, 23 – 24, 55, 94, 99 – 100, 108, 120,
123, 127 – 28, 130 – 33, 141, 147, 151 – 52,
160, 173, 178 – 79, 188 – 90, 192, 194,
197 – 98, 201 – 4, 207, 214
– apodictic   11
– as written in the heart   178, 192, 194, 204,
207
– casuistic   11
– Deuteronomic   188, 197, 202
– holy   173
– moral law   23
– natural law(s)   133, 141
– of monolatry   99 – 100
– punitive   152
– retributive   120, 123, 127 – 28, 130 – 32,
179, 203
Leviticus   6, 64, 77, 127
literalism   128, 140, 144, 146
logic of topos   14, 58 – 59, 107 – 8, 115
logos   80 – 84, 87 – 88, 110, 112
love   27, 30, 38, 42, 44, 46 – 47, 51, 54 – 56,
59 – 60, 63 – 69, 81 – 82, 84, 104, 109 –
10, 113, 121, 124, 126 – 27, 129 – 30, 142 –
46, 148, 151 – 56, 160, 197
– according to Aristotle   81 – 82, 84, 110
– agape   63 – 65, 69
– eros   63
– love of neighbor   64
– magnetic field of   130, 143 – 46, 148, 151 –
52, 154, 156, 160
– of Abraham   1, 27 – 28, 30, 38, 42, 44, 47,
51, 55 – 56
– of God   see God, love of
loyalty   53, 68

Maimonides   54
Manasseh   220
Marcion   122
Marduk   103, 105
matsebet   164, 167

meaninglessness 28, 85, 113–14, 123, 150
mercy 124, 127
messiah, messianic 74, 153, 165–67, 175–76, 179, 217
metaphor 71, 115, 143, 164
metaphysics 148
Micah 24, 32, 56, 95
midrash 34, 45
misfortune 96, 120, 136, 150, 183, 186, 199, 202–3
mishpaṭ 75
mission(s) 92, 127
modernism 130
Moloch 23, 25, 32
money 83, 130, 181–82
monolatry 97, 99, 100, 108
monotheism 1, 14–15, 90–93, 97–101, 104, 106–7, 113–16, 218, 224
– and prophets 1, 14, 97–98, 100–1, 104, 106, 108, 114
– criticism against 1, 14, 90, 93–94, 113, 116, 218, 225
– egoistic nature of 91–92, 113, 115
– essence of 107, 113, 115
– exclusive 14, 97, 99–100, 114
– formation of 98, 100–1, 104, 106
– in the modern world 1, 14, 90
– reconstruction of 14, 90, 113, 115
– source of 1, 14, 90, 106
– Yahwistic 98–101, 104, 106
morality 88, 131, 135, 203
morals 134–36, 154, 228
mōrēs 134
Moriah 27, 31, 42–43, 58
Moses 10, 28, 77, 104, 120–21, 125–28, 132, 177
Moses und Aron (Opera) 120
murder 10–13, 49, 55, 58, 122, 126, 135–36, 138–39, 141–44, 150–52, 155–56, 159–60, 199, 217
music 120–21, 125, 155–56, 181–82
mystical experience 86
myth, mythological language 81, 92, 107–8, 115, 128, 133, 149, 217

narrative identity 28
Nathan 216

nationalism 12, 36, 61, 70
nature 119, 130, 132–34, 142, 149–50, 159, 176, 225
– pregivenness of 141–42, 150, 157; also see existence, givenness of
Nazis 122, 132
Nebuchadnezzar 103–4
negation 54, 57–58, 60, 69, 108
– self-negation 55, 57–63, 67–69, 108–9, 113, 115
– also see self-denial
Neo-Babylonian Empire 95
new covenant 167, 176, 178–80, 192–94, 196–98, 200–1, 204–7, 218
nihilism 120, 123–25, 129, 206, 217
Nirvana 87
Noah 39, 167
nomological knowledge 214
non-ontological 123–24, 129–31
nūs 82–84, 110

obedience 22, 24–25, 40, 45, 49, 55, 66, 69, 71, 173, 180, 188–89; also see Abraham, obedience of; Isaac, obedience of
objectivity 62, 225, 228
ontology, ontological 27–28, 123–24, 130, 225
opera 120–21, 125, 155–56
otherness 33, 35, 40
ownership 29, 33

pagan, pagans 95, 98, 103, 105, 114–15, 126, 173, 187
pain, painful 43, 51, 68, 136
Palestine 36, 93
Palestinians 12
pantheism 57
paramārtha 100, 110
pariah 62, 76
pastors, pastoral ministry 212, 225–30
paternalism 71
patriarchal 34, 214
Paul 27, 79, 193
peace 62, 75, 87, 93–94, 154, 165–67, 174, 177, 186, 189, 191, 199
Pentateuch 23, 36, 126, 214, 227

personality 34, 49
pesticides 149, 158
philautos 82
Philistines 102
philology 1, 3, 70–71, 200, 218, 221, 223–24
philosophical dialogues 80–81
philosophical hermeneutics 11, 13–14, 72, 144, 146, 217–18
Plato 2, 80–81, 83, 110, 146–48
pleasure 42, 82–83, 96, 110, 123–24, 157
plundering, ideology of 91–95, 97, 113
pluralism 92, 94, 100
poetry 104, 196, 223, 225
politics 94, 113–14, 147, 152–54, 160, 216, 224
pollution 13, 149
polytheism 97–101
post-enlightenment rationality
postmodernism, postmodernists 137–38, 143, 146, 159
poverty 76, 83
prayer 46, 48, 64, 68, 77, 85–86, 89, 97, 127, 130, 132, 197, 199, 202
preaching 120, 137, 153, 188, 226
pregivenness 141, 144, 150, 158–59
primogeniture 216
privatization 28
prophecy 62, 94–95, 103–4, 122, 164–68, 172, 174, 176, 178–80, 183, 185–86, 192, 196–98, 200–1, 204–5, 216, 218, 222
– false 174–75, 182–86, 188, 191, 201
– fulfillment of 114, 167–68, 176, 178, 186
– messianic 74, 165–67, 176, 179
– of New Covenant see new covenant
– true 182–83, 186, 205
prophets 2, 10, 14, 38, 76, 93–95, 97–98, 100–2, 104–6, 108, 114, 124, 126, 172, 174–75, 177–78, 181, 183, 186, 188, 191, 199, 201, 203, 215, 220, 222, 224
Protestantism 89, 145–46
providence 52, 54
Pseudepigrapha 212
pseudonymous texts 122
Puccini, Giacomo 155

punishment, divine 57, 76, 80, 95, 126–27, 188, 190, 200, 203
Puritans 92

qere 5, 173
Qohelet 1, 95–96, 119–20, 123–26, 128–30, 206, 216–17
– nihilism of 95, 120, 123–25, 129, 206, 216–17

Rashi 54
rationality 35, 60, 203
ratsach 11–12
reason 82–85, 111, 134, 136, 139, 142, 151, 157
rebellion 75, 135, 180, 185, 200
reciprocity 26, 29, 32
redactor 37, 182, 185, 217
relationship(s) 27, 31, 33, 40, 47, 49, 53, 57, 60–63, 69, 100, 104, 106, 119, 124, 134, 144, 173, 187, 193, 203, 207, 222
relativism 136–38
religion see Japan, religion
Rembrandt 19
remnant 164, 175–76, 180
respect 82, 137, 147, 154, 222
responsibility 13, 25–27, 95–96, 146
ressentiment of the weak 88, 131
resurrection 78, 205
retribution 36, 61, 96, 120, 124–28, 130–32, 179, 188, 191, 203–4, 206–7
revelation 109, 206, 221–22
reward 36, 39, 57, 61, 66, 69–70, 84, 175
ri (order, reason) 134, 136, 139, 142, 144, 158–59
righteous servant(s) 73–74, 76–78, 96, 110, 120–21, 123–24, 127–28, 170, 175, 191, 204, 217
– redemptive work of 79, 84, 110, 127, 132, 170–71, 217
– suffering of 73–77, 110, 124, 127, 170, 172, 217
righteousness 75–77, 96, 121, 126–27, 129, 165, 175–76, 203
– self-righteousness 114
– unrighteousness 127, 187
rinri (ethics) 131, 134, 139

riro (ordered path) 134
ro (path, paths) 134, 136, 144

Sabbath 11, 188
sacrifice 1, 3, 19 – 20, 22 – 27, 29 – 32, 37,
    43, 45 – 46, 48 – 49, 54 – 56, 58, 62, 67,
    77, 83, 86, 89, 110, 112, 122, 127, 144,
    156, 176 – 77, 188, 191, 218, 223
– of Isaac 1, 3, 19, 22, 62, 218, 223; also
    see Akedah
– of the firstborn 19, 23 – 24, 56, 122
– self-sacrifice 45, 67, 86, 112
salvation 2, 61 – 62, 65, 76, 85 – 88, 111 – 12,
    114, 142 – 43, 163, 165, 167 – 68, 173 –
    74, 176, 179 – 80, 183, 185 – 86, 188 –
    89, 191, 199 – 204, 214 – 15, 218
– history of 2, 218
Sarah 27
sarcasm 186
Sarin Gas Attack 135
Sarkozy 135
Saul 215
savior 105, 114, 166, 176
scholarly research 3, 15, 70, 226 – 28
– accountability of 3, 14, 217, 224
schools 123, 134 – 35, 144, 148, 157, 159
science 12, 129 – 30, 132 – 33, 139 – 41,
    149 – 50, 160, 225 – 26, 228
scientists 150
Second Isaiah 13, 73, 74, 75, 76, 77, 78, 80,
    84, 85, 86, 89, 101, 104, 105, 106, 109,
    110, 114, 127, 131, 143, 163, 164, 168,
    169, 176, 180, 200, 221, 217, 221; also
    see Isaiah
Selbsthingabe 87; also see *Hingabe*
self-abandonment 85, 111
self-abasement 76
self-absolutization 28
self-awareness 78 – 79, 84, 91, 218
self-consciousness 12, 78, 92, 225
self-contradiction 56, 59, 69, 154
self-denial 53, 58 – 59, 111, 113 – 14; also
    see negation, self-negation
self-devotion 87
self-differentiation 28
self-dissolution 29, 34
self-emptying 29

self-enlightenment 85, 86, 111
self-giving 87
self-identity see identity
self-interest 87, 112
self-negation see negation, self-negation
self-salvation 180, 202
self-satisfaction 169
selflessness 87, 112
servant song(s) 74 – 76, 78, 109 – 10, 168 –
    69, 171 – 72, 221
Sesshū 181 – 82
Shinran 86
shōgi 100, 110
sin(s) 13, 32, 59 – 60, 66, 68 – 69, 76 – 78,
    80, 86, 88, 95, 109, 111, 126 – 27, 131 –
    32, 156, 170 – 71, 178 – 80, 187 – 88,
    190 – 91, 193, 198 – 205, 207, 217; also
    see iniquity
– original 109, 180, 190, 200 – 3
– sinners 64, 88, 109, 131, 171
Sinai 127, 145, 204
Sinaitic Manuscript 174
skepticism 104, 119, 136 – 38, 143, 146, 225
societal structures 13, 95
societal order 144, 147
Society for Old Testament Study in Japan 2,
    19, 90, 211 – 13, 215, 221, 224 – 30
Socrates 1, 80 – 84, 89, 109 – 10
Solomon 42, 97
soteriology 2, 139, 142 – 45, 180
spirit 3, 82, 87, 91, 114, 145, 166 – 67, 208,
    214, 220
spiritual, spirituality 70, 80, 91 – 92
St. John's Passion 156
stoic 36, 70
struggle, struggling 29, 63, 71, 127, 158,
    179 – 80, 201, 203 – 5, 214, 218
subjectivity 12 – 13, 25, 38, 62, 70 – 71, 75,
    103, 114, 216 – 17, 222, 225
substitutionary atonement 75 – 78, 80, 114 –
    15, 128, 171
suffering 1, 2, 21 – 22, 27, 30, 56, 73 – 77,
    80 – 89, 106, 109, 110 – 12, 127, 131 – 32,
    136, 138, 168, 170, 172, 191, 199, 217,
    221, 223
– according to Aristotle 1, 73, 81, 84, 109 –
    10

– irrational 75–76
– paradox of 73–74, 77, 88–89
– unjust 73–74, 76–77, 81–82, 84–85,
  110–11
suicide 124, 156, 199
supra-ethical acts 14
symbols, symbolism 58, 71, 74, 88–89,
  106, 108, 113, 115, 126, 129–30, 140,
  185, 216–17
syncretism 97–98, 101, 187
Syro-Ephraimite War 95, 165, 167, 220
systematic theology 54, 71

Talmud 165
Targum 173
tariki 85, 89, 111
technology 91, 141
teleological suspension of the ethical 20,
  27, 30
temple 42, 74, 98, 103, 173, 175, 199
temptation 37, 113
Ten Commandments see Decalogue
terebinth 163–64, 168
terrorists, terrorism 14, 89, 92, 135
thanksgiving 129, 140
thaumazein 148
theft 10, 199
theism 109
theodicy 54, 73, 75–79, 203, 208, 217, 223
Theodizee des Leidens 73
theological interpretation 30, 197, 205, 218
Tiglath-pileser 102, 165
Tokyo National Museum in Ueno 181
tragedy 14, 44, 46, 130, 156
transcendence, transcendency 14, 86,
  104–6, 111, 149, 216
trial(s) 39, 49, 52, 54, 61, 80, 174
tsaddiq 176
tsedaqa 176
tsemach 176
Turandot 155–56

U.S.A. 5, 89, 92, 125, 132, 152–53, 223
Ugarit 99

ultimate meaning 100, 110, 182
ultra-egoist(ic) 91–92, 113
unbelief 51, 59, 128
unethical, unethicality 1, 25, 27, 30, 32, 35,
  55–56, 61, 68–69, 71, 135, 137
Unheilstheodizee 73
universal(ism) 11–12, 20–21, 61–65, 69,
  74, 76, 104–7, 115, 143, 145, 205, 218,
  222, 228–30
unrighteous(ness) 77, 95, 127, 170–72, 180,
  187, 200, 207

value-freedom 3, 71
values 3, 63, 71, 83, 88, 94, 109–10, 124,
  131, 135, 137, 225, 228, 230
vanity 96, 120, 123–24, 206
Vatican Manuscript 174
vengeance 62, 64, 152, 191
victimizers 86, 135, 152
victims 13, 89, 121, 135–36, 138, 152

war 11–14, 46, 48, 62, 89, 93–95, 103,
  124, 131–32, 151, 165, 167, 186, 211,
  220, 227
wisdom 88, 96, 98–99, 157–59, 166–67,
  199, 228
wonder 140–41, 148–51
worship 48–50, 98–99, 105–6, 122, 126,
  187–88, 227

Yahweh 27, 33–35, 37–38, 53–55, 58, 60,
  65–66, 69, 74–75, 78, 93, 95, 97–106,
  114, 121, 126, 142–43, 165–71, 173–76,
  178–80, 183, 185–88, 190–94, 197–
  98, 202–3, 207, 219
Yahweh-alone-movements 95, 99, 104
Yahwism 101
Yamanaka, Shinya 141
Yehimilk Inscription 99
Yomiuri Shimbun 154

Zedekiah 176, 184, 189
Zion 74, 174
– inviolability of 174

Author Index

Abelard, Peter 54–55
Arieti, S. 52, 56
Auerbach, Erich 41

Baltzer, Klaus 78, 104
Barth, Hermann 10
Barth, Karl 54, 71, 85, 86, 111, 145
Barton, John 4
Becking, Bob 101
Bieber, Marianus 22
Bonhoeffer, Dietrich 54, 71
Brickhouse, Thomas C. 81
Bright, J. 194
Buber, M. 24–25, 30, 32, 35, 68, 122, 168, 222
Budde, K. 164
Burnet, John 80

Calvin, J. 49
Carson, Rachel 149–50
Causse, Jean-Daniel 33
Coats, George W. 39
Cohen, Menachem 49, 54
Collingwood, R. G. 217

de Moor, Johannes Cornelis 101
Delitzsch, F. 30–31, 50
Derrida, Jacques 1, 26–28, 30–31, 35, 55, 68, 71, 122
Dever, William G. 102
Dilworth, David A. 107
Dōgen Zenji 131
Doi, Kenji 218
Duhm, Bernhard 196–98

Ebach, Jürgen 22
Elliger, K. 5

Feuerbach, Ludwig 91, 109
Fink, Eugen 123
Fohrer, Georg 10
Fox, Michael V. 198
Fujisawa, Norio 147
Funayama, Shin'ichi 91

Furuya, Yasuo 212

Gadamer, Hans-Georg 12, 72, 146, 216
Gesenius, Wilhelm 38
Gilkey, L. 94
Goulder, M. 217
Gunkel, Hermann 23, 214, 222

Hatano, S. 217
Havel, Václav 149–50
Hegel, Georg Wilhelm Friedrich 35, 57–58, 60, 68, 91, 131, 217
Heidegger, Martin 120, 123, 217
Hermanni, F. 22
Heschel, Abraham Joshua 132, 145
Hick, John 92, 94
Hisamatsu, Shin'ichi 146
Holladay, William L. 186, 196

Ibn Shmuel, Yehuda 54
Ibn Tibbon, R. Samuel 54
Ikeda, Yutaka 221, 225
Imamichi, Tomonobu 142, 205–6
Inoue, Yōji 122
Ishida, Tomoo 215–16, 226
Ishikawa, Ritsu 221
Itō, Susumu 79
Iwata, Yasuo 82

Jacob, Benno 41
Jepsen, A. 11
Joüon, Paul 42, 221
Jung, Carl G. 1, 121–22, 128–29, 132, 203, 206–7

Kamitō, Keiko 150
Kant, Immanuel 1, 20, 22–24, 30, 35, 55–57, 68, 71, 122, 131, 216–17
Katō, Shinrō 82
Katō, Takashi 102
Kautzsch, E. 38
Kawai, Hayao 92
Keel, Othmar 101
Kennan, George F. 153–54

Kida, Ken'ichi   212, 221–22, 224, 228
Kierkegaard, Søren   1, 20–28, 30–32, 35,
    41, 48, 50–52, 55, 58, 67–68, 122
Kita, Hiroshi   230
Knitter, Paul F.   92, 94
Kobayashi, Hideo   181, 208
Kohata, Fujiko   220
Kohn, Murray J.   34
Kolakowski, L.   22
Krašovec, Jože   198
Kratz, Reinhard G.   4
Kume, Hiroshi   12
Kuske, Martin   54

Lacan, J.   33
Lemaire, André   19
Lequier, G.   22
Levin, Christoph   197, 227
Levinas, Emmanuel   1, 25–26, 28, 30–31,
    35, 68, 122, 131
Levine, Baruch A.   103
Locke, John   2, 151–52
Luscombe, D. E.   55
Luther, Martin   45, 86
Luz, Ulrich   85, 111, 146

Mahnke, Allan W.   101
Maritain, R.   22
Masuda, Keizaburō   20
Matsushita, Ryōhei   136–37
McKane, William   183–86, 194, 197–98, 208
Meinhardt, Jack   101
Michel, Diethelm   23
Miller, Patrick D.   101
Miyamoto, Hisao   27–30, 32–35, 40, 49, 53,
    68, 200, 204, 223, 225
Miyashita, Satoko   122
Mizugaki, Wataru   212
Moberly, R. Walter L.   36–37
Mori, Arimasa   44, 46, 55, 71
Mori, Kazurō   91–93
Moriizumi, Kōji   145
Morimura, Susumu   112
Moriya, Akio   218, 221
Motomura, Ryōji   102
Mowinckel, Sigmund   198
Mukōda, Kuniko   208

Muraoka, Takamitsu   221

Nahmanides, Moses   49
Nakazawa, Kōki   164, 212, 221
Nakazawa, Shin'ichi   92
Namiki, Kōichi   90, 212, 221–25
Neef, Heinz-Dieter   23–24
Nicholson, E. W.   186
Niebuhr, Reinhold   153
Nietzsche, Friedrich   88, 120, 123, 131, 217
Nishida, Kitarō   1, 3, 35, 56–60, 62, 68,
    107–9, 115, 146, 225
Nishimura, Toshiaki   212, 217, 221, 223, 230
Nomoto, Shinya   217, 230
Nomura, Mikiko   121
Noth, M.   222

Odashima, Tarō   220
Oeming, Manfred   101, 103
Ōnuki, Takashi   28, 79, 212
Ōshima, Chikara   230
Ōsumi, Yūichi   220
Ōtomo, Satoru   218–19, 221

Panikkar, R.   92
Parfit, Derek   112
Polish, David   52
Popper, Karl R.   112

Ricœur, Paul   12, 72, 146, 216–17
Ro, Johannes Unsok   230
Robinson, H. Wheeler   34
Rosenau, Hartmut   22
Rudolph, W.   5, 194, 197

Sakon, Kiyoshi   212, 221, 229
Sakon, Yoshishige   212
Sasaki, Kei   12
Sasaki, Tetsuo   218
Schelling, F. W. J.   22–23
Schestow, L.   22
Schmid, Konrad   28, 101, 103, 198
Schmidt, Ludwig   23
Schmidt, W. H.   98–99, 106, 126, 197
Schniewind, Julius D.   64
Schoenberg, Arnold   1, 120–21, 125–26,
    128–29, 131–32

Schweizer, Eduard   64
Seki, Hajime   153
Sekine, Masao   65, 79, 164, 168–70, 177, 186, 192, 194, 212–15, 224–25
Sekine, Seizō   11–12, 41, 50–51, 53, 59, 64, 74, 76, 82, 88, 96, 98, 114–15, 122, 125, 129, 131, 139, 147, 163, 172, 178, 212, 216
Seow, Choon-Leong   4
Shanks, Hershel   101
Shibuya, Haruyoshi   106, 150, 156
Short, J. Randall   4, 5, 36
Smith, Mark S.   101, 104
Smith, Michael B.   25
Smith, Nicholas D.   81
Steck, Odil Hannes   10
Steenblock, V.   22
Susman, Margarete   223
Suzuki, Yoshihide   223

Takata, Saburō   82
Takeuchi, Seiichi   98, 106
Takizawa, Katsumi   143
Tanaka, Michitarō   80–81
Teshima, Izaya   228
Tetsuya, Takahashi   27
Thiel, Winfried   2, 173–75, 177, 183–90, 192–96, 198–206, 208, 219
Tigay, Jeffrey H.   101
Tillich, Paul   88, 130, 146, 217
Tilliette, Xavier   22
Tōbō, Yoshinobu   212, 228
Tödt, Ilse   54
Tsuchido, Kiyoshi   212, 229
Tsukimoto, Akio   90–91, 98, 102–7, 114, 212, 217, 220–21
Tsumura, Toshio   221

Uchida, Tatsuru   122
Uchida, Yoshiaki   73

Uchimura, Kanzō   45
Uelinger, Christoph   101
Ukai, Nobushige   151

van der Horst, Pieter Willem   101
van der Toorn, Karel   101
Volz, P.   194, 197
Von Rad, Gerhard   23, 30, 36–38, 41, 43–44, 49–52, 55, 59, 65, 70, 222

Wakabayashi, Judy   4, 12, 64, 82, 96, 122, 147, 206, 216
Wanke, Gunther   189
Watanabe, Jirō   90
Watanabe, Zenta   212
Watsuji, Tetsurō   122, 134, 216, 225
Weber, Max   14, 62, 71, 73, 75–77, 214, 217
Weippert, Manfred   101, 186
Wellhausen, J.   222
Wellisch, Erich   56
Wenham, Gordon J.   37, 39, 40, 43, 45, 49, 52–53, 55, 71
Westermann, Claus   21–22, 35–36, 38, 40, 55, 71, 103
Witte, Markus   4, 28
Wolf, Susan   112
Würthwein, Ernst   182

Yagi, Seiichi   85, 111–13, 131, 143, 146, 212
Yamaga, Tetsuo   10, 21, 90, 98, 219–20, 223, 226
Yamamoto, Takashi   28
Yanaihara, Tadao   131–32
Yoshida, Hidekazu   181–82, 206
Yoshizawa, Denzaburō   123
Yuasa, Yasuo   203, 206–7
Yusa, Michiko   58, 107

Zevit, Ziony   101

Ancient Sources Index

Old Testament

Genesis
1   129
1:1–2   60
1:3 ff.   60
1:28–30   167
3:6   169
6:9   171
7:1   171
9:1–17   39
9:2–3   167
12   37–39, 49, 51
12:1   39, 42
12:1–3   37
12:3   38, 40
12:7   37–38
12:11 ff.   52
13:14–16   37
14   39
14:22   60
15   38, 49
15:2   51
15:7   37
15:8   51
15:18   37
15:18–21   38–39
16   52
17   49
17:16–19   39
17:17   46
17:18   51
18:23 ff.   51
20   52
21:3   46
21:9 ff.   52
21:16   42
21:18   39
21:25 ff.   36
21:28 ff.   36
21:31   36
21:31–34   40
22   19–72, 214

22:1   22, 30, 35, 38, 45, 48
22:1–14   38
22:1–19   19
22:2   22, 28, 39, 42, 44, 49–50
22:2–4   42
22:3   42–43, 48–49
22:3–4a   28
22:4   42–43, 48, 52
22:4–5   48
22:5   29, 33, 48–50, 52, 56
22:5a   48
22:6   36, 44, 46, 49
22:7   44–45, 48–49
22:7–8   45
22:8   29–31, 34, 36, 45, 48–50, 52, 56
22:9   42–43, 46, 52
22:9–10   52
22:10   34, 52
22:11   48
22:12   22, 29, 33, 36, 49, 53
22:12 ff.   24
22:13   34
22:14a   40
22:14   36–37, 40, 54, 61, 65–67, 69–70
22:15   35, 69
22:15–18   21, 29, 33, 36, 40, 44
22:15–19   35–41, 61, 65, 67, 70
22:16   33, 35–36, 38
22:17   33, 36, 39, 61
22:18   29, 33, 36, 39–40, 61, 66–67
22:19   33, 36, 40
24:7   37
26:3   37
26:4   37
26:23 ff.   36
26:24   37, 103
31:22   49
32:23–33   214
32:42   167
32:53   167
40:20   49
42:18   49
49:13   165

Exodus
2:11–15   126
2:16–17   127
3–14   220
3:18   49
4:10   127
4:24–26   214
5:3   49
6:7   196
13:12–13   24, 56
14:31   104
15:25b   37
16:32   171
16:33   171
17:1–7   127
19:11   49
19:16   49
20   10
20:3   99
20:4   121
20:5–6   126
20:13   22
22:28   23, 55
23:25–29   127
31:13   54
32:3–32   127
32:9–13   127
32:13   38
32:32   77
34:14   22
34:19–20   24, 56

Leviticus
1:5 ff.   177
3:2   42
3:6 ff.   177
3:16   42
5:14–6:7   127
7:1–9   127
19:17–18   64
19:18   64

Numbers
3:44 ff.   24, 56
11:15   28
12:7   104
14:19   179, 194

14:20   179, 194
21:14   93
21:35   93
28   42
28–29   177
29   42
35:30   11

Deuteronomy
2:34   93
3:3   93
4:24   22
5   10
5:7   99
5:8   121
5:9–10   126
6:6   194, 197
6:15   22
7:6 ff.   106
7:21   167
10:16   197
11:18   194, 197
13:2 ff.   183
13:6   185
13:15   93
18:9 ff.   183
18:15–19   177
26:17   179, 194
26:18   179, 194
28:1–14   172
29:12   179, 194, 195
29:19   194
30:6   194, 197
30:11–14   197
30:14   194
34:10   177

Joshua
6:24   93
10–11   93
10:20   93
22:28   171

Judges
5   93
6:25   97
13:5   33

13:7   33
13:24   33

1 Samuel
2:21   33
8:5   215
16   167
16:13   167
16:18   167
17:55   33
17:58   33
18:5   169
18:14   169
18:15   169
18:17   93
18:27   215
18:30   169
24   215
26   215

2 Samuel
3:18   104
7   93
7:24   179, 194
10:4 – 5   75
12   217
13:32   33
23:2 – 3   167
23:5   93
24:1   25

1 Kings
2:3   169
8:30   179, 194
8:34   179, 194
8:36   179, 194
8:39   179, 194
8:50   179, 194
10:26   93
11:4 ff.   97
14:23   173
18:19 ff.   173
18:21   97
18:36   104

2 Kings
3   220

3:4 – 27   219
5:18   194
8:31 – 32   37
16   220
16:9   102
17:10   173
18:7   169
23:4 ff.   98
23:15 ff.   98

1 Chronicles
21:1   25

2 Chronicles
3:1   42 – 43
11:5 – 12   93
16:7 – 9   219
17:3 – 6   219
19:2 – 3   219
20   219 – 20
20:1 – 30   95
20:37   219
25:7 – 9   219
28   220

Nehemiah
1:5   167
4:14   167

Job
1:8   104
1:21   53
2:3   61
2:10   61
3:1 ff.   199
9   128
34:35   169
38 ff.   128 – 29, 206
38:2   121
42:10 – 17   39

Psalms
2:6 – 7   166
5:2   99
14:5   171
22   79
24:6   171

32:8 169
36:4 169
51 217
66:10 61
69:17 [MT 18] 104
88:10 – 13 84
123:2 104
139:21 – 23 64
139:23 – 24 61

Proverbs
1:3 169
1:7 167
7:7 33
9:10 167
10:3 120
10:5 169
10:19 169
14:35 169
15:33 167
16:23 169
17:2 169
19:14 169
25:21 – 22 64

Ecclesiastes
1:2 120
3:11 120
3:12 – 14 96, 123
3:16 – 17 96
3:17 120
3:22 96, 123
5:18 96, 123
8:14 96, 120
8:15 96, 123
9:7 123
9:7 – 9 96
9:10 84
12:13 167

Isaiah
1:24 38
2:2 – 4 94
3:15 38
3:16 – 23 172
5:11 – 12 172
5:16 99

5:26 ff. 95
6 176, 214
6:5 167
6:13 163 – 64, 167
7 95
7:4 – 9 220
7:6 167
7:9b 220
7:17 166
7:17 ff. 95
7:20 75
8:16 167 – 68
8:23 165 – 66
8:23 – 9:6 165
9 106, 167, 176
9:1 165 – 66
9:1 – 6 166
9:2 165
9:5 165 – 66
9:6 165 – 66, 176
9:7 167
10 102
10:5 102 – 3
10:19 164
10:25 103
11 166, 176
11:1 166, 176
11:1 – 2 166
11:1 – 9 166
11:2 166
11:4 – 5 176
11:6 – 9 167
11:8 166
11:8 – 9 166
11:9 166, 179
14:22 38
14:23 38
16:5 167
30:1 – 5 220
30:16 95
31:1 – 3 220
40 – 55 74
41:8 104
41:8 – 9 200
41:13 – 14 200
41:20 169
41:25 114

41:25a   114
42:1–4   74
43:1   200
43:5   200
44:1   104
44:2   104
44:9–20   105, 126
44:18   169
44:19   105
44:21   104
44:28   104–5
45:1   104–5
45:3   114
45:3–5   114
45:4   104, 114
45:5   114
45:6–7   104
45:21–22   105
47   62
49–55   114
49:1–6   74
50:4   168
50:4–9   74
50:6   74
52:13   78, 85, 169–71
52:13–15   169
52:13–53:12   64, 74, 109, 115, 127, 168
53   106, 214
53:1–10aα   169
53:3   75
53:4b   79
53:5–6   75
53:7   79, 85
53:7a   75
53:8   75, 78, 171
53:9   171–72
53:10   172
53:10–11   78
53:10aβ   170
53:10aβ–12   169
53:10b   78, 170
53:10b–11   78, 110
53:10b–12aα   170
53:11   78–79, 169
53:11a   170
53:11b   170
53:11–12   169

53:12   77–78, 110, 169
53:12aα   171
53:12aβ   170–71
53:12b   170
53:12bα   171
53:12bβ   171
54:13   168
55:13   168
56–66   3, 216
65:25   167

Jeremiah
1:1–3   173
1:4   177
1:7bβ   173
1:9–10   173
1:13–15   187
1:16–19   173
2:2   173, 178, 187
2:5b   173
2:8   187
2:9   199
2:11   187
2:13   187
2:17–19   187
2:19   199
2:20   172–73, 187
2:20b   173
2:23–24   97
2:23–25   187
2:24   168
2:25   173
2:26b   173
2:27–37   187
2:28   126
2:33   173
2:35   199
3:1ff.   97
3:1–5   187
3:4–5   199
3:6–13   173
3:12aβ   173
3:13bα   173
3:14–18   173
3:20–21   187
3:22   191
3:23–25   199

3:25   186, 188, 191
4:3 – 4   173
4:4   200, 202
4:5 – 18   199
4:8   191
4:9 – 10   188
4:10   174 – 75, 191
4:14   187
4:19 – 20   186, 190, 199
4:19 – 31   199
4:22   187
4:27   188, 191
4:28   188
4:31   191
5:1 – 5   191, 199
5:5 – 8   187
5:6   199
5:6 – 9   199
5:7   179, 194
5:8   179
5:9   199
5:9b   179
5:10b   179
5:12 – 13   199
5:13   179
5:15   179
5:15 – 17   199
5:18 – 19   173
5:26 – 31   191, 199
5:31   188
6:4   199
6:7   199
6:10   180, 200
6:10 – 11   199
6:13 – 14   188
6:13 – 15   191
6:15   199
6:18 – 19   173
6:19   179, 190
6:20   188
6:22 – 26   199
6:24   191
6:26   191
7:1 – 3   179, 189
7:1 – 8:3   173
7:4   173, 188, 199
7:5 – 7   179, 190

7:5 – 8   189
7:7   199
7:9   11, 199
7:9a   173
7:9b   189
7:10a   173, 188
7:10b   189
7:12   173
7:13   189
7:14   173, 199
7:15   189
7:16   190, 203
7:18abα   173
7:21   176
7:21b   173, 177
7:21 – 26   176 – 77
7:21 – 29   177
7:22   176
7:23   176, 179, 194
7:24   177, 194
7:24 – 26   177
7:25   177
7:26   177 – 79, 188, 202
7:28b   173, 177
7:29   173, 177
8:1 – 2   98
8:6   191
8:6 – 7   199
8:8   188
8:8 – 12   199
8:10 – 12   191
8:11   188, 199
8:14   199
8:14 – 16   191
8:15 – 17   199
8:18 – 19a   186, 190, 199
8:19b   173
8:20   191
8:20 – 23   186, 190, 199
9:1 – 5   199
9:7   199
9:7 – 8   191
9:9 – 10   186, 190
9:10   199
9:11 – 15   173
9:12 – 15   179, 190
9:16 – 21   186, 190, 199

9:17 – 21   191
9:22 – 23   186, 191, 199
9:24   169
9:24 – 25   180, 200
9:25b   202
10:1 – 16   174
10:13   190
10:17 – 22   190
10:18   200
10:19 – 22   199
10:21   199
10:21 – 22   191
10:23 – 24   180, 190, 200
10:24   207
10:27   190
11   201 – 2
11:1 – 13   179, 190
11:1 – 14   174, 179, 189
11:2   179
11:3   179
11:3b   202
11:4   179, 194
11:4b   202
11:5   202
11:6   179
11:8   179
11:10   179
11:10b   202
11:11   202
11:14   179, 190, 202 – 3
11:15 – 12:6   174
11:18 – 12:6   174
11:21 – 23   174
12:1b   204
12:1 – 4   190
12:1 – 5   174
12:1 – 6   199
12:14 – 17   174
12:16 – 17   190
13:9   199
13:10a   174
13:11   174, 177
13:12 – 14   174
13:15   199
13:17   186, 190, 199
13:18   186, 191
13:18 – 19   187

13:21   191
13:22   199
13:23   168, 180, 190, 200
13:26   199
14:1 – 15:4   174, 183
14:2 – 10   174
14:2 – 6   199
14:7   191, 199
14:7 – 9   193
14:8 – 9   190
14:10   199
14:10 – 16   175
14:11 – 12   190, 203
14:13 – 16   183
14:14   174
14:21   193, 195
15:1   190, 203
15:6 – 9   199
15:10 – 21   174, 199
15:11   186, 190, 203
15:17   191
15:18   190
16:3b   174
16:4a   199
16:4b   174
16:9   199
16:10 – 13   174, 179, 190
16:12   179, 188, 202
16:12 – 13a   204
16:13a   203
16:16 – 18   174
16:19 – 21   174
17:1   190
17:3 – 4   199
17:9   180, 190, 200, 207
17:12 – 18   174
17:14 – 18   199
17:19 – 27   174, 179, 189
17:21 – 27   188
18:1   174
18:6   199
18:7 – 10   203
18:7 – 11   174
18:8   188
18:8 – 10   179, 189
18:12   174
18:16   199

18:18 174
18:18 – 23 199
18:20 186, 190, 203
19:2b–9 174
19:4 179, 190
19:11b–15 174
19:19 – 23 174
20:1 174
20:6 174
20:7 – 18 174, 199
20:11 169
20:14 – 18 199
21 201 – 2
21:1 – 10 174
21:8b 202
21:8 ff. 95
21:8 – 10 179, 189
21:9 95
21:9a 202
21:12 199
21:13 199
21:14 199
22:1 – 5 174
22:3 179, 190, 199
22:6 – 7 199
22:8 – 9 174
22:9 179
22:11 – 12 174
22:17b 174
22:23 191
22:25 – 27 174
22:28 174
22:29 174
22:30b 174
23 176
23:1 175
23:1 – 2 175
23:1 – 4 174
23:2 175
23:2 – 6 175
23:3 175
23:5 167, 175 – 76
23:6 175 – 76
23:7 175
23:7 – 8 174
23:8 175
23:9 – 32 183

23:9 – 40 175
23:10 199
23:11 – 15 191
23:11 – 16 199
23:16 188
23:17 174, 183
23:18 – 22 199
23:25 – 31 188, 199
23:32 174, 183
23:34 – 40 174
24 179, 194
24:1 – 10 174
24:7 179, 194 – 95, 198
25 102
25:1 – 38 174
25:4 177
25:8 ff. 95
25:9 102, 104
26 – 29 198
26:3 174, 179, 188 – 89
26:4 – 6 179, 190
26:4b 174
26:4b–6 179, 189
26:5 174, 177
26:6 174
26:13 174, 188
26:19 177
27 184
27 – 29 175, 183
27:1 184
27:1 – 4 187
27:2 186
27:5 – 10 174
27:6 104
27:8 186
27:9 ff. 183
27:11 187
27:12 – 15 174
27:16 – 22 174
28 174, 183 – 85
28:1 184
28:1aα 174, 185
28:1b–16bα 188
28:1 – 17 184
28:5 184
28:6 184
28:6 – 9 186

28:9 199
28:10 184, 186
28:11 184, 186, 191
28:12 184
28:15 184
28:16bβ 174, 183, 185
28:17 184, 188
29 183
29:1 192
29:2 174
29:3 – 4a 192
29:4b 174
29:5 – 7 189, 192
29:8 – 9 183
29:8 – 24 174
29:12 – 14 179, 189
29:15 183
29:16 – 30 188
29:19 177
29:21 – 23 183
29:24 – 32 183
29:25 174
29:31aβb 174
29:32 185
29:32aβb 174
30 – 31 198
30:1 – 3 174
30:5 – 8 200
30:6 191
30:7 – 31 191
30:10 – 11 200
30:10 – 31:26 189
30:11 191
30:12 – 24 200
30:21 191
30:22 195
30:26 191
31 176, 179, 194 – 95, 197, 204
31 – 33 198
31 – 34 198
31:1 179, 194 – 95
31:1 – 14 200
31:5 – 6 198
31:11 191
31:15 – 20 198
31:18 197
31:21 197

31:27 – 34 174, 205
31:29 – 30 188
31:31 178, 192, 197
31:31 – 34 178 – 80, 189, 192 – 95
31:32 178, 192, 198, 207
31:33 178 – 80, 192, 194 – 95, 197, 200, 207
31:33b 178, 194
31:34 167, 178 – 80, 192 – 94, 198, 200, 207
31:35 – 40 174
32:1 – 6a 174
32:15 191
32:16 – 44 174
32:18 – 19 188
32:38 179, 194 – 95
33 174
34 – 35 198
34:1 174
34:2ab 174
34:3 – 7 192
34:8 179
34:8a 174
34:8b 192
34:9a 192
34:9aβb 174
34:10 179
34:10 – 11 192
34:12b 174
34:13b – 17 174
34:18 179
34:18aβ 174
34:19 – 22 174
35 184
35:1 174
35:2 – 7a 192
35:7bβ 174
35:8 – 11 192
35:13 – 18 174
35:15 177
36 182
36 – 41 198
36:2b 174
36:3 174, 179, 194
36:7 174
36:29 – 30 199
36:31 174
37:1 – 2 174
37:3 203

37:19 174
37:21 191
38:2 174, 179, 189
38:15 191
38:17–18 189
38:22–23 174
39:1–2 174
39:4–10 174
39:13 174
39:15b 174
39:16aβ 174
39:17 174
39:18b 174
40:1 174
40:2b–3 174, 204
42:1–9 192
42:10 ff. 188
42:10–16 174
42:17aβbβ 174
42:18–22 174
42:21–22 179, 189
43:1 174
43:4 174
43:7 174
43:10 104
43:13 174
44:1–14 174
44:4 177
44:15 174
44:17aβ 174
44:18b 174
44:20–23 174
44:24aαb 174
44:25a 174
44:25aßb 192
44:26a 174
44:26b 192
44:27 174
44:28b 174
44:29–30 192
45:1b 174
45:2 174
45:3–5 192
45:5a 199
45:5bα 174
46:10 94
46:15–16 94

46:25–26 94
46:27–28 200
47:4 94
47:6–7 94
48:10 94
48:12 94
48:25–26 94
48:42 94
48:44 94
49:2 94
49:5 94
49:8 94
49:15 94
49:20–22 94
49:27 94
49:35–38 94
50 62
50:9–16 94
50:18 94
50:19–20 200
50:21 94
50:24–40 94
50:34 191
51 62
51:1–2 94
51:11 94
51:20–24 94
51:36 94
51:55–58 94

Lamentations
3:42 194

Ezekiel
8:5 ff. 98
11:19 198
14:11 196
16:15 ff. 97
23:3 ff. 97
36–37 198
36:26 198

Daniel
12:3 169

Hosea
1:7 95

2:4 ff.   97
2:20   167
2:25   196
4:2   11
4:13 ff.   97
4:14   173
5:13   220
7:11   220
8:6   126
11:1   33

Amos
1:5   102
2:7   194
5:21 – 27   177
6:4 – 6   172
8:4 – 6   172
9:7   102

Micah
4:1 – 4   94
4:5   100
5:9   95
6:8   25
6:7 – 8   56

Nahum
1   62

Habakkuk
2:14   167

Zechariah
3:8   176
6:12   176
8:8   196

Old Testament Apocrypha & Pseudepigrapha

Sirach (Ecclesiasticus)
45:1 ff.   126

1 Enoch
48:10   166

52:4   166

Psalms of Solomon
17:32   166
18:5   166
18:7   166

New Testament

Matthew
4:1 – 11   113
5   13
5:43 – 44   64
14:23 – 25   178
20:28   79
22:39   64
26:28   79
26:39   85
27:46   79, 110

Mark
10:15   112
10:45   79
14:24   79
15:34   79, 110

Luke
14:26   27

John
1:17   126
1:18   141
6:23 ff.   126

Romans
4:25   79

1 Corinthians
15:3 – 5   79

2 Corinthians
3:5 – 18   178
3:6   193

Galatians
2:20   87

Hebrews
8:8 – 12   178

James
1:2 – 4   61

Early Jewish Sources

Jewish Antiquities
1.225   52
1.227   45
1.229 – 31   47 – 48, 68
1.230 – 32   46
1.231 – 32   46
1.232   46

Bereshit Rabbah   45

Classical Greek Sources

Apology of Socrates
23BC   83
24C   80, 110
29DE   83

40C   80, 81
40Eff.   81
41C   81

Crito
48B   80

Metaphysics
I, 2, 982b12   148

Nicomachean Ethics   64, 82 – 83, 109 – 10

Phaedrus
250 A   148

Poetics   156

Republic
539Bff.   81
591ff.   147

Theaetetus
155D   148

Qur'an

37:95 – 113   49